BEYOND DECODING

BEYOND DECODING

The Behavioral and Biological
Foundations of Reading Comprehension

Edited by
RICHARD K. WAGNER
CHRISTOPHER SCHATSCHNEIDER
CAROLINE PHYTHIAN-SENCE

THE GUILFORD PRESS
New York   London

© 2009 The Guilford Press
A Division of Guilford Publications, Inc.
72 Spring Street, New York, NY 10012
www.guilford.com

Printed in the United States of America

This book is printed on acid-free paper.

Last digit is print number: 9   8   7   6   5   4   3   2   1

Library of Congress Cataloging-in-Publication Data

Beyond decoding : the behavioral and biological foundations of reading
comprehension / edited by Richard K. Wagner, Christopher Schatschneider,
and Caroline Phythian-Sence.
       p. cm.
  Includes bibliographical references and index.
  ISBN 978-1-60623-310-8 (hardcover : alk. paper)
  1. Reading comprehension.   2. Reading comprehension—Psychological aspects.
3. Cognitive learning.   I. Wagner, Richard K.   II. Schatschneider, Christopher.
III. Phythian-Sence, Caroline.
  LB1050.45.B5 2009
  418′.4019—dc22

                                                                        2009017351

About the Editors

Richard K. Wagner, PhD, is Robert G. Lawton Distinguished Research Professor of Psychology at Florida State University and Associate Director of the Florida Center for Reading Research. His major area of research interest is the acquisition of complex cognitive knowledge and skills, which he has pursued in two domains. In the domain of reading, Dr. Wagner's research has focused on the role of reading-related phonological processing abilities in the normal and abnormal development of reading skills; the prediction, prevention, and remediation of dyslexia; and understanding the origins of individual and developmental differences in reading comprehension. In the domain of human intelligence, his research has focused on the role of practical knowledge and intelligence in intellectual performance manifested outside the classroom setting. Dr. Wagner's work has addressed a variety of measurement issues and practical considerations involving the assessment of constructs in the domains of language, reading, and intelligence. He has coauthored a test of practical intelligence called the Tacit Knowledge Inventory for Managers and is coauthor of tests of phonological processing (Comprehensive Test of Phonological Processes in Reading), reading (Test of Word Reading Efficiency), and early literacy (Test of Preschool Early Literacy). He has been elected Chair of the Advisory Board of the National Institute for Literacy.

Christopher Schatschneider, PhD, is a Professor of Psychology at Florida State University and Associate Director of the Florida Center for Reading Research. His research focuses on early reading development and reading disabilities and has been supported by the National Institute of Child Health and Human Development and the Institute of Education Sciences. Dr. Schatschneider is also a trained methodologist who frequently provides assistance to investigators around design and analysis issues that arise when designing experiments and analyzing data from studies of early reading development. He is the Editor of *Annals of Dyslexia* and serves on the editorial boards of numerous journals.

Caroline Phythian-Sence, PhD, engages in research and pilot development for Reading Is Fundamental, UK, at the National Literacy Trust, in London, England. Previously, Dr. Phythian-Sence was a doctoral student of Richard Wagner at Florida State University and the Florida Center for Reading Research, where she studied vocabulary knowledge and its relation to comprehension.

Contributors

Stephanie Al-Otaiba, PhD, College of Education and Florida Center for Reading Research, Florida State University, Tallahassee, Florida

Rebecca S. Betjemann, PhD, Department of Psychology, Regis University, Denver, Colorado

Emily Bigelow, MEd, Department of Teaching and Learning, Vanderbilt University, Peabody College, Nashville, Tennessee

Kate Cain, DPhil, Department of Psychology, Fylde College, Lancaster University, Lancaster, United Kingdom

Sarah Carlson, MA, Department of Educational Psychology, University of Minnesota, Minneapolis, Minnesota

Jose M. Castillo, EdS, Florida Problem Solving/Response to Intervention Project, University of South Florida, Tampa, Florida

Donald L. Compton, PhD, Department of Special Education, Vanderbilt University, Peabody College, Nashville, Tennessee

Jacqueline M. Coyle, BS, Department of Psychology, Florida State University, Tallahassee, Florida

Laurie E. Cutting, PhD, Kennedy Krieger Institute, Baltimore, Maryland

G. Nicole Davis, PhD, Department of Special Education, Vanderbilt University, Peabody College, Nashville, Tennessee

Sarah H. Eason, MS, Kennedy Krieger Institute, Baltimore, Maryland

Amy M. Elleman, MEd, Department of Special Education, Vanderbilt University, Peabody College, Nashville, Tennessee

Jennifer K. Gilbert, BS, Department of Special Education, Vanderbilt University, Peabody College, Nashville, Tennessee

Lisa Glover, BA, Department of Psychology and Florida Center for Reading Research, Florida State University, Tallahassee, Florida

Lynn Huestegge, PhD, Institute of Psychology, RWTH Aachen University, Aachen, Germany

John L. Jones, MA, Department of Psychology, Florida State University, Tallahassee, Florida

Michael P. Kaschak, PhD, Department of Psychology, Florida State University, Tallahassee, Florida

Janice M. Keenan, PhD, Department of Psychology, University of Denver, Denver, Colorado

Panayiota Kendeou, PhD, Department of Educational and Counselling Psychology, Faculty of Education, McGill University, Montreal, Quebec, Canada

Jane Lawrence, MEd, Department of Special Education, Vanderbilt University, Peabody College, Nashville, Tennessee

Kate Nation, DPhil, Department of Experimental Psychology, University of Oxford, Oxford, United Kingdom

Jane Oakhill, DPhil, Department of Psychology, Life Sciences, University of Sussex, Falmer, East Sussex, United Kingdom

Natalie G. Olinghouse, PhD, Department of Educational Psychology, Neag School of Education, University of Connecticut, Storrs, Connecticut

Richard K. Olson, PhD, Department of Psychology, University of Colorado, Boulder, Colorado

Stephen A. Petrill, PhD, Department of Human Development, The Ohio State University, Columbus, Ohio

Caroline Phythian-Sence, PhD, National Literacy Trust, London, United Kingdom

Kelly A. Powell-Smith, PhD, NCSP, Dynamic Measurement Group, Eugene, Oregon

Kanu Priya, MA, MS, Department of Management, Terry College of Business, University of Georgia, Athens, Georgia

Ralph Radach, PhD, Department of Psychology and Florida Center for Reading Research, Florida State University, Tallahassee, Florida

Keith Rayner, PhD, Department of Psychology, University of California, San Diego, La Jolla, California

Christopher Schatschneider, PhD, Department of Psychology and Florida Center for Reading Research, Florida State University, Tallahassee, Florida

Christiane Schmitten, MSc, Institute of Psychology, RWTH Aachen University, Aachen, Germany

Andrea Sell, BS, Department of Psychology, Florida State University, Tallahassee, Florida

Timothy J. Slattery, PhD, Department of Psychology, University of California, San Diego, La Jolla, California

Joseph K. Torgesen, PhD, Department of Psychology and Florida Center for Reading Research, Florida State University, Tallahassee, Florida

Paul van den Broek, PhD, Department of Education and Child Studies, University of Leiden, Leiden, The Netherlands

Richard K. Wagner, PhD, Department of Psychology and Florida Center for Reading Research, Florida State University, Tallahassee, Florida

Mary Jane White, PhD, Department of Educational Psychology, University of Minnesota, Minneapolis, Minnesota

Preface

Reading is a unique accomplishment. It requires the coordinated orchestration of just about every perceptual, linguistic, and cognitive process that has been identified. Because of its relatively recent origin in the time line of human history, we know that reading has emerged without the direct benefit of evolutionary pressure. It has done so by conscripting the services of organs and functions related to vision, speech, and language that have proved beneficial to human existence over the years. Yet, unlike walking or the ability to vocalize, reading simply is not possible unless one is taught (or teaches oneself) how to do it.

The only purpose for reading is to comprehend the author's message. Yet most of what we know about reading concerns the mechanics of decoding individual words. For a long while, it was assumed that a near-exclusive focus on decoding individual words was appropriate because that was the clear bottleneck for poor reading. Once a reader was able to identify the words on a page, comprehension of the text would follow automatically. That has not turned out to be the case. Intervention programs, for example, that have been found to improve decoding accuracy substantially have been found to have modest, at best, effects on reading comprehension.

Adequate decoding appears to be necessary, but not sufficient, for successful reading comprehension. *What, then, are the foundations of suc-*

cessful reading comprehension, and what are promising approaches to finding them? This book addresses these questions by including contributing chapters that present both behavioral and biological approaches to understanding the foundations of reading comprehension.

Beginning with behavioral approaches, three perspectives are represented. The first is a cognitive perspective that addresses the underlying processes and knowledge structures that support reading comprehension. Kaschak, Jones, Coyle, and Sell (Chapter 1) approach reading comprehension from the perspective of embodiment theory. According to embodiment theory, much of comprehension is grounded in perception and action. Rather than being an exclusively abstract phenomenon that is limited to the frontal lobes, comprehension involves the body as well. Rayner and Slattery (Chapter 2) use precise measurements of eye movements or, more accurately, where the eyes are parked and for how long when individuals read carefully constructed sentences for comprehension. Their review of their own and others' studies presents a convincing case for the promise of eye movement studies for investigating reading comprehension. Compton et al. (Chapter 3) report the results of randomized cluster trials of interventions designed to improve the acquisition of vocabulary and declarative knowledge of struggling late elementary-age students. They report aptitude × treatment interactions in the effectiveness of several intervention conditions they examined.

The second behavioral approach is represented by a developmental perspective. Radach, Schmitten, Glover, and Huestegge (Chapter 4) review the application of eye movement methodologies to the study of developing readers. They argue that it is important to establish a data base of eye movement data for normally developing readers. In addition to the importance of describing normal development, these data would serve as baseline data for comparing the eye movements of impaired readers. van den Broek, White, Kendeou, and Carlson (Chapter 5) review the development of cognitive processes involved in reading comprehension. They argue that most education practice focuses on the products of reading comprehension to the neglect of the processes of reading comprehension that underlie the resulting products. Priya and Wagner (Chapter 6) review the roles of fluent decoding and vocabulary in the development of reading comprehension. They suggest that it is important to consider not only person variables, like fluent decoding and vocabulary, but also variables associated with the text, the comprehension task, and the context when designing studies.

The final behavioral perspective is represented by an individual-differences perspective. Cain and Oakhill (Chapter 7) identify correlates of reading comprehension. They then proceed to differentiate skills that appear to play a causal role in comprehension, and hence are promising targets for intervention for the purpose of improving comprehension, from those that are more likely to be byproducts or correlates of comprehension. Nation (Chapter 8) uses studies of individuals with poor reading comprehension to identify deficits in reading- and language-related areas that are associated with poor reading comprehension, and focuses on the important role of vocabulary. Castillo, Torgesen, Powell-Smith, and Al-Otaiba (Chapter 9) compare alternative fluency-based measures for identifying individuals at risk for poor reading comprehension.

Turning to biological approaches, two perspectives are represented. The first is focused on genetic bases of reading comprehension. Keenan, Olson, and Betjemann (Chapter 10) used genetically informed research designs to investigate biological and behavioral origins of individual differences in reading comprehension. Using the Colorado twin sample, they report independent genetic influences on decoding and listening comprehension, which are two of the best predictors of reading comprehension. Petrill (Chapter 11) describes genetic and environmental influences on the development of reading skills. In most behavioral genetic studies, environmental influences on development are not measured directly but rather are inferred from the patterns of relations shown by identical and fraternal twins. A key advance in an ongoing study of genetic and environmental influences on reading is making home visits to measure environmental variables directly.

The second biological perspective is represented by neuroimaging studies. Eason and Cutting (Chapter 12) describe results from neuroimaging studies of individuals reading sentences for comprehension. The patterns of activation reported suggest more extensive activation compared with that observed for reading single words, including more right hemisphere activation and activation of the inferior frontal gyrus and the posterior, superior, and middle temporal gyri. They argue for more fully incorporating both behavioral and neurobiological findings for the purpose of developing a more complete understanding of the normal development of reading comprehension and of observed impairments.

In a concluding chapter, Wagner, Schatschneider, and Phythian-Sence (Chapter 13) describe some promising directions for the future that lie at the interface of the perspectives that have been covered.

ACKNOWLEDGMENT

The idea for this volume emerged at a conference on reading comprehension funded by the Florida Center for Reading Research, and its preparation has been supported by Grant No. P50 HD052120 from the National Institute of Child Health and Human Development and by Grant No. R305G030104 from the Institute of Education Sciences.

Contents

III. INDIVIDUAL-DIFFERENCES APPROACHES

IV. BIOLOGICAL-BASED APPROACHES

PART I

COGNITIVE APPROACHES

1

Language and Body

Michael P. Kaschak, John L. Jones,
Jacqueline M. Coyle, *and* Andrea Sell

What is language comprehension? What does it mean to say that we understand a word, a sentence, or a text? The contributors to this book offer a range of perspectives on questions such as these. In the following pages, we explore the *embodiment hypothesis*, which posits that language is understood through the same mechanisms that allow us to understand the objects, actions, and events that occur around us. Specifically, language comprehension is grounded in our bodies' systems of perception and action planning. We begin with a broad discussion of the embodied approach to cognition and lay out some ideas for how understanding (in a general sense) is grounded in perception and action. Then we review the growing body of literature suggesting that language comprehension is grounded in perception and action. We conclude by considering the ways in which an embodied theory of language comprehension may develop and some potential applications of this theoretical orientation.

EMBODIMENT

Glenberg, Jaworski, and Rischal (2007) point out that the presence or absence of a nervous system in an organism depends not on the complexity of that organism but on whether or not the organism moves. Complex organisms that do not move (e.g., trees) do not have nervous systems; simple organisms that do move (e.g., sea squirts) do have nervous systems. This observation illustrates the starting point of the embodied approach to cognition: Cognition is an adaptation that evolved to support organisms' ability to successfully plan and execute action in the world. As such, it is proposed that cognitive systems are grounded in the bodily systems responsible for perception and action planning.

Embodied approaches to cognition have only recently begun to gain traction within the mainstream of cognitive psychology and cognitive science. Nonetheless, the intellectual foundations of this approach have existed in psychology and related disciplines for quite some time. Within psychology, three separate research programs presaged important components of the embodied approach. The first of these is Piaget's research on child development (e.g., Piaget, 1926). A central principle of Piaget's approach is the claim that children's ability to think about complex concepts grows out of their bodily interactions with the world. As we see at several points in this chapter, the idea that an understanding of complex (and abstract) concepts is rooted in bodily interactions in the world is an important component of the embodied approach to language comprehension.

A second important precedent for the embodied research program is James Gibson's (1979) ecological approach to perception. Gibson argued that visual perception could best be understood by considering the interaction between an organism and its environment. Rather than proposing that organisms perceive the environment in terms of abstract features (e.g., geons; Biederman, 1985), Gibson claimed that organisms perceive the environment in terms of *affordances*, or possibilities for interaction. Affordances are jointly determined by the nature of one's body and the nature of one's environment. For example, whereas humans have arms and hands and, therefore, perceive "graspability" in the environment, other organisms (e.g., worms) lack such appendages and, therefore, do not perceive this affordance in the environment. As demonstrated in several recent studies (e.g., Tucker & Ellis, 1998; Bub, Masson, & Cree, 2008), it appears that affordances are routinely perceived (or activated in memory) when objects are perceived or thought about. The notion of affordances plays a key role in some embodied approaches to language comprehension (e.g., Glenberg & Robertson, 2000; Kaschak & Glenberg, 2000).

A third (and sometimes unacknowledged) precedent for embodiment in cognitive psychology is the proceduralist approach to memory (e.g., Kolers & Roediger, 1984). Proceduralists claim that memory is stored within the sensory modalities that were relevant to the processing of a given stimulus. Memory for a visual stimulus is stored in the visual stimulus, just as memory for auditory stimuli is stored in auditory cortex, and memory for complex stimuli may be distributed over several processing stores (see Crowder, 1993, for a discussion). The claim that memory storage is essentially *modal* (as opposed to *amodal* representations, which are claimed to be abstracted away from particular perceptual modalities; see Glenberg, 1997, and Glenberg & Robertson, 2000, for a discussion) has been featured heavily in arguments in favor of an embodied approach to cognition (e.g., Barsalou, 1999).

The roots of embodiment in psychology can also be found in philosophy and linguistics. Philosophers have long debated the *symbol grounding problem*, or the problem of how arbitrary symbols (such as words) can become meaningful (e.g., Searle, 1980; Harnad, 1990; Glenberg, 1997). Harnad (1990) illustrates the problem with his Chinese airport example. Imagine disembarking from a plane at a Chinese airport armed with no knowledge of Chinese other than what can be found in a Chinese dictionary. Once off the plane, you decide to read one of the signs. You see the first word on the sign but do not know its meaning. You look up the meaning of this word, only to find that its definition is written entirely in Chinese. In order to understand the definition, you look up the meaning of the first word of the definition in your dictionary only to find that this definition is also written in Chinese. Under such circumstances, it is clear that no matter how hard you try, you are never going to figure out what the sign means. This is Harnad's (1990) symbol grounding theory: Arbitrary symbols (such as words) cannot be understood in terms of other arbitrary symbols (more words). Their meaning needs to be grounded in something that is understood on a more basic level.

One solution to the symbol grounding problem is to claim that understanding is grounded in our body and its interactions with the world (e.g., Newton, 1996). The idea is that, on a fundamental level, we understand the way our bodies interact with the world. For instance, when we reach out and grasp an object, we understand our action on many levels (e.g., the intention behind the grasp, the subsequent actions that can be taken). This understanding of our own bodies and our own actions provides the bedrock on which our understanding of other things (such as words) can be developed. As one example, our understanding of the word *give* is not rooted in an abstract understanding of concepts such as "transfer" but rather is understood in terms of action (e.g., the arm actions involved in the execution of "giving" actions; see Glenberg & Kaschak, 2002).

The notion that an understanding of our own bodies and our own actions serves as the general foundation for our ability to understand the world has received support from the discovery and subsequent studies of mirror neurons in primates (e.g., Di Pellegrino, Fadiga, Fogassi, Gallese, & Rizzolatti, 1992; Rizzolatti & Craighero, 2004). Mirror neurons are neurons located in premotor cortex that fire both when the organism performs an action and when the organism sees a conspecific performing the same action. Although the mirror system has been most directly and extensively studied in nonhuman primates (see Rizzolatti & Craighero, 2004, for a review), positron emission tomography (PET) and functional magnetic resonance imaging (fMRI) studies suggest the presence of a similar kind of system in humans (e.g., Koski, Wohlschlager, Bekkering, Woods, Bubeau, Mazziotta, et al., 2002). The mirror system provides a mechanism through which an organism can understand the actions of others: Organisms understand what other organisms are doing because they understand what *they* would be doing if they were performing the same action. Several authors have trumpeted the mirror system as a broad foundation for understanding, particularly in areas of social cognition (e.g., Keysers & Perrett, 2004). Although this hypothesis is clearly within the range of viable possibilities, some caution should be taken in assessing these claims. For example, whereas mirror neurons have been directly recorded in primates, their presence can only be inferred from fMRI and PET studies in humans. It is likely that mirror neurons do exist in humans, but it is important to note that direct evidence of this is currently lacking (Gernsbacher, Stevenson, & Schweigert, 2007).

The final root of embodiment to be considered here is the metaphor-based approach to cognitive linguistics developed by Lakoff and Johnson (1980, 1999). Lakoff and Johnson argue that our understanding of many abstract concepts are grounded in physical experience through a process of metaphor. For example, it is suggested that "anger" is understood through a metaphor to heated fluid in a container. This metaphor is evidenced by the ubiquity of phrases such as "He blew his top" and "My emotions boiled over," which relate anger and its consequences to the behavior of heated fluid in a container. Similarly, it is suggested that we understand abstract concepts such as social harm through metaphors to physical harm (e.g., "He stabbed me in the back"; "That was a slap in the face"). In demonstrating the pervasiveness of metaphorical understanding of concepts (see Lakoff & Johnson's, 1980, 1999, extensive discussions), Lakoff and Johnson lend support to the notion that concrete experiences in the world (particularly, but not exclusively, those involving our own bodies) provide a central foundation for our ability to understand the world.

The embodied approach to language comprehension that we explore in the next section of this chapter has been shaped by a diverse set of theoretical proposals from psychology, philosophy, and linguistics. The brief overview provided here does not do justice to any of the particular approaches, nor to the ways that they have directly or indirectly affected current thinking in embodied cognition. Limited as it may be, we hope that this overview helps to demonstrate that, whereas "embodiment" has a somewhat short history as a buzzword in cognitive psychology and cognitive science, the ideas at the core of this approach have a long tradition within the field.

THE EMBODIED APPROACH
TO LANGUAGE COMPREHENSION

The embodied approach to language comprehension holds that language is understood through sensorimotor simulations of the objects, actions, and events being described. The term "simulation" is borrowed from Barsalou (1999). It refers to the notion that one can think about things that are not present by reinstating the patterns of neural activity that occur when the real objects, actions, or events are witnessed. For example, a certain pattern of neural activity occurs when we see a coffee mug, and we can think about coffee mugs at a later point in time by reinstating this pattern of activity. Following the indexical hypothesis developed by Glenberg and colleagues (e.g., Glenberg & Robertson, 1999, 2000; Kaschak & Glenberg, 2000), we suggest that there are three overlapping stages of language comprehension. First, words and phrases in the linguistic input retrieve perceptual and motor information from memory. Second, affordances (i.e., possibilities for interaction) are derived from the perceptual information that is retrieved. Third, the perceptual information (and accompanying affordances) and motor traces are integrated into a coherent simulation of the situation that is described.

To illustrate the embodied approach to language comprehension, consider the following example:

1. The chef pulled an apple pie from the oven.

The noun phrases in the sentence (the chef, the apple pie, and the oven) trigger the retrieval of perceptual information about their referents. For example, one would simulate a human adult for the chef; would simulate the shape, texture, smell, and weight of the pie; and would simulate the appearance and heat of the inside of the oven. The verb (*pulled*) triggers the retrieval of particular motor plans. Comprehending the entire sentence is accomplished by combining the perceptual and motor information into a simulation of the event: You simulate the experience of reaching into the oven to lift out the pie. Note that a simulation can be as skeletal or detailed as required based on the reader's goal. If the reader is interested in achieving only a shallow level of understanding, the simulation may involve only basic information about the pie (i.e., its shape and weight) and the action needed to remove it from the oven. On the other hand, if the comprehender is interested in achieving a more detailed understanding of the situation, the simulation can include additional details (such as the smell of the pie or the heat of the oven). Indeed, one of the strengths of positing that sensorimotor representations underlie language comprehension is that the same information can be used to derive several levels of detail as needed (see Zwaan & Kaschak, 2008, for a discussion). Thus, the same visual percept of the pie can trigger the activation of particular affordances for action in the context of removing it from an oven and a different set of affordances in the context of needing something to throw at someone (see Glenberg & Robertson, 2000; Kaschak & Glenberg, 2000, for demonstrations).

The embodied approach to language comprehension is similar in some regards to the constraint-satisfaction approach to comprehension (e.g., MacDonald, Pearlmutter, & Seidenberg, 1994; McRae, Spivey-Knowlton, & Tanenhaus, 1998). The constraint-based account of sentence comprehension suggests that comprehenders consider multiple sources of probabilistic information (e.g., the likelihood of particular words occurring in particular sentence structures) in order to generate the most likely interpretation of the current sentence. This probabilistic information is considered online as the incoming sentence unfolds. Consider sentence 2:

2. The horse raced past the barn fell.

After encountering, "The horse raced...," the most likely interpretation of the sentence is that "raced" is the main verb of the sentence, indicating the action taken by the horse. This interpretation remains likely until the comprehender encounters the verb "fell" at the end of the sentence. At this point, the comprehender must revise his or her understanding of the sentence to the most likely interpretation given the new evidence available in the linguistic input. In this case, the most likely revised interpretation is that "The horse fell" is the main clause of the sentence and "raced past the barn" is a reduced relative clause modifying "the horse." We believe that a similar kind of online consideration of multiple sources of information characterizes the embodied approach to language comprehension. Based on one's experiences with the world, the entities that are mentioned at the beginning of the sentence will trigger the retrieval of particular perceptual or motor information. This information will constrain the sensorimotor information that is retrieved to simulate later entities in the sentence and will also dispose the comprehender to simulate a certain likely event sequence. For instance, we would simulate the removal of a pie from the oven in terms of the common occurrence (for most of us) of removing something from a household oven. On the other hand, a baker may have a different simulation of this event based on his or her more specific experiences with other kinds of ovens and other kinds of baking scenarios.

The embodied and constraint-based approaches to sentence comprehension both view sentence processing as a dynamically unfolding event in which multiple levels of probabilistic information that have been derived from experience shape the ultimate understanding at which the comprehender arrives. There is a clear difference in the informational currency in which each approach trades, with the constraint-based approach focusing on a more linguistic level of information (e.g., word co-occurrence frequencies and structural frequencies) and the embodied approach focusing more on the phenomenal elements of experience (e.g., the perceptual and motor components of removing a pie from an oven). Given the similarities that are present, there is the intriguing possibility that the two approaches may ultimately be subsumed under a larger common framework. It is not clear at this point that such a unification will work, but exploring this idea may be a useful way to develop and further constrain both of these theoretical approaches.

The embodied approach to language comprehension is less than a decade old, but there is already a growing body of literature supporting the notion that the understanding of language is grounded in our bodies' systems of perception and action planning. This evidence comes from both behavioral studies (Glenberg & Kaschak, 2002; Kaschak et al., 2005; Zwaan & Taylor, 2006; Richardson, Spivey, Barsalou, & McRae, 2003) and research using neuroimaging techniques (e.g., Kan, Barsalou, Solomon, Minor, & Thompson-Schill, 2003; Pulvermuller, 1999). We now present an overview of this evidence.

Perceptual Effects

The embodied approach to language comprehension proposes that language comprehension involves the use of systems of perception and action planning to simulate the events that are being described. This hypothesis leads to several straightforward predictions. First, the comprehension of language (particularly language for which perceptual details are important) should involve the activation of perceptual representations. Second, processing perceptual information should affect the comprehension of language. Finally, the comprehension of language should affect the operation of the perceptual system. There is evidence for all three predictions.

Some of the earliest studies in the perceptual domain were reported by Zwaan and colleagues (Stanfield & Zwaan, 2001; Zwaan, Stanfield, & Yaxley, 2002). The experiments were a variant of the sentence–picture verification task. Participants were asked to read sentences of the following sort:

3. The eagle is in the sky.
4. The eagle is in the nest.

The important distinction between these sentences is that the perceptual details of the eagle are different in each scenario. In sentence 3, the eagle will have its wings spread out, but in sentence 4 the eagle will have its wings folded in by the side of its body. After reading each sentence, participants were shown a picture of the object (in this case, the eagle) that was described in the sentence. In some cases, the picture matched the perceptual details of the scenario described by the sentence. For instance, sentence 3 could be followed by a picture of an eagle with outstretched wings. In other cases, the picture mismatched the details of the sentence. After sentence 3, this would be a picture in which the eagle's wings were folded in. Zwaan and colleagues show that participants are faster to respond to the picture when the perceptual details match the content of the sentence than when they do not match. Note that the relevant information to produce this effect (i.e., the position of the eagle's wings) is never explicitly mentioned in the sentence. Thus, the idea is that comprehenders are simulating the situation described in the sentence, and certain perceptual details are represented as a part of running that simulation (see Zwaan, Madden, Yaxley, & Aveyard, 2004, for a demonstration of this sort involving the presentation of dynamic stimuli rather than static pictures after the end of the sentence).

Another early set of studies on the relationship between perception and language comprehension is reported by Richardson et al. (2003), who were interested in exploring the representation of particular kinds of verbs. Following theoretical proposals from cognitive linguistics (e.g., Lakoff & Johnson's, 1980, discussion of orientational metaphors), they proposed that verbs are represented in part via spatial schemas. Verbs such as "lift," whose action typically occurs in an up–down manner, are represented as a vertically oriented schema. Verbs such as "push," whose action typically occurs in a toward–away plane, are represented as a horizontally oriented schema. Richardson et al. (2003) support the idea that visuospatial schemas underlie the representation of certain kinds of verbs by showing that the processing of sentences containing those verbs affects one's ability to perceive shapes presented on a computer screen. Specifically, when a verb involving an up–down schema is processed, participants show a decreased ability to perceive shapes presented at the top and bottom of the computer screen (i.e., dots presented in the location of the visual schema). When a verb involving a horizontally oriented schema is processed, participants show a decreased ability to perceive shapes on the left and right ends of the screen. Richardson et al. (2003; cf. Bergen, Lindsay, Matlock, & Narayanan, 2007) demonstrate that the processing of verbs can affect visual perception. Meteyard, Bahrami, and Vigliocco (2007) provide further evidence for the claim that language processing can affect visual perception. Participants were asked to engage in a task in which they detected motion in a visually presented stimulus. While performing this task, the participants heard motion words that were irrelevant to their main task. The motion words affected participants' ability to detect motion. When the words indicated motion in a direction incongruent with the direction of the visually presented motion, participants' perceptual sensitivity to that motion was impaired.

Kaschak and colleagues (2005, 2006) report a separate line of studies exploring the interaction between perception and language processing. Kaschak et al. (2005) asked participants to process sentences describing motion in a particular direction:

5. The car approached you. [Toward]
6. The squirrel ran away from you. [Away]

7. The confetti fell on the parade. [Down]
8. The rocket blasted off. [Up]

Participants listened to these sentences and made sensibility (or gram-maticality) judgments on them. While doing so, the participants viewed percepts depicting motion toward them, away from them, upward, or downward. During the processing of any given sentence, the percept moved either in the same direction as the motion described in the sentence (toward sentence, toward percept) or in the opposite direction as the motion described in the sentence (toward sentence, away percept). The results of this study demonstrate that the processing of a visual motion percept interferes with the processing of sentences describing motion in the same direction. That is, participants have more difficulty processing "toward" sentences when viewing a toward percept than when viewing an away percept.

The studies reviewed to this point demonstrate a relatively consistent pattern of results. When participants process sentences and visual percepts in succession, congruency effects occur: Participants are faster to respond when the information described by the sentence matches that presented in the visual percept. When participants are asked to process sentences and percepts at the same time, interference occurs: Participants are faster to respond when the content of the sentence mismatches the content of the percept, and their perceptual acuity is reduced when the perceptual stimuli that are presented are congruent with the content of the language with respect to content or spatial location. Although this is a reasonably coherent story, it is not the whole story. Kaschak et al. (2006) report one of the few studies of the perception–language interaction that does not involve visually presented percepts and show that the presence of congruence or interference effects may be affected by the perceptual modality through which the linguistic and perceptual stimuli are presented.

Kaschak et al. (2006) presented participants with sentences similar to sentences 5 to 8. Participants listened to (or read) these sentences while also listening to auditory motion stimuli. As in Kaschak et al. (2005), the auditory stimuli depicted motion toward participants, away from participants, upward, and downward. When the participants listened to the critical sentences, a congruence effect was observed: Participants were faster to comprehend sentences when the direction of motion described in the sentence matched the direction depicted by the auditory stimulus. However, when participants read the critical sentences, the opposite effect emerged: Participants were slower to comprehend sentences when the direction of motion described by the sentence matched the direction of motion depicted by the motion stimulus. Kaschak et al. (2006) interpreted these results in the context of recent explorations of perceptual distractor effects (e.g., Lavie, 2005).

Lavie (2005) reviewed a collection of studies showing that the effects of distractor stimuli on perceptual task performance depends on the difficulty of the perceptual task and whether the distractor is presented in the same perceptual modality as the stimuli for the primary task. When the perceptual task is easy, distractor stimuli always affect task performance. When the perceptual task is difficult, distractor stimuli presented in the same modality do not affect task performance, but stimuli presented in a different modality do. Lavie (2005) argued that such effects show that attentional capacity is limited within a particular perceptual modality but not across modalities. This literature provides a straightforward explanation of the data reported by Kaschak et al. (2006). Sentence processing is a complex, attention-demanding task. Thus, when the participant is listening to (and making judgments on) sentences, he or she may not have the attentional capacity needed to also process the auditory motion stimulus. In this case, it is as though the participant is listening to the motion stimulus and then (sequentially) hearing the sentence (i.e., as though the sentence and stimulus are presented sequentially rather than simultaneously). As seen previously, this is the case when one observes congruence effects. When the participant is reading the sentence, he or she is consuming visual attention but not auditory attention. Similarly, when the participant is listening to the sentence, he or she is consuming auditory, but not visual, attention (as in Kaschak et al., 2005). In both cases, the participant is able to process the linguistic stimuli and the perceptual stimuli at the same time. As noted previously, this is the case when one observes faster processing when the sentence and percept depict mismatching situations.

The behavioral studies reviewed previously show that language comprehension involves the activation of perceptual information. This information comes in the form of abstract visual schemas (e.g., Richardson et al., 2003), coding of the shape (Stanfield & Zwaan, 2001), orientation (Zwaan et al., 2002), direction of motion (Zwaan et al., 2004; Kaschak et al., 2005, 2006), and color and visual texture (e.g., Connell, 2007; Yaxley & Zwaan, 2007) of the objects and situations that are described. The studies also show that the interaction of language and perception is bidirectional: Language processing affects perception, and perceptual processing affects language comprehension. These outcomes are supported by the results of neuroimaging studies showing that the processing of perceptually relevant words (such as color adjectives) activates areas of the brain known to be involved in perceptual processing (e.g., Pulvermuller, 1999). Thus, the overall picture is consistent with the embodied approach to language comprehension: The comprehension of at least some kinds of language is grounded in our perceptual systems.

Motor Effects

As in the case of the perceptual modalities, the embodied approach to language comprehension proposes that there should be an interaction between language processing and motor planning. The main predictions are the same as in the case of perception: Language comprehension should involve the activation of motor representations, the processing of language should affect the operation of the motor planning system, and the planning of action should affect the language processing system. There is support for each of these predictions.

A number of studies have focused on the word level of processing. The main question of interest in these studies concerns the kinds of information that are activated when a word is processed. In one study, Glover, Rosenbaum, Graham, and Dixon (2004) asked participants to reach out and grasp an object. The reach for a particular object will have particular kinematic properties. For example, the aperture of the hand as it approaches the object will be different depending on the size of the object. While participants were performing their reaches, they also saw names of objects printed on the object that they were to grasp (e.g., a grape is a small object, but an apple is a larger object). The results show that the processing of the word affects the characteristics of the grasp that is being undertaken. If the named object is small, the hand aperture on the executed action is smaller than would be expected based on the actual object that is being acted on. If the named object is large, the opposite effect occurs. It appears that processing the name of an object activates motor information relevant to acting on that object. Boulenger, Roy, and Paulignan (2006) report a similar result: The processing of an action verb during the execution of an action affects one's ability to produce that action.

Bub et al. (2008) take a more detailed look at the motor representations that are active during language processing. Bub et al. (2008) distinguish between volumetric gestures (e.g., the motor plan needed to simply grasp an object) and functional gestures (e.g., the motor plan needed to use an object for its intended use). As one illustration, the volumetric gesture for a calculator would be an open-handed grasp, and the functional gesture for that same object would be a single-finger poke (i.e., the way you would use a finger to press the individual keys of the calculator). Bub et al. (2008) trained participants on a set of gestures that corresponded to the functional and volumetric gestures related to a critical set of objects (e.g., calculator, stapler). After this training, participants were shown pictures of the objects (e.g., a stapler) and then executed a gesture based on some feature of the object (e.g., its color). For instance, participants were told to execute the "poke" gesture when they saw a green object. The gesture executed could thus be the functional gesture for the pictured object, the volumetric gesture for the pictured object, or irrelevant for the use of the pictured object. Participants were faster to execute the action when it was the functional or volumetric gesture for the pictured object than when it was irrelevant to the object. In a subsequent experiment, Bub et al. (2008) show that the same effect arises when the name of the object (rather than the picture) is presented on the screen. Thus, the processing of a word seems to evoke the motor representations needed to act on that object. Interestingly, whereas activation of the functional gestures appears to arise almost immediately upon the processing of the word, activation of the volumetric gestures appears to arise somewhat later in processing, if at all (see Masson, Bub, & Newton-Taylor, 2008). This suggests that action-relevant information is more readily accessed in the context of language processing.

The interaction between motor planning and language processing has also been explored on the sentence level of processing. Glenberg and Kaschak (2002) report a finding called the action-sentence compatibility effect (ACE). Participants were asked to read sentences that describe action toward the body or action away from the body:

 9. Open the drawer. [Toward]
10. Close the drawer. [Away]
11. Mike gave you a pen. [Toward]
12. You gave Mike a pen. [Away]

Participants were also asked to make sensibility judgments on the sentences. When participants wished to indicate that the sentence made sense, half of the time they were asked to generate a motor response toward their body and half of the time they were asked to generate a motor response away from their body. Thus, the motor response required to respond to the sentence either matched or mismatched the direction of the motor act described in the sentence. Glenberg and

Kaschak (2002) demonstrated that participants were faster to respond when the direction of their motor response matched the direction of the action described in the sentence. Thus, the comprehension of sentences about action affects one's ability to plan and execute action in the world.

An interesting outcome in Glenberg and Kaschak's (2002) study is that the motor compatibility effect was observed not only for sentences describing concrete actions (such as sentences 9–12) but also for sentences describing abstract kinds of action (e.g., "Jenni sang you a song"). Glenberg and Kaschak (see also Kaschak & Glenberg, 2000; Glenberg, Sato, Cattaneo, et al., 2008) suggest that one explanation for this effect is that particular motor patterns may be related to particular kinds of grammatical constructions. The abstract sentences in Glenberg and Kaschak (2002) use the dative constructions in English, which is canonically associated with descriptions of transfer acts (Goldberg, 1995). These constructions are acquired in the context of real transfer events (e.g., being asked to give something to your parents), and thus the construction and related verbs (e.g., "give" is a verb that frequently occurs in dative forms) may become associated with particular motor acts, such as moving one's arm away from one's body. Once this relationship among verbs, sentence constructions, and motor acts are learned for concrete actions, this understanding can be the grounding through which abstract actions (such as abstract kinds of transfer) can be understood. This proposal is similar to Lakoff and Johnson's (1980) claims about the understanding of abstractions through metaphorical extension of concrete situations.

A number of subsequent studies have attempted to take a finer look at the temporal and linguistic dynamics of the ACE. Borreggine and Kaschak (2006) replicated the Glenberg and Kaschak (2002) study but varied the time point at which participants were told what the nature of their motor response would be. These studies show that the ACE arises only when participants know which direction their motor response will go while they are processing the sentence; when their knowledge of the direction of action is delayed until after the end of the sentence, participants show no hint of the ACE.

Zwaan and Taylor (2006) report the first online studies of the ACE. Participants were asked to read sentences describing manual rotation: For example,

13. While listening to his stereo, Larry turned down the volume.

Participants read these sentences phrase by phrase and moved from phrase to phrase by rotating a knob in a clockwise or counterclockwise direction. The direction in which the knob was rotated was either consistent or inconsistent with the act of manual rotation described in the sentence. Zwaan and Taylor (2006) show the standard ACE (i.e., faster rotation when the direction of rotation matches the direction of the action in the sentence) but demonstrate that this effect only arises on the verb ("turned down"). Thus, the motor information is activated as soon as it is relevant to the comprehension of the sentence, which in this case is as soon as the verb reveals the nature of the action that needs to be simulated. It is interesting to note that the motor compatibility effect dissipates quickly: by the next word ("volume"), all signs of the effect are gone.

In a follow-up study, Taylor and Zwaan (2008) replicated the basic manual rotation paradigm, but altered the sentences such that the last word of the sentence was an adverb that directed the comprehender's attention either to the nature of the act being described ("turned down the volume *quickly*") or the nature of the actor ("turned down the volume *obediently*"). When the adverb described the action itself, the motor compatibility effect reemerged while processing the adverb; when the adverb described the actor, the motor compatibility effect did not reemerge. This suggests the possibility that motor compatibility effects emerge during sentence processing whenever the incoming lexical items focus the comprehender's attention on the motor act itself (see also Taylor & Zwaan, 2008), whether that be on the verb of the sentence or on some other lexical item. Studies from our own lab (e.g., Kaschak & Borreggine, 2008; Jones & Kaschak, 2008) confirm this basic intuition, showing that motor compatibility effects on sentences such as those used by Glenberg and Kaschak (2002) arise not on the verb of the sentence but on the next word. The idea is that the verb occurs so early in these sentences that the participant does not yet have enough information to know exactly what the described action will be like (contrast this to Zwaan and Taylor's sentences, when the verb appeared at the end of the sentences). Thus, the motor effect is delayed until the next word, which serves to clarify the nature of the action that is being described in the sentence.

The interpretation of these online motor compatibility effects bears some similarity to the theoretical approach that has emerged around constraint-based approaches to sentence comprehension. Numerous studies using the visual world paradigm show that comprehenders activate information relevant to the comprehension of sentences (e.g., Chambers, Tanenhaus, & Magnuson, 2004) and the processing of words (e.g., Dahan & Tanenhaus, 2005) as early as possible during online comprehension. The motor compatibility effects also seem to arise as early as possible during sentence processing, namely at the point at which the sentence has revealed enough information for the participant to know enough details about the action being described to construct a simulation.

The behavioral studies described previously are complemented by numerous reports from neuroscience (e.g., Isenberg et al., 1999; Kan et al., 2003; Martin & Chao, 2001; Pulvermuller, 1999). The processing of motor verbs and nouns describing tools activates motor cortex (e.g., Pulvermuller, 1999, 2005). This motor activation is relatively fine grained. Hauk, Johnsrude, and Pulvermuller (2004) report that verbs such as "kick," "pick," and "lick" activate different areas of motor cortex, particularly those areas associated with the legs, hands, and mouth, respectively. Virtually all of these studies have shown that language processing affects motor processing. Glenberg and colleagues have shown that the opposite is true: Motor processing can affect language comprehension. For example, Glenberg, Sato, and Cattaneo (2008) demonstrate that fatiguing the motor system with respect to performing a given action (e.g., actions moving away from the body) impairs the comprehension of sentences describing actions that have the same direction of action.

In short, the available evidence shows that the comprehension of language involves the activation of motor information. Language comprehension affects our ability to plan and execute actions, and the planning and execution of actions affects language comprehension. These data provide strong support for an embodied approach to language comprehension.

A THEORY OF EMBODIED
LANGUAGE COMPREHENSION?

Thus far, we have considered the growing body of evidence that supports the primary claims of the embodied approach to language comprehension: Language comprehension should involve the use of sensorimotor representations, sensorimotor processing should affect language comprehension, and language comprehension should affect sensorimotor processes. Interactions between sensorimotor systems and language processing have been observed in cases of both visual (and auditory) perception and motor planning and more recently have been observed in the case of the processing of emotions (Havas, Glenberg, & Rinck, 2007). We have said comparatively little about the overarching embodied theory of language comprehension, particularly with regard to the fine details of the processing mechanisms that would support such comprehension. This lapse points to a present weakness of the embodied approach, namely a lack of specificity in delimiting the mechanisms that give rise to the effects reported previously. Next, we discuss some reasons why theoretical developments of this sort are currently lacking and speculate on some directions in which the embodied theory might develop.

Constructing a detailed embodied account of language comprehension requires a consideration of several levels of processing. First, one needs to consider the mechanics of language processing itself, including the mechanisms through which speech or written text is decoded and fed into higher level comprehension processes. Second, one needs to consider the memory retrieval mechanisms that are needed to draw out the perceptual and motoric information relevant for the simulation of the content of the current sentence. Third, one needs to consider the workings of the perceptual or motor planning system that is being tapped in the particular experiment that is being conducted. Understanding the ACE, for example, requires an understanding of the events that occur as an action is planned and then executed (absent language processing) and an understanding of how and when the language processing system interfaces with the motor planning process to develop a simulation. Finally, one needs to consider how perception, action, and language comprehension work together in real time to allow the understanding of language to occur.

Research on language comprehension, perception, and motor planning can lay the groundwork for assessing each of the levels of theorizing described in the preceding paragraph. There are large numbers of studies devoted to speech perception, syntactic parsing, motor planning, and so on. It is in combining these different domains (and different levels of theorizing) that the problems arise. The problems come both in extending our thinking about language comprehension toward theoretical proposals in perception and action planning and in extending what is known about perception and action planning to language comprehension. Hommel, Musseler, Aschersleben, and Prinz's (2001) theory of event coding (TEC) provides a precise account of the temporal dynamics of perception and action planning, but this account is built around the results of experiments in which the presentation of stimuli and the execution of motor responses is fairly well circumscribed. It is not clear how this account can be extended to a somewhat less circumscribed kind of task such as language comprehension (but see Borreggine & Kaschak, 2006, for a discussion). At the same time, so little is known about the process of constructing simulations during language comprehension that it is difficult to know where to begin in adopting a theory of perception or action planning.

Although the challenges involved in developing an embodied theory of language comprehension that is similar in computational or mechanistic rigor to what is seen in other areas of language comprehension research are large, we nonetheless believe that this is a tractable research problem. One important step to developing a theory of this sort will be to move beyond the kinds of paradigms that are currently used in most "embodied" studies of language comprehension. These studies typically involve the use of gross measures of processing (e.g., whole sentence reading times, word reading times, judgment times) that conflate several layers of processing and decision making (see Meteyard et al., 2007, for a discussion of this issue). If we are to understand how and when sensorimotor information is used to ground language comprehension, we need to develop experimental paradigms that are more sensitive to the layers of processing (e.g., early perceptual processes as opposed to later occurring strategic decision-making effects) that may be tapped in a given task. Meteyard et al. (2007) provide an example of one such paradigm. Along the same lines, it may be necessary to develop detailed task analyses for the experimental paradigms that are used in an effort to understand how different sorts of processing (e.g., motor processing and language processing) interact. Borreggine and Kaschak (2006; Kaschak & Borreggine, 2008) attempt such an analysis with their discussion of how TEC might explain the data from studies of motor compatibility effects. This description is far from a broad account of the role of motor processes in language comprehension, but it indicates how analysis of particular experiments can help bridge the gap between theorizing in the domains of study relevant to the embodied approach to language comprehension.

What will the embodied theory of language comprehension that emerges from this research look like? It is tempting to think that the theory will develop along the lines of current constraint-based approaches to language comprehension. As discussed throughout this chapter, there are many parallels between the two approaches, and it is possible that a common framework may ultimately encompass both areas of research and theorizing. Whereas we believe that the embodied theory that develops will have many of the characteristics of a constraint-based approach to language comprehension, it is our sense that theorizing on the embodied approach will become more strongly identified with theories of perception and motor planning than with current theories of language comprehension. As one example of this, current work on motor planning emphasizes the role of prediction in planning and executing action (e.g., Wolpert's hierarchical modular selection and identification for control, or H-MOSAIC, model of motor control; Wolpert, Doya, & Kawato, 2003). Similar ideas are beginning to be applied to thinking about language production and comprehension (e.g., Pickering & Garrod, 2007; see Ferreira, 2003, and Townsend & Bever, 2001, for a discussion of similar design features in perceptual processing and language processing). How much of language comprehension will ultimately be explained by theories of perception and action planning remains to be seen. We suspect that most, if not all, of the work done by current theories of language processing will ultimately be subsumed by theories of perception and action planning.

THE EMBODIED APPROACH
AND TRANSLATIONAL RESEARCH

As a science, psychology is well positioned to provide a framework for both basic research and applications of this basic research to a range of real-world problems. Within the past decade, the field has witnessed a growing interest in what is termed "translational research" (Ericsson & Williams, 2007), or research that translates principles of basic research to applied settings. One reason for this interest in translational research may be a function of funding priorities: Taxpayers clearly have an interest in seeing that the science they support leads to some practical outcomes. A second reason for the interest in translational research is the belief that the application of basic research to applied settings provides an excellent mechanism for testing the basic theories. As such, it is fair to ask whether the contributions of the embodied approach to language comprehension will translate to applied settings.

There has not been a lot of translational research under the banner of embodied cognition, but some efforts have been made. Within the domain of language comprehension, Glenberg, Gutierrez, Levin, Japuntich, and Kaschak (2004) present an intervention designed to raise the reading comprehension performance of young children (kindergarten and first- and second-grade students). On the basis of the idea that language comprehension involves the simulation of the actions described in the linguistic input, Glenberg et al. (2004) asked students to either act out or imagine acting out the actions described in a set of short stories. The acting (or imagined acting) was done based on a set of props adapted for use with the stories. Glenberg et al. (2004) demonstrate that both real action and imagined action improve young children's ability to remember what they read and to draw inferences from what they read. Follow-up studies have shown that action has beneficial effects in other reading situations and in other educational settings (such as science education; Glenberg et al., 2007). The success of Glenberg and colleagues' translational projects suggests that the embodied approach to language comprehension may hold promise for designing interventions aimed at improving educational practice. Glenberg and Robertson's (1999) work further suggests that the design of instructions and instructional materials is another area in which the embodied approach can be fruitfully applied.

More broadly, the central concepts of embodied cognition are finding their way into a discussion of issues relevant to clinical psychology (e.g., Lindeman & Abramson, 2008) and social psychology (e.g., Neidenthal, Barsalou, Winkielman, Krauth-Gruber, & Ric, 2005; Schubert, 2004, 2005; Maner, Kaschak, & Jones, in press). The basic premise of this work is that the operation of the motor system (e.g., the preparation of approach and avoidance actions) can provide windows through which the bodily nature or grounding of clinically relevant or social issues can be understood. As these ideas continue to develop, it is likely that embodied constructs will play a role in the creation of assessments and interventions that will be of practical value.

CONCLUSION

This chapter has presented an overview of the embodied approach to language comprehension, which proposes that the comprehension of language is tantamount to the construction of sensorimotor simulations of the objects, actions, and events that are described in the linguistic input. Whereas theorizing in this area is still in its early stages, empirical support for this approach is growing. By grounding the comprehension of language in our bodies' systems of perception and action planning, we believe that the embodied approach to comprehension allows us to answer the most basic questions about language: What is meaning? How do we understand? How does language relate to the rest of the cognitive system? The answers to these questions await further explorations of the sort described here.

REFERENCES

Barsalou, L. W. (1999). Perceptual symbol systems. *Behavioral and Brain Sciences, 22,* 577–660.

Bergen, B. K., Lindsay, S., Matlock, T., & Narayanan, S. (2007). Spatial and linguistic aspects of visual imagery in sentence comprehension. *Cognitive Science, 31,* 733–764,

Biederman, I. (1985). Recognition by components: A theory of human image understanding. *Psychological Review, 94,* 115–147.

Borreggine, K. L., & Kaschak, M. P. (2006). The action-sentence compatibility effect: It's all in the timing. *Cognitive Science, 30,* 1097–1112.

Boulenger, V., Roy, A. C., & Paulignan, Y. (2006). Cross-talk between language processes and overt motor behavior in the first 200 msec of processing. *Journal of Cognitive Neuroscience, 18,* 1607–1615.

Bub, D. N., Masson, M. E. J., & Cree, G. S. (2008). Evocation of functional and volumetric gestural knowledge by objects and words. *Cognition, 106,* 27–58.

Chambers, C. G., Tanenhaus, M. K., & Magnuson, J. S. (2004). Actions and affordances in syntactic ambiguity resolution. *Journal of Experimental Psychology: Learning, Memory, and Cognition, 30,* 687–696.

Connell, L. (2007). Representing object color in language comprehension. *Cognition, 102,* 476–485.

Crowder, R. G. (1993). Systems and principles in memory theory: Another critique of pure memory. In A. F. Collins, S. E. Gathercole, M. A. Conway & P. E. Morris (Eds.), *Theories of memory.* Hillsdale, NJ: Erlbaum.

Dahan, D., & Tanenhaus, M. K. (2005). Looking at the rope when looking for the snake: Conceptually mediated eye movements during spoken-word recognition. *Psychonomic Bulletin and Review, 12,* 453–459.

Di Pellegrino, G., Fadiga, L., Fogassi, L., Gallese, V., & Rizzolatti, G. (1992). Understanding motor events: A neurophysiological study. *Experimental Brain Research, 91,* 176–180.

Ericsson, K. A., & Williams, A. M. (2007). Capturing naturally occurring superior performance in the laboratory: Translational research on expert performance. *Journal of Experimental Psychology: Applied, 13,* 115–122.

Ferreira, F. (2003). The misinterpretation of noncanonical sentences. *Cognitive Psychology, 47,* 164–203.

Gernsbacher, M. A., Stevenson, J. L., & Schweigert, E. K. (2007, November). *Mirror neurons in humans?* Paper presented at the 48th Annual Meeting of the Psychonomic Society, Long Beach CA.

Gibson, J. J. (1979). *The ecological approach to visual perception.* New York: Houghton Mifflin.

Glenberg, A. M. (1997). What memory is for. *Behavioral and Brain Sciences, 20,* 1–19.

Glenberg, A. M., Gutierrez, T., Levin, J. R., Japuntich, S., & Kaschak, M. P. (2004). Activity and imagined activity can enhance young children's reading comprehension. *Journal of Educational Psychology, 96*, 424–436.

Glenberg, A. M., Jaworski, B. E., & Rischal, M. (2007). What brains are for: Action, meaning, and language comprehension. In D. S. McNamara (Ed.), *Reading comprehension strategies: Theories, interventions, and technologies.* New York: Routledge.

Glenberg, A. M., & Kaschak, M. P. (2002). Grounding language in action. *Psychonomic Bulletin and Review, 9*, 558–565.

Glenberg, A. M., & Robertson, D. A. (1999). Indexical understanding of instructions. *Discourse Processes, 28*, 1–26.

Glenberg, A. M., & Robertson, D. A. (2000). Symbol grounding and meaning: A comparison of high-dimensional and embodied theories of meaning. *Journal of Memory and Language, 43*, 379–401.

Glenberg, A. M., Sato, M., & Cattaneo, L. (2008). Use-induced motor plasticity affects the processing of abstract and concrete language. *Current Biology, 18*, 1290–1291.

Glenberg, A. M., Sato, M., Cattaneo, L., Riggio, L., Palumbo, D., & Buccino, G. (2008). Processing abstract language modulates motor system activity. *Quarterly Journal of Experimental Psychology, 61*, 905–919.

Glover, S., Rosenbaum, D. A., Graham, J., & Dixon, P. (2004). Grasping the meaning of words. *Experimental Brain Research, 154*, 103–108.

Goldberg, A. E. (1995). *Constructions: A construction grammar approach to argument structure.* Chicago: University of Chicago Press.

Harnad, S. (1990). The symbol grounding problem. *Physica D, 42*, 335–346.

Hauk, O., Johnsrude, I., & Pulvermuller, F. (2004). Somatotopic representation of actions words in human motor and premotor cortex. *Neuron, 41*, 301–307.

Havas, D. A., Glenberg, A. M., & Rinck, N. (2007). Emotion simulation during language comprehension . *Psychonomic Bulletin and Review, 14*, 436–441.

Hommel, B., Musseler, J., Aschersleben, G., & Prinz, W. (2001). The theory of event coding (TEC): A framework for perception and action planning. *Behavioral and Brain Sciences, 24*, 849–937.

Isenberg, N., Silbersweig, D., Engelien, A., Emmerich, K., Malavade, K., Benti, B., et al. (1999). Linguistic threat activates the human amygdala. *Proceedings of the National Academy of Sciences, 96*, 10456–10459.

Jones, J. L., & Kaschak, M. P. (2008). *More on the temporal dynamics of the action–sentence compatibility effect.* Manuscript in preparation.

Kan, I. P., Barsalou, L. W., Solomon, K. O., Minor, J. K., & Thompson-Schill, S. L. (2003). Role of mental imagery in a property verification task: fMRI evidence for perceptual representation of conceptual knowledge. *Cognitive Neuropsychology, 20*, 525–540.

Kaschak, M. P., & Borreggine, K. L. (2008). Temporal dynamics of the action–sentence compatibility effect. *Quarterly Journal of Experimental Psychology, 61*, 883–895.

Kaschak, M. P., & Glenberg, A. M. (2000). Constructing meaning: The role of affordances and grammatical constructions in language comprehension. *Journal of Memory and Language, 43*, 508–529.

Kaschak, M. P., Madden, C. J., Therriault, D. J., Yaxley, R. H., Aveyard, M., Blanchard, A. A., et al. (2005). Perception of motion affects language processing. *Cognition, 94,* B79–B89.

Kaschak, M. P., Zwaan, R. A., Aveyard, M. ,& Yaxley, R. H. (2006). Perception of auditory motion affects language processing. *Cognitive Science, 30,* 733–744.

Keysers, C., & Perrett, D. I. (2004). Demystifying social cognition: A Hebbian perspective. *Trends in Cognitive Sciences, 8,* 501–507.

Kolers, P. A., & Roediger, H. L. (1984). Procedures of mind. *Journal of Verbal Learning and Verbal Behavior, 23,* 425–449.

Koski, L., Wohlschlager, A., Bekkering, H., Woods, R. P., Dubeau, M. C., Mazziotta, J. C., et al. (2002). Modulation of motor and premotor activity during imitation of target-directed actions. *Cerebral Cortex, 12,* 847–855.

Lakoff, G., & Johnson, M. (1980). *Metaphors we live by.* Chicago: University of Chicago Press.

Lakoff, G., & Johnson, M. (1999). *Philosophy in the flesh.* New York: Basic Books.

Lavie, N. (2005). Distracted and confused? Selective attention under load. *Trends in Cognitive Sciences, 9,* 75–82.

Lindeman, L. M., & Abramson, L. Y. (2008). The mental simulation of motor incapacity in depression. *Journal of Cognitive Psychotherapy, 22,* 228–249.

MacDonald, M. C., Pearlmutter, N. J., & Seidenberg, M. S. (1994). Lexical nature of syntactic ambiguity resolution. *Psychological Review, 101,* 676–703.

Maner, J. K., Kaschak, M. P., & Jones, J. L. (in press). Social power and the advent of action. *Social Cognition.*

Martin, A., & Chao, L. L. (2001). Semantic memory and the brain: Structure and process. *Current Opinion in Neurobiology, 11,* 194–201.

Masson, M. E. J., Bub, D. N., & Newton-Taylor, M. (2008). Language-based access to gestural components of conceptual knowledge. *Quarterly Journal of Experimental Psychology, 71,* 869–882.

McRae, K., Spivey-Knowlton, M. J., & Tanenhaus, M. K. (1998). Modeling the influence of thematic fit (and other constraints) in on-line sentence comprehension. *Journal of Memory and Language, 38,* 283–312.

Meteyard, L., Bahrami, B., & Vigliocco, G. (2007). Motion detection and motion verbs—Language affects low-level visual perception. *Psychological Science, 18,* 1007–1013.

Newton, N. (1996). *Foundations of understanding.* Philadelphia: Johns Benjamins.

Niedenthal, P. M., Barsalou, L. W., Winkielman, P., Krauth-Gruber, S., & Ric, F. (2005). Embodiment in attitudes, social perception, and emotion. *Personality and Social Psychology Review, 9,* 184–211.

Piaget, J. (1926). *The language and thought of the child.* New York: Routledge & Kegan Paul.

Pickering, M. J., & Garrod, S. (2007). Do people use language production to make predictions during comprehension? *Trends in Cognitive Sciences, 11,* 105–110.

Pulvermuller, F. (1999). Words in the brain's language. *Behavioral and Brain Sciences, 22,* 253–279.

Pulvermuller, F. (2005). Brain mechanisms linking language and action. *Nature Reviews Neuroscience, 6,* 576–582.

Richardson, D. C., Spivey, M. J., Barsalou, L. W., & McRae, K. (2003). Spatial representations active during real-time comprehension of verbs. *Cognitive Science, 27,* 767–780.

Rizzolatti, G., & Craighero, L. (2004). The mirror-neuron system. *Annual Review of Neuroscience, 27,* 169–192.

Schubert, T. (2004). The power in your hand: Gender differences in bodily feedback from making a fist. *Personality and Social Psychology Bulletin, 30,* 757–769.

Schubert, T. (2005). Your highness: Vertical positions as perceptual symbols of power. *Journal of Personality and Social Psychology, 89,* 1–21.

Searle, J. R. (1980). Minds, brains, and computers. *Behavioral and Brain Sciences, 3,* 417–457.

Stanfield, R. A., & Zwaan, R. A. (2001). The effect of implied orientation derived from verbal context on picture recognition. *Psychological Science, 12,* 153–156.

Taylor, L. J., & Zwaan, R. A. (2008). Motor resonance and linguistic focus. *Quarterly Journal of Experimental Psychology, 61,* 896–904.

Townsend, D. J., & Bever, T. G. (2001). *Sentence comprehension.* Cambridge, MA: MIT Press.

Tucker, M., & Ellis, R. (1998). On the relations between seen objects and components of potential actions. *Journal of Experimental Psychology: Human Perception and Performance, 24,* 830–846.

Wolpert, D. M., Doya, K., & Kawato, M. (2003). A unifying computational framework for motor control and social interaction. *Philosophical Transactions of the Royal Society of London Series. B, Biological Sciences, 358,* 593–602.

Yaxley, R. H., & Zwaan, R. A. (2007). Simulating visibility during language comprehension. *Cognition, 105,* 229–236.

Zwaan, R. A., & Kaschak, M. P. (2008). Language comprehension as a means of "re-situating" oneself. In P. Robbins & M. Aydede (Eds.), *The Cambridge handbook of situated cognition.* Cambridge, UK: Cambridge University Press.

Zwaan, R. A., Madden, C. J., Yaxley, R. H., & Aveyard, M. E. (2004). Moving words: Dynamic mental representations in language comprehension. *Cognitive Science, 28,* 611–619.

Zwaan, R. A., Stanfield, R. A., & Yaxley, R. H. (2002). Language comprehenders mentally represent the shape of objects. *Psychological Science, 13,* 168–171.

Zwaan, R. A., & Taylor, L. J. (2006). Seeing, acting, understanding: Motor resonance in language comprehension. *Journal of Experimental Psychology: General, 135,* 1–11.

2

Eye Movements and Moment-to-Moment Comprehension Processes in Reading

Keith Rayner *and* Timothy J. Slattery

Two important and critical components of skilled reading are rate (how fast we read) and comprehension (how well we understand the text). It is relatively easy to measure reading rate, and fairly reliable methods for assessing comprehension are currently in use. Comprehension can be assessed informally by asking students to summarize a passage or answer open-ended questions. And many standardized tests assess comprehension with multiple-choice questions. Although passage comprehension can be assessed fairly accurately, it is not clear how to identify the factors that contribute to comprehension failure. Yet a low comprehension score on a standardized test does not identify the underlying difficulties that contribute to it. Thus, identifying the factors that contribute to impaired comprehension remains a challenge.

In this chapter, we argue that monitoring eye movements during reading can provide valuable information regarding moment-to-moment comprehension processes (see also Rayner, 1997, 1998; Rayner, Chace, Slattery, & Ashby, 2006). We begin by first reviewing some basic characteristics of eye movements during reading and then review data on using eye movements to infer moment-to-moment comprehension processes. We note at the outset that our review is largely biased toward work reported from our lab, but we also think that the conclusions we reach are fairly consistent with the views of other workers in the field of eye movements and reading.

BASIC CHARACTERISTICS OF EYE MOVEMENTS DURING READING

There are three major components of eye movements during reading: saccades, fixations, and regressions. Although it feels like our eyes glide smoothly across the page of text during reading, in reality we make a series of movements (saccades) from one place to another in the text separated by pauses (fixations) that typically last 200 to 250 msec It is only during the fixations that new information is encoded, because vision is suppressed during saccades. For skilled readers, the eyes typically move about seven to nine letter spaces with each saccade. An important point, however, is that the values just cited (200–250 msec for fixations and seven to nine letter spaces for saccades) are averages, and there is considerable variability in both of these measures. It is fairly clear that much of the variability in both of these measures is related to the ease or difficulty associated with understanding the text (see Rayner, 1998). Thus, as text gets more difficult, fixations get longer and saccades get shorter. About 10 to 15% of the time, skilled readers make a regression (or a saccade that moves the eyes backward in the text) to read material that they have previously encountered. Just as fixations get longer and saccades get shorter as the text gets more difficult, readers make more regressions when reading is difficult.

When children first start reading, their eye fixations tend to be quite long (and average more than 350 msec in first grade), and they make as many as two fixations per word. In addition, about 30% of their fixations are regressions. However, by fourth or fifth grade, fixation durations and saccade lengths have stabilized (as long as the reading material is age appropriate; Rayner, 1986). But the rate of regressions continues to decline up through college age. Just as younger readers have longer fixations, shorter saccades, and more regressions than skilled readers, poor readers and dyslexic readers at all ages are characterized by longer fixations, shorter saccades, and more regressions (Ashby, Rayner, & Clifton, 2005; Chace, Rayner, & Well, 2005). Despite this fact, it is important to realize that for the most part eye movements do not cause reading problems. Rather, eye movements reflect the difficulties that less skilled readers have in encoding the words and understanding the text.

An important issue with respect to eye movement research is how to appropriately measure processing time. If it were the case that readers always made one and only one fixation on a word, then there would be no problem because the average fixation duration on a word could be computed. However, the reality is that readers sometimes skip words (about two-thirds of the words are typically fixated, with short words and predictable words often skipped), and they sometimes make more than one fixation on a word before moving to another word. Thus, when the unit of analysis is a single word, eye movement researchers typically report a number of related measures such as first-fixation duration (the duration of the first fixation on a word independent of the number of fixations on the word), single-fixation duration (when only one fixation is made on a word), gaze duration (the sum of all fixations on a word before moving to another word), and total fixation time (the sum of all fixations, including regressions, on a word). In addition, the probability of fixating on the word and the frequency of regressions out of the word are also reported.

When the unit of analysis is larger than a single word, then first-pass reading time (the sum of all first pass fixations before leaving a region) and total reading time (the sum of all fixations in the region) are typically computed. An additional very useful measure is the go-past time (the sum of all fixations from first entering a region until exiting in the forward direction). This measure is also sometimes called the regression-path duration and includes any regression out of the region before moving forward in the text. This go-past measure has also been used recently when the unit of analysis is a single word and basically reflects the amount of time from when a given region or word is first fixated until when the reader moves forward beyond this word or region in the text.

It is important to note that studies dealing with comprehension differ in terms of which of these measures is most useful in analyzing the data. Our argument is that when readers have difficulty understanding text, they make more fixations (and hence shorter saccades) and longer fixations as well as more regressions. This argument is quite easy to sustain with respect to lexical processing. This is because it is abundantly clear that lexical variables strongly influence how long readers fixate on a word. We document this assertion in more detail later in this chapter. Here we note that a computational model of eye movements in reading, the E–Z Reader model (Pollatsek, Reichle, & Rayner, 2006; Rayner, Reichle, & Pollatsek, 1998, 2005; Reichle, Pollatsek, Fisher, & Rayner, 1998; Reichle, Rayner, & Pollatsek, 2003), does a very good job of accounting for eye movements during reading based largely on the premise that lexical processing (word recognition) is driving the eyes through the text. Furthermore, there is good reason to believe that higher order comprehension processes influence eye movements primarily when something does not compute (Clifton, Staub, & Rayner, 2007; Staub & Rayner, 2007): When skilled readers encounter an anomalous word (Rayner, Warren, Juhasz, & Liversedge, 2004; Staub, Rayner, Pollatsek, Hyona, & Majewski, 2007; Warren & McConnell, 2007; Warren, McConnell, & Rayner, 2008) or when they are garden-pathed by syntactic ambiguity (Binder, Duffy, & Rayner, 2001; Boland & Blodgett, 2001; Clifton et al., 2003; Frazier & Rayner, 1982; Rayner, Carlson, & Frazier, 1983; Rayner & Frazier, 1987; Rayner, Garrod, & Perfetti, 1992), their fixations get longer and they often make shorter saccades and more regressions (Altmann, Garnham, & Dennis, 1992; Rayner & Sereno, 1994). In cases such as this, higher order comprehension processes can override the normal default situation in which lexical processing is driving the eyes and result in longer fixations or regressions back to earlier parts of the text. It is also the case that readers pause longer at the ends of clauses and sentences (Hirotani, Frazier, & Rayner, 2006; Rayner, Sereno, Morris, Schmauder, & Clifton, 1998; Rayner, Kambe, & Duffy, 2000) either to integrate the semantic information or for implicit prosody. The point we make here, and which is reinforced later in this chapter, is that, consistent with models like E–Z Reader, eye movements seem to be largely driven by lexical processing with semantic processing in the background (as far as eye movements per se are concerned) and such processing primarily influences eye movements when something does not compute and at other strategic points (like the ends of clauses and sentences).

Our goal is not to discuss models of eye movement control in this chapter, especially because there are many such models that have recently appeared. The most prominent of the alternatives to the E–Z Reader model are the SWIFT (Saccade generation with inhibition by foveal targets; Engbert, Longtin, & Kliegl, 2002; Engbert, Nuthmann, Richter, & Kliegl, 2005) and Glenmore (Reilly & Radach, 2006) models. For the most part, all of the models do a good job of accounting for basic eye movement data. They do, however, differ on a number of dimensions that are beyond the scope of the present chapter.

BACKGROUND ISSUES TO USING EYE MOVEMENTS TO STUDY COMPREHENSION PROCESSES

An interesting question is, can eye movements be used to effectively study on-line comprehension processes during reading? Most standard experiments dealing with discourse processes and comprehension have typically used more gross measures such as sentence reading time. Or they have used tasks that disrupt the normal reading process in some way, such as self-paced reading and probe tasks. There is nothing wrong with these tasks, and depending on exactly the question one is interested in, they provide useful data. However, if the goal is to know something about when a given variable has an effect or about the time course of processing, then eye movements offer considerable promise. But eye movement data are also fairly complicated, and there are a few background issues that have to be answered before one could know whether eye movement data would aid in understanding comprehension processes. We turn now to these issues.

There are two critical questions:

1. How much useful information does a reader obtain during an eye fixation?
2. How tight is the link between the eye and the mind?

Secondarily, is the variability in the eye movement record that we mentioned earlier associated with moment-to-moment comprehension processing?

The Perceptual Span

The question of how much useful information readers obtain during an eye fixation is directly related to the perceptual span (or the area of effective vision during a fixation). This issue is important because eye movement data would be more or less valuable depending on how much information can be processed on a single eye fixation. If readers can process all of the information on a single line (or over multiple lines) in a single fixation, then eye movement data would not be very informative because the researcher would not know specifically which words were being processed at any particular point in time. Of course, as we have already outlined, the reality is that readers typically move their eyes seven to nine letter spaces, so this mere fact makes it unlikely that information can be obtained from all of the words on a line. Perhaps a more reasonable possibility is that readers can process the meanings of a number of words (e.g., three or four) simultaneously within a single fixation. This possibility would render eye movement data somewhat uninformative because once again it would not be obvious which words were being processed when. At the other extreme, if readers can only obtain information from the currently fixated word and process only the meaning of that word, then eye fixations would be particularly informative about moment-to-moment processing. Interestingly, the word-by-word self-paced reading paradigm pretty much forces this on the reader. However, the main problem with self-paced reading is that it significantly slows the rate of reading (so reading speed is reduced up to as much as half the normal rate). Furthermore, with self-paced reading, the reader loses the capability of looking back in the text when needed for comprehension. Fortunately, a great deal of research on the perceptual span when reading English demonstrates quite conclusively that readers obtain information from only a limited region on each fixation. Much of the time, readers only process the meaning of the fixated word, although when words are highly predictable or when short words appear in succession the meaning of more than one word can be processed on a fixation.

Although we have the impression that we can see an entire line of text or even an entire page of text, this is an illusion. This fact has been clearly demonstrated by studies that use a gaze-contingent moving window paradigm (see Figure 2.1), introduced by McConkie and Rayner (1975; Rayner & Bertera, 1979). The logic behind the gaze-contingent moving window paradigm is that we can determine how much of the text is being processed by varying the window size in which the text appears normal. Therefore, the amount of information available to a reader is determined by how large the window (showing the normal text) has to be for readers to read normally or, conversely, how small the window can be before there is disruption to reading. In this paradigm, the text within the window is normally presented, but the text outside the window is manipulated by either replacing the correct letters with other letters or replacing them all with Xs. Studies using this paradigm have demonstrated that English readers acquire useful information from an asymmetrical region around the fixation point (extending three to four character spaces to the left of fixation and about 14 to 15 character spaces to the right). Furthermore, if the fixated word and the word to the right of fixation are normal and all other letters are replaced with visually similar letters, readers are not aware that the words outside of the window have been changed, and their reading speed only decreases by about 10%. If two words to the right of fixation are normally displayed, there is very little slowdown in reading. Research has also found that readers do not use information from the words on the line below the currently fixated line (Rayner, 1998). Finally, the moving window paradigm can be reversed to produce a moving mask paradigm (Rayner & Bertera, 1979; Rayner, Inhoff, Morrison, Slowiaczek, & Bertera, 1981). In this case, a mask moves with the eyes on each fixation, covering the letters in the center of vision (Figure 2.1). From this paradigm, results demonstrate that reading while the central region is masked (when only letters in parafoveal vision are presented normally) is almost impossible.

Another gaze-contingent display change paradigm (see Figure 2.1)—the boundary paradigm (Rayner, 1975)—has been used to investigate the degree to which information outside the fixated region is processed. In this paradigm, a target word immediately to the right of the currently fixated word is replaced with another word, a nonword, or random string of letters (creating an invalid preview). When the readers' eyes cross an invisible boundary located between the two words, the invalid preview changes to the target word; because vision is suppressed during the eye movement, with readers not aware of the change. This invalid preview condition is then compared with a valid preview condition in which the target word is presented normally. When readers have an invalid preview of the word to the right of fixation, they spend

Normal Line:
Where do people look while reading passages of text?

Moving Window Paradigm (13-character window):
Xxxxx xx xxxxxe look while xxxxxxx xxxxxxxx xx xxxx?
                            *

ﹾ Xxxxx xx xxxxxx xxxx xxxle reading paxxxxxx xx xxxx?
                          *

Moving Mask Paradigm (7-character mask):
Where do people look wxxxxxxxading passages of text?
                       *

Where do people look while rexxxxxxxassages of text?
                             *

Boundary Paradigm:
Where do people look while feeding passages of text?
                          *

Where do people look while reading passages of text?
                          *

FIGURE 2.1. Examples of a normal line of text, a moving window (with a 13-character window), a moving mask (with a 7-character mask), and the boundary paradigm. In the boundary paradigm, when the reader's eye movement crosses an invisible boundary location (the letter *e* in *while*), the preview word (*feeding*) changes to the target word (*reading*). The asterisk represents the location of the eyes in each example.

about 30 to 50 msec more fixating that word (following a saccade to it) than when they have a valid preview. It is also interesting to note that, using this technique, studies have revealed that readers do not combine a literal representation of the visual information across saccades, but rather abstract (and phonological) information is integrated across eye fixations (McConkie & Zola, 1979; Rayner, McConkie, & Zola, 1980).

From these gaze-contingent display change experiments, we can conclude that readers are obtaining useful information no more than 14 to 15 letter spaces to the right of fixation. However, information about the meaning of the word is limited to a region extending about three to four letter spaces to the left of fixation to, on most fixations, no more than five to eight letter spaces to the right. The region to the right is somewhat variable depending on the lengths of the words. Thus, if two or three short words are in succession, they can be identified on a single fixation. Furthermore, if the upcoming word is highly predictable from the preceding context, readers are more likely to skip over the word (Altaribba, Kroll, Sholl, & Rayner, 1996; Balota, Pollatsek, & Rayner, 1985; Ehrlich & Rayner, 1981; Rayner & Well, 1996). However, this does not mean that the word is not processed. Rather, it is processed on the fixation before the skip. Thus, the duration of the fixation before the skip is inflated, as is sometimes the duration of the fixation after the skip (Drieghe, Rayner, & Pollatsek, 2005; Hogaboam, 1983; Pollatsek, Rayner, & Balota, 1986).

The Eye–Mind Span

How tight is the link between the eyes and the mind? Like the issue of the perceptual span, this is important because if the eyes were ahead of the mind an appreciable amount, like the eyes are ahead of the voice in oral reading by two to three words (Rayner, 1998), then eye movements might not be particularly informative with respect to moment-to-moment comprehension problems. However, the data suggest that the link between the eyes and the mind is fairly tight: It is not perfect, because readers do get preview information about words before fixating on them (as noted in the prior section) and there are spillover effects (Rayner & Duffy, 1986) in which the fixation duration following a given target word will be increased because of the difficulty of processing the target word. However, lexical manipulations of target words have revealed that such manipulations strongly and predominantly influence the duration of the fixations on the target word itself (Rayner, Pollatsek, Drieghe, Slattery, & Reichle, 2007).

As briefly noted previously, the difficulty of the text being read has an impact on eye movement patterns (fixation duration, saccade length, and frequency of regressing to previously read text). Specifically, it has become very clear that the length of time the eyes remain in place is influenced by a host of linguistic factors, including the frequency of the fixated word (Inhoff & Rayner, 1986; Rayner & Duffy, 1986; Rayner, Sereno, & Raney, 1996; Slattery, Pollatsek, & Rayner, 2007), the predictability of the fixated word (Ehrlich & Rayner, 1981; Rayner & Well, 1996), the number of meanings the fixated word has (Duffy, Morris, & Rayner, 1988; Rayner, Cook, Juhasz, & Frazier, 2006; Sereno, O'Donnell, & Rayner, 2006), when the meaning of the word was acquired (Juhasz & Rayner, 2003, 2006), semantic relations between the word and prior words (Carroll & Slowiaczek, 1986; Morris, 1994), and the familiarity of the word (Williams & Morris, 2004). For a more in-depth review of these factors and others, see Rayner (1998).

The most compelling evidence that cognitive processes drive the eyes through text comes from experiments in which the fixated word either disappears or is masked after 50 to 60 msec (Ishida & Ikeda, 1989; Liversedge et al., 2004; Rayner et al., 1981; Rayner, Liversedge, & White, 2006; Rayner, Liversedge, White, & Vergilino-Perez, 2003). In these studies, readers are allowed to see the fixated word for 50 to 60 msec before it disappears. Under these conditions, they read quite normally; however, if the word to the right of fixation also disappears or is masked, then reading is disrupted (Rayner, Liversedge, & White, 2006). This result indicates quite strongly that the word to the right of fixation is very important in reading. For the present purposes, it is important to note that when the fixated word disappears after 60 msec, the fixation duration on the space initially occupied by the word is still determined by the frequency of the word: If it is a low-frequency word, the eyes remain in place longer (Rayner et al., 2003; Rayner, Liversedge, & White et al., 2006). So, even though the word is no longer visible, the length of time the eyes remain fixated is determined by that word's frequency. This evidence is very compelling and supports the notion that the cognitive processes associated with a fixated word are what drive eye movements through the text.

To summarize, it is clear that readers obtain information from a limited region during a fixation (extending to about 14 to 15 character spaces to the right of fixation). Information used for word identification is obtained from an even smaller region (extending to about five to eight character spaces to the right of fixation). Furthermore, the word to the right of fixation is important and some information about that word is processed, as shown by preview benefit from that word. On some fixations, readers process the meaning of the fixated word and the word to the right of fixation and will subsequently skip the word to the right of fixation. Finally, the ease or difficulty associated with processing the fixated word strongly affects how long readers look at that word.

Although much evidence suggests that lexical processing controls eye movements during reading, it would be foolish to argue that higher level comprehension processes do not also have an influence. We now discuss such processes.

EYE MOVEMENTS AND ONLINE COMPREHENSION PROCESSES

In the remainder of this chapter, we first review some data on eye movements from passage reading in which the difficulty of the passage is varied. We demonstrate that the global aspects of eye movements reflect passage difficulty (and hence, presumably, how easy or difficult the passage is to comprehend). We then present a couple of specific examples in which comprehension processes influence eye movements of skilled readers (both in terms of longer fixations and more regressions).

Eye Movements Reflect Global Passage Difficulty

Rayner, Chace, et al. (2006) had college undergraduates read passages that had been rated for overall difficulty as their eye movements were recorded. On a 7-point scale, passage difficulty ranged from 2.78 (relatively easy reading) to 6.63 (relatively difficult reading). The average passage length was 564 words.

Table 2.1 shows the correlations among the various measures. Not surprisingly, the highest correlation is between the average number of fixations per passage and the total time needed to read the passage. It has been argued in the past that reading rate can only be modified by varying the number of fixations and that fixation duration is relatively stable. However, Rayner (1978) presented data that contradicted this claim, demonstrating that fixation durations increase with passage difficulty. Data from the Rayner, Chace, et al. (2006) study reaffirm this claim, because the range of average fixation duration correlated with passage difficulty: As passage difficulty increased, so did average fixation duration and the average number of fixations per word. In general, as passage difficulty increases, readers make more fixations (which

TABLE 2.1. Correlations of Average Fixation Duration, Number of Fixations, Total Reading Time, and Average Time per Word with Passage Difficulty.

Variable	Avg. FD	Num. fix.	Read time	Avg. time/word
Difficulty	.379*	.421**	.446**	.323*
Avg. FD		.539**	.676**	.618**
Num. fix.			.984***	.794***
Total time				.826***

Note. Avg. FD, average fixation duration; Num. fix., number of fixations. Data from Rayner, Chace, Slattery, and Ashby (2006). $*p = .05$; $**p = .01$; $***p = .001$.

also translate into shorter saccade lengths) and longer fixations. These results thus provide further confirmation that eye movement measures reflect global passage difficulty.

Eye Movements Reflect Local Syntactic Difficulty

There are obviously a number of ways in which local text difficulty can be manipulated, but one such manipulation is via syntactic ambiguity. As noted previously, many studies have clearly demonstrated immediate effects of syntactic ambiguity. When readers are led down a garden path, their eye movements clearly reflect that they have difficulties processing the sentence when the encounter the disambiguating information. Consider structurally ambiguous sentences such as the following:

1a. John put the book on the table and went to sleep.
1b. John put the book on the table into his briefcase.
2a. The woman rushed to the hospital and forgot her laundry.
2b. The woman rushed to the hospital had a pretty baby girl.

These sentences are typically referred to as garden path sentences (see Frazier & Rayner, 1982). In sentence 1, the prepositional phrase (PP) "on the table" is ambiguous as to whether it should be attached to the verb (as in sentence 1a, "put the book on the table") or to the noun (as in sentence 1b, "put the book into his briefcase"). Thus, there is a temporary syntactic ambiguity involving how to parse the PP, and sentence 1a is typically easier to understand than sentence 1b. In sentence 2, there is likewise an ambiguity and the garden path seems intuitively stronger. Here (in sentence 2b), the reduced relative (RR) clause "rushed to the hospital," which is comprehensible in its unreduced form (who was rushed to the hospital), is initially misparsed (as the woman in a hurry). The correct interpretation of sentence 2b is usually delayed until the following disambiguating region ("had a pretty baby girl") is read.

What happens when readers encounter this type of disambiguating information (i.e., the text immediately following the ambiguous PP or RR clause)? Basically, the first-pass reading time for the disambiguating region will be considerably longer for the b-sentence versions than for the a-sentence versions. Furthermore, readers will be much more likely to regress from the disambiguating region in the b-sentence versions than the a-sentence versions. Thus, it is clear that eye movements reflect local syntactic processing difficulty.

Eye Movements Are Influenced by Inconsistencies in Text

A common way to explore the effects of inconsistencies in text is to examine the disruption that occurs when an anaphor and its antecedent (i.e., what it refers to) do not agree. Rayner, Chace, et al. (2006) had readers read passages of text while their eye movements were recorded. Embedded sentences contained a target anaphor; half of the passages contained anaphors that were consistent with their antecedents while the other half contained inconsistent anaphors. In addition, the antecedent and the anaphor were near to each other (as in sentence 3), or some distance was introduced between the two by inserting filler material; this was done by simply adding additional sentences between the antecedent and the anaphor. In sentence 3a, the information in the two sentences is consistent, as Alison ordered celery sticks and that is what the waiter brought her. However, in sentence 3b, the antecedent information is inconsistent with the anaphor; Alison ordered celery sticks, but the waiter brought her carrot sticks.

> 3a. Alison decided to order some celery sticks to snack on. The waiter brought her some water and the celery sticks after only a few minutes.
> 3b. Alison decided to order some celery sticks to snack on. The waiter brought her some water and the carrot sticks after only a few minutes.

Generally, readers looked longer at the inconsistent anaphor than the consistent anaphor, indicating that the inconsistent anaphors were more difficult to process. Longer reading times for the inconsistent anaphor suggest that comprehension processes typically detected the inconsistency immediately.

Regressions and Comprehension Processes

Regressions are an important characteristic of eye movements in reading, but they are poorly understood. This is partly because it is difficult (if not impossible) to experimentally induce regressions (see Inhoff & Weger, 2005, for an interesting exception to this generalization). Whereas regressions are often assumed to reflect some type of breakdown of comprehension processes, in reality most regressions are rather short and take the eyes back to the immediately preceding word. Such short regressions are most likely due to either oculomotor errors (i.e., perhaps the eyes overshot the intended saccade target on the prior saccade) or lexical processes (i.e., was it really that word?). However, longer regressions largely reflect comprehension failures. The relative rarity of long-distance regressions suggests that readers avoid looking very far back in the text unless it is absolutely necessary. In this context, it is interesting that when readers do make long regressions, they are fairly accurate in finding that portion of the text where their understanding went astray (see Frazier & Rayner, 1982; Meseguer, Carreiras, & Clifton, 2002; see Mitchell, Shen, Green, & Hodgson, 2008, and Weger & Inhoff, 2007, for interesting discussions of regressions and the extent to which long-range regressions are accurate).

The study by Rayner, Chace, et al. (2006) included long passages of text and thus provides an excellent opportunity to examine the effect of inconsistency on skilled readers' regressions. Interestingly, when the anaphor was separated from its antecedent by additional text (far condition) readers were no more likely to regress back from the anaphor when it was inconsistent. However, readers were more likely to regress from the spillover region in the near-inconsistent condition than in the near-consistent condition.

The results of the Rayner, Chace, et al. (2006) study demonstrate that near inconsistencies resulted in both longer fixations on the inconsistent anaphor and more regressions from the words immediately after the anaphor back to the antecedent. Interestingly enough, when there was some distance introduced between the antecedent and the anaphor, the effect of the inconsistency on processing time was delayed (appearing on the word after the anaphor) and no effect of inconsistency was observed on the probability of making a regression. So, although the inconsistency was noted, it did not result in more regressions back to the antecedent. In general, this finding—that it is quite difficult to get readers to regress far in the text—is consistent with observations from other studies (Rayner, 1998). We point out, however, that in studies in which comprehension breakdowns are more extreme, long-distance regressions should be more prevalent.

CONCLUDING COMMENTS

The studies described in the prior section document that (1) eye movements are sensitive to global text difficulty; (2) eye movements are affected by immediate local processing difficulties in terms of longer fixations on text that resolves temporary syntactic ambiguity as well as on text that includes an inconsistency between an anaphor and its prior antecedent; and (3) regressions are sensitive to immediate antecedent-anaphor inconsistencies. We further noted that long-distance regressions are rather difficult to invoke. Even when comprehension was somewhat difficult as in the far-inconsistent condition of Rayner, Chace, et al. (2006), readers did not like to make long-distance regressions. We are fairly certain, however, and prior research demonstrates (see Rayner, 1997, 1998), that when comprehension completely breaks down, readers will make long-distance regressions.

Typically, research on comprehension processes or discourse comprehension has relied on rather gross reading time measures. Such research is certainly justifiable if the researcher does not care when a given effect is occurring. However, if there is concern about exactly when an effect appears, then eye movements are an excellent measure of moment-to-moment comprehension processes. Eye movement data afford the researcher valuable temporal information about exactly when in the reading record a given manipulated variable had an effect. Although there are a few studies (see, e.g., Cook & Myers, 2004; Garrod, O'Brien, Morris, & Rayner, 1990; Garrod & Terras, 2000; O'Brien, Raney, Albrecht, & Rayner, 1997; O'Brien, Shank, Myers, & Rayner, 1988) in which eye movements were monitored to assess immediate comprehension in discourse processing, the number of such studies pales in comparison to the number of studies that used more gross reading time measures. This stands in stark contrast to the study of moment-to-moment lexical processing and syntactic parsing, where eye movement data have become more or less the gold standard for measuring the time course of effects. Our view is that the time is ripe for more comprehension studies to use eye movement data to understand discourse processing.

ACKNOWLEDGMENTS

Preparation of this chapter was supported by Grant No. HD17246 from the National Institutes of Health and by a grant from the Microsoft Corporation.

REFERENCES

Altarriba, J., Kroll, J. F., Sholl, A., & Rayner, K. (1996). The influence of lexical and conceptual constraints on reading mixed-language sentences: Evidence from eye fixations and naming times. *Memory & Cognition, 24,* 477–492.

Altmann, G. T. M., Garnham, A., & Dennis, Y. (1992). Avoiding the garden path: Eye movements in context. *Journal of Memory and Language, 31,* 685–712.

Ashby, J., Rayner, K., & Clifton, C. (2005). Eye movements of highly skilled and average readers: Differential effects of frequency and predictability. *Quarterly Journal of Experimental Psychology, 58A,* 1065–1086.

Balota, D. A., Pollatsek, A., & Rayner, K. (1985). The interaction of contextual constraints and parafoveal visual information in reading. *Cognitive Psychology, 17,* 364–390.

Binder, K. S., Duffy, S. A., & Rayner, K. (2001). The effects of thematic fit and discourse context on syntactic ambiguity resolution. *Journal of Memory and Language, 44,* 297–324.

Boland, J. E., & Blodgett, A. (2001). Understanding constraints on syntactic generation: Lexical bias and discourse congruency effects on eye movements. *Journal of Memory and Language, 45,* 391–411.

Carroll, P. J., & Slowiaczek, M. L. (1986). Constraints on semantic priming in reading: A fixation time analysis. *Memory & Cognition, 14,* 509–522.

Chace, K. H., Rayner, K., & Well, A. D. (2005). Eye movements and phonological parafoveal preview: Effects of reading skill. *Canadian Journal of Experimental Psychology, 59,* 209–217.

Clifton, C., Staub, A., & Rayner, K. (2007). Eye movements in reading words and sentences. In R. van Gompel, M. H. Fischer, W. S. Murray, & R. L. Hill (Eds.), *Eye movements: A window on mind and brain* (pp. 341–372). New York: Elsevier.

Clifton, C., Traxler, M. J., Mohamed, M. T., Williams, R. S., Morris, R. K., & Rayner, K. (2003). The use of thematic role information in parsing: Syntactic processing autonomy revisited. *Journal of Memory and Language, 49,* 317–334.

Cook, A. E., & Myers, J. L. (2004). Processing discourse roles in scripted narratives: The influences of context and world knowledge. *Journal of Memory and Language, 50,* 268–288.

Drieghe, D., Rayner, K., & Pollatsek, A. (2005). Eye movements and word skipping during reading revisited. *Journal of Experimental Psychology: Human Perception and Performance, 31,* 954–969.

Duffy, S. A., Morris, R. K., & Rayner, K. (1988). Lexical ambiguity and fixation times in reading. *Journal of Memory and Language, 27*, 429–446.

Ehrlich, S. F., & Rayner, K. (1981). Contextual effects on word perception and eye movements during reading. *Journal of Verbal Learning and Verbal Behavior, 20*, 641–655.

Engbert, R., Longtin, A., & Kliegl, R. (2002). A dynamical model of saccade generation in reading based on spatially distributed lexical processing. *Vision Research, 42*, 621–636.

Engbert, R., Nuthmann, A., Richter, E., & Kliegl, R. (2005). SWIFT: A dynamical model of saccade generation during reading. *Psychological Review, 112*, 777–813.

Frazier, L., & Rayner, K. (1982). Making and correcting errors during sentence comprehension: Eye movements in the analysis of structurally ambiguous sentences. *Cognitive Psychology, 14*, 178–210.

Garrod, S., O'Brien, E. J., Morris, R. K., & Rayner, K. (1990). Elaborative inferencing as an active or passive process. *Journal of Experimental Psychology: Learning, Memory, and Cognition, 16*, 250–257.

Garrod, S., & Terras, M. (2000). The contribution of lexical and situational knowledge to resolving discourse roles: Bonding and resolution. *Journal of Memory and Language, 42*, 526–544.

Hirotani, M., Frazier, L., & Rayner, K. (2006). Punctuation and intonation effects on clause and sentence wrap-up: Evidence from eye movements. *Journal of Memory and Language, 54*, 425–443.

Hogaboam, T. W. (1983). Reading patterns in eye movement data. In K. Rayner (Ed.), *Eye movements in reading* (pp. 309–332). New York: Academic Press.

Inhoff, A. W., & Rayner, K. (1986). Parafoveal word processing during eye fixations in reading: Effects of word frequency. *Perception and Psychophysics, 40*, 431–439.

Inhoff, A. W., & Weger, U. W. (2005). Memory for word location in reading: Eye movements to previously read words are spatially selective but not precise. *Memory & Cognition, 33*, 447–461.

Ishida, T., & Ikeda, M. (1989). Temporal properties of information extraction in reading studied by a text-mask replacement technique. *Journal of the Optical Society. A, Optics and Image Science, 6*, 1624–1632.

Juhasz, B. J., & Rayner, K. (2003). Investigating the effects of a set of intercorrelated variables on eye fixation durations in reading. *Journal of Experimental Psychology: Learning, Memory, and Cognition, 29*, 1312–1318.

Juhasz, B. J., & Rayner, K. (2006). The role of age-of-acquisition and word frequency in reading: Evidence from eye fixation durations. *Visual Cognition, 13*, 846–863.

Liversedge, S. P., Rayner, K., White, S. J., Vergilino-Perez, D., Findlay, J. M., & Kentridge, R. W. (2004). Eye movements while reading disappearing text: Is there a gap effect in reading? *Vision Research, 44*, 1013–1024.

McConkie, G. W., & Rayner, K. (1975). The span of the effective stimulus during a fixation in reading. *Perception & Psychophysics, 17*, 578–586.

McConkie, G. W., & Zola, D. (1979). Is visual information integrated across successive fixations in reading? *Perception & Psychophysics, 25*, 221–224.

Meseguer, E., Carreiras, M., & Clifton, C. (2002). Overt reanalysis strategies and eye movements during the reading of garden path sentences. *Memory & Cognition, 30,* 551–561.

Mitchell, D. C., Shen, X., Green, M. J., & Hodgson, T. L. (2008). Accounting for regressive eye-movements in models of sentence processing: A reappraisal of the Selective Reanalysis hypothesis. *Journal of Memory and Language, 59,* 266–293.

Morris, R. K. (1994). Lexical and message-level sentence context effects on fixation times in reading. *Journal of Experimental Psychology: Learning, Memory, and Cognition, 20,* 92–103.

O'Brien, E. J., Raney, G. E., Albrecht, J. E., & Rayner, K. (1997). Processes involved in the resolution of explicit anaphors. *Discourse Processes, 23,* 1–24.

O'Brien, E. J., Shank, D. M., Myers, J. L., & Rayner, K. (1988). Elaborative inferences during reading: Do they occur on-line? *Journal of Experimental Psychology: Learning, Memory, and Cognition, 14,* 410–420.

Pollatsek, A., Rayner, K., & Balota, D. A. (1986). Inferences about eye movement control from the perceptual span in reading. *Perception and Psychophysics, 40,* 123–130.

Pollatsek, A., Reichle, E. D., & Rayner, K. (2006). Tests of the E–Z Reader model: Exploring the interface between cognition and eye-movement control. *Cognitive Psychology, 52,* 1–56.

Rayner, K. (1975). The perceptual span and peripheral cues in reading. *Cognitive Psychology, 7,* 65–81.

Rayner, K. (1978). Eye movements in reading and information processing. *Psychological Bulletin, 85,* 618–660.

Rayner, K. (1986). Eye movements and the perceptual span in beginning and skilled readers. *Journal of Experimental Child Psychology, 41,* 211–236.

Rayner, K. (1997). Understanding eye movements in reading. *Scientific Studies in Reading, 1,* 301–323.

Rayner, K. (1998). Eye movements in reading and information processing: 20 years of research. *Psychological Bulletin, 124,* 372–422.

Rayner, K., & Bertera, J. H. (1979). Reading without a fovea. *Science, 206,* 468–469.

Rayner, K., Carlson, M., & Frazier, L. (1983). The interaction of syntax and semantics during sentence processing: Eye movements in the analysis of semantically biased sentences. *Journal of Verbal Learning and Verbal Behavior, 22,* 358–374.

Rayner, K., Chace, K. H., Slattery, T. J., & Ashby, J. (2006). Eye movements as reflections of comprehension processes in reading. *Scientific Studies of Reading, 10,* 241–255.

Rayner, K., Cook, A. E., Juhasz, B. J., & Frazier, L. (2006). Immediate disambiguation of lexically ambiguous words during reading: Evidence from eye movements. *British Journal of Psychology, 97,* 467–482.

Rayner, K., & Duffy, S. A. (1986). Lexical complexity and fixation times in reading: Effects of word frequency, verb complexity, and lexical ambiguity. *Memory & Cognition, 14,* 191–201.

Rayner, K., & Frazier, L. (1987). Parsing temporarily ambiguous sentences. *Quarterly Journal of Experimental Psychology, 39A,* 657–673.

Rayner, K., Garrod, S. C., & Perfetti, C. A. (1992). Discourse influences during parsing are delayed. *Cognition, 45,* 109–139.

Rayner, K., Inhoff, A. W., Morrison, R. E., Slowiaczek, M. L., & Bertera, J. H. (1981). Masking of foveal and parafoveal vision during eye fixations in reading. *Journal of Experimental Psychology: Human Perception and Performance, 7,* 167–179.

Rayner, K., Kambe, G., & Duffy, S. A. (2000). Clause wrap-up effects on eye movements during reading. *Quarterly Journal of Experimental Psychology, 53,* 1061–1080.

Rayner, K., Liversedge, S. P., & White, S. J. (2006). Eye movements when reading disappearing text: The importance of the word to the right of fixation. *Vision Research, 46,* 310–323.

Rayner, K., Liversedge, S. P., White, S. J., & Vergilino-Perez, D. (2003). Reading disappearing text: Cognitive control of eye movements. *Psychological Science, 14,* 385–389.

Rayner, K., Pollatsek, A., Drieghe, D., Slattery, T. J., & Reichle, E. D. (2007). Tracking the mind during reading via eye movements: Comments on Kliegl, Nuthmann, and Engbert (2006). *Journal of Experimental Psychology: General, 136,* 520–529.

Rayner, K., McConkie, G. W., & Zola, D. (1980). Integrating information across eye movements. *Cognitive Psychology, 12,* 206–226.

Rayner, K., & Sereno, S. C. (1994). Regressive eye movements and sentence parsing: On the use of regression-contingent analyses. *Memory & Cognition, 22,* 281–285.

Rayner, K., Sereno, S. C., & Raney, G. E. (1996). Eye movement control in reading: A comparison of two types of models. *Journal of Experimental Psychology: Human Perception and Performance, 22,* 1188–1200.

Rayner, K., Reichle, E. D., & Pollatsek, A. (1998). Eye movement control in reading: An overview and a model. In G. Underwood (Ed.), *Eye guidance in reading and scene perception* (pp. 243–268). Oxford, UK: Elsevier.

Rayner, K., Reichle, E. D., & Pollatsek, A. (2005). Eye movement control in reading and the E–Z Reader Model. In G. Underwood (Ed.), *Cognitive processes in eye guidance* (pp. 131–162). Oxford, UK: Oxford University Press.

Rayner, K., Sereno, S. C., Morris, R. K, Schmauder, A. R., & Clifton, C. (1989). Eye movements and on-line language comprehension processes. *Language and Cognitive Processes, 4*(Special issue), 21–49.

Rayner, K., Warren, T., Juhasz, B. J., & Liversedge, S. P. (2004). The effect of plausibility on eye movements in reading. *Journal of Experimental Psychology: Learning, Memory, and Cognition, 30,* 1290–1301.

Rayner, K., & Well, A. D. (1996). Effects of contextual constraint on eye movements in reading: A further examination. *Psychonomic Bulletin & Review, 3,* 504–509.

Reichle, E., Pollatsek, A., Fisher, D. L., & Rayner, K. (1998). Toward a model of eye movement control in reading. *Psychological Review, 105,* 125–157.

Reichle, E. D., Rayner, K., & Pollatsek, A. (2003). The E–Z Reader model of eye movement control in reading: Comparison to other models. *Behavioral and Brain Sciences, 26,* 445–476.

Reilly, R., & Radach, R. (2006). Some empirical tests of an interactive activation model of eye movement control in reading. *Cognitive Systems Research, 7,* 34–55.

Sereno, S. C., O'Donnell, P. J., & Rayner, K. (2006). Eye movements and lexical ambiguity resolution: Investigating the subordinate bias effect. *Journal of Experimental Psychology: Human Perception and Performance, 32,* 335–350.

Slattery, T. J., Pollatsek, A., & Rayner, K. (2007). The effect of the frequencies of three consecutive words on eye movements during reading. *Memory & Cognition, 35,* 1283–1292.

Staub, A., & Rayner, K. (2007). Eye movements and on-line comprehension processes. In G. Gaskell (Ed.), *The Oxford handbook of psycholinguistics* (pp. 327–342). Oxford, UK: Oxford University Press.

Staub, A., Rayner, K., Pollatsek, A., Hyona, J., & Majewski, H. (2007). The time course of plausibility effects on eye movements during reading. *Journal of Experimental Psychology: Learning, Memory, and Cognition, 33,* 1162–1169.

Warren, T., & McConnell, K. (2007). Investigating effects of selectional restriction violations and plausibility violation severity on eye-movements in reading. *Psychonomic Bulletin & Review, 14,* 770–775.

Warren, T., McConnell, K., & Rayner, K. (2008). Effects of context on eye movements when reading about possible and impossible events. *Journal of Experimental Psychology: Learning, Memory, and Cognition, 34,* 1001–1010.

Weger, U. W., & Inhoff, A. W. (2007). Long-range regressions to previously read words are guided by spatial and verbal memory. *Memory & Cognition, 35,* 1293–1306.

Williams, R. S., & Morris, R. K. (2004). Eye movements, word familiarity, and vocabulary acquisition. *European Journal of Cognitive Psychology, 16,* 312–339.

3

The Influence of In-Text Instruction on Declarative Knowledge and Vocabulary Learning in Struggling Readers

How IQ Confounds the Story

Donald L. Compton, Amy M. Elleman,
Natalie G. Olinghouse, Jane Lawrence, Emily Bigelow,
Jennifer K. Gilbert, *and* G. Nicole Davis

The process of comprehending written material requires the coordination of a complex set of skills, and as a consequence there are a number of potential sources of comprehension failure (Cain, Oakhill, & Bryant, 2000; Leach, Scarborough, & Rescorla, 2003; Mastropieri & Scruggs, 1997; National Center for Learning Disabilities, 1999; Oakhill, Cain, & Yuill, 1998; Paris & Oka, 1989; Perfetti, Marron, & Foltz, 1996; Pressley, 2000; Stanovich, West, Cunningham, Cipielewski, & Siddiqui, 1996; Torgesen, 1998). Gough's "simple view of reading" (Gough, 1996; Gough & Tunmer, 1986) postulates that two general types of skill are required for good reading comprehension: (1) the ability to accurately and fluently identify the words in print and (2) general language comprehension ability. Others have expanded on the "simple view of reading" by recognizing the importance of more specific knowledge (e.g., vocabulary, declarative) and active application of specific reading strategies required to maximize reading comprehension (e.g., Baker, 1979; Baker & Brown, 1984; Cain & Oakhill, 1999; Mastropieri & Scruggs, 1997; National Center for Learning Disabilities, 1999; Palincsar & Brown, 1984; Perfetti et al., 1996; Stanovich, Cunningham, & West, 1998; Stanovich & West, 1989). For instance, Cain and Oakhill (1999) and Perfetti et al. (1996) have suggested that the ability to make inferences and monitor comprehension processes also varies with comprehension skill. Children who are poor comprehenders have been shown to have difficulty spontaneously engaging in active strategies to enhance understanding and retention of information and to circumvent comprehension failures (Baker & Anderson, 1982; Deshler, Ellis, & Lenz, 1996; Palincsar & Brown, 1984; Pazzaglia, Cornoldi, & DeBeni, 1995; Yuill & Oakhill, 1991). These highly strategic processes have been referred to as comprehension-fostering and comprehension-monitoring processes and are considered important metacognitive skills that allow the reader to construct and retain a coherent representation of information contained in text (Garner, 1987; Palincsar & Brown, 1984). Thus, evidence indicates that individual differences in various skills, ranging from lower level word recognition skills to advanced language and metacognitive skills, are associated with reading comprehension variance in developing readers. Additionally, deficits in each of these areas have been implicated as a significant contributor to comprehension failure, appreciably decreasing children's ability to use text as a means of gaining information and knowledge (see Perfetti et al., 1996; Pressley, 2000).

Consequently, designing instruction to ameliorate the reading comprehension problems of struggling readers requires a set of instructional procedures that address a diverse range of literacy skills. Effective reading programs designed to improve struggling readers' comprehension skills must provide integrated work across decoding and word recognition, reading fluency, vocabulary and knowledge development, and reading comprehension strategy use (see Pressley, 2000). However, multiple consensus reports provide converging evidence that teachers have difficulty integrating multiple instructional components in an effective manner to teach reading to struggling readers (National Institute of Child Health and Human Development, 2000; RAND Reading Study Group, 2002; Snow, Burns, & Griffin, 1998). Additionally, few studies have systematically studied the effects of multicomponent reading programs on the reading skills of struggling readers. Our long-term research objective is to develop multicomponent reading programs to address the diverse needs of late elementary school students who are struggling readers. With this in mind, we have been examining the effects of in-text reading activities, embedded within multicomponent reading programs, on struggling readers' ability to construct and retain vocabulary and declarative knowledge from text. These text-based knowledge-building instructional procedures were combined with previously validated instruction in decoding and word recognition, reading fluency, and oral reading of text to form a multicomponent reading program to address the diverse needs of late elementary school students who are struggling readers.

THE PRIVILEGED RELATION BETWEEN TEXT READING AND KNOWLEDGE ACQUISITION

The relation among vocabulary knowledge, declarative knowledge, and reading comprehension is well documented (e.g., Anderson & Freebody, 1985; Anderson & Pearson, 1984; Anderson, Reynolds, Schallert, & Goetz, 1977; Beck, Perfetti, & McKeown, 1982; Blachowicz & Fisher, 2000; Nagy, Anderson, & Herman, 1987). Given that poor comprehenders tend to have impoverished vocabulary and declarative knowledge, it is widely accepted that background knowledge and vocabulary are important components of generally effective reading comprehension instruction for struggling readers (see National Institute of Child Health and Human Development, 2000; RAND Reading Study Group, 2002). Previous research (e.g., Anderson, Spiro, & Anderson, 1978; Perfetti et al., 1996; Stanovich, 2000) has demonstrated that increased knowledge positively impacts other important processes needed for text comprehension. In particular, knowledge increases seem to positively influence the control of comprehension monitoring processes and also the mechanisms that trigger inference making (see Perfetti et al., 1996; Stanovich & Cunningham, 1993). However, there is disagreement about how instruction should be designed to develop declarative knowledge and vocabulary in struggling readers. Some contend that direct instruction of relevant knowledge and vocabulary is an important means of developing the specific knowledge needed for struggling readers to comprehend text (e.g., Beck, McKeown, & Kucan, 2002; Carnine, Silbert, & Kame'enui, 1997; Tomesen & Aarnoutse, 1998; Kamil, 2004; White, Graves, & Slater, 1990). Others assert that context should be used as the primary means of inducing knowledge and vocabulary development (e.g., Adams, 1990; Landauer & Dumais, 1996; Kintsch, 1998; Stanovich et al., 1996; Sternberg, 1987).

Considering vocabulary first, knowing the meanings, relationships, and contextual interpretations of new vocabulary words enhances comprehension of context-area text (Baumann & Kame'enui, 1991). It is estimated that the rate of vocabulary acquisition in children during elementary through high school years is between 3,000 and 5,000 words per year (Nagy et al., 1987; Smith, 1941), which translates into 10 to 15 new words per day. To achieve this rate of vocabulary learning, it has been argued that most new words are added to the lexicon through reading (Cunningham & Stanovich, 1991; Landauer & Dumais, 1996; Stanovich & West, 1989). Compared with oral language, written text is considerably more lexically rich with significantly more low-frequency words (referred to as "rare" words) per 1,000 (Hayes & Ahrens, 1988). For example, children's books contain approximately 50% more rare words compared with adult prime-time television (Cunningham & Stanovich, 1998). This relative difference in word rarity has direct implications for vocabulary development. Opportunities to acquire new words occur when an individual is exposed to a word outside his or her current oral vocabulary. Reading text significantly increases the probability that children will encounter and incorporate new words into their evolving lexicons. Further, the more children read, the greater the probability they will encounter new words.

However, just reading more may not be sufficient to ensure expanded vocabulary knowledge through increased exposure to new words. Proponents of the cognitive efficiency hypothesis (e.g., Sternberg, 1985) argue that exposure alone through text reading is not enough to explain individual differences in vocabulary development. The cognitive efficiency hypothesis contends that, in addition to differences in exposure, differences in the ability to infer meaning from context accounts for vocabulary differences across individuals. Supporting this position is the fact that written context lacks many of the features of oral language that support learning new word meanings, such as intonation, body language, and shared physical surrounds (Beck et al., 2002). Studies estimate that of 100 unfamiliar words met in reading, between 5 and 15 will be learned (Nagy, Herman, & Anderson, 1987; Swanborn & de Glopper, 1999). Thus, although text reading appears to significantly increase the possibility that children will encounter new words, it is a far less supportive vehicle than oral language for inferring the meaning of new words (see Jenkins, Matlock, & Slocum, 1989). Compounding the problem is the fact that children who are poor readers tend to have limited declarative knowledge and vocabulary, and this interferes with the process of inducing meaning from context (see

Perfetti et al., 1996). In addition, children who are poor readers typically do not read widely or engage in effective word-learning strategies that facilitate the learning of word meanings (Baker, Simmons, & Kame'enui, 1995).

From an instructional standpoint, it appears that poor comprehenders would benefit from exposure to the rich vocabulary afforded by text if it were linked with a set of strategies that increased the probability that the meaning of an unknown word could be successfully derived. To address this need, we developed an instructional dialogue, set of strategies, and materials that would allow poor readers to derive the meaning of unfamiliar words encountered in expository text and also provided them with a set of antonyms and synonyms and glossary-type definitions to help strengthen the semantic network in which the word is embedded (see Kintsch, 1998; Landauer & Dumais, 1996).

A similar case has been made for declarative knowledge. Perfetti et al. (1996) have argued that "the component that may be the most important [to reading comprehension] and least interesting is domain knowledge" (p. 142). Numerous studies (Anderson et al., 1977; Anderson et al., 1978; Spilich, Vesonder, Chiesi, & Voss, 1979) provide evidence that declarative knowledge influences reading comprehension. Readers who possess high levels of declarative knowledge consistently exhibit better comprehension and retention than readers with low levels of knowledge (Chiesi, Spilich, & Voss, 1979; Langer & Nicolich, 1981; Pearson, Hanson, & Gordon, 1979). Good and poor readers differ not only in the amount of knowledge they have available but also in how they make use of their knowledge to facilitate comprehension (Bransford, Stein, Shelton, & Owings, 1981; Oakhill, 1984). There are also reports that when poor readers are prompted to use their prior knowledge or are provided with activities to build prior knowledge, their reading comprehension improves (e.g., Dole, Valencia, Greer, & Wardrop, 1991; Neuman, 1988; Recht & Leslie, 1988).

When translated into classroom instructional strategies, prior knowledge training usually takes the form of teacher-directed prereading activities to help students activate or build background knowledge (Graves, Cooke, & Laberge, 1983; Langer, 1984; McCormick, 1989). Although providing prereading instructional procedures to improve poor readers' use of prior knowledge has considerable face validity, some have questioned the efficacy of prior knowledge instruction as a means of improving reading comprehension. For instance, Stanovich (2000) has questioned the dominant unidirectional causal model that postulates that individual differences in knowledge (e.g., vocabulary and declarative) and lower level cognitive subprocesses (e.g., working memory, lexical processing, inference making, comprehension monitoring) determine reading comprehension ability. Instead, Stanovich has proposed a reciprocal or bidirectional causal model in which individual differences in exposure to print affect both the development of the cognitive processes and declarative knowledge bases that support further gains in comprehension growth. Similar to arguments made for vocabulary, text is considerably richer in terms of its declarative knowledge content compared with oral language. As a result, Stanovich and colleagues (Stanovich & Cunningham, 1993; West, Stanovich, & Mitchell, 1993) have argued, "Print is a unique source of declarative knowledge, not replaceable by electronic media or oral sources" (Stanovich et al., 1996, p. 17). Therefore, text appears exceptionally well suited for promoting knowledge acquisition in struggling readers. However, for poor readers to take advantage of the increased knowledge density contained in text, they must actively construct and reflect on the knowledge contained in the text. Simply requiring children who are struggling readers to read more connected text is not sufficient to build their general declarative knowledge. One reason is that poor-reading children routinely find themselves with reading materials that are far too difficult (Stanovich, 1986). Another is that a majority of children who are struggling readers fail to actively construct meaning as they read (e.g., National Center for Learning Disabilities, 1999; Palincsar & Brown, 1984; Yuill & Oakhill, 1991).

From an instructional standpoint, it again appears that poor comprehenders would benefit from exposure to the rich declarative knowledge afforded by text if it were linked with a set of strategies that increased the probability that the knowledge in the text could be integrated into the children's declarative knowledge. To examine the efficacy of in-text instruction on struggling readers' ability to acquire declarative knowledge from text, we based our in-text dialogue and strategies on the reciprocal teaching and transactional instructional methods developed by Palincsar and Brown (1984) and Pressley (2000), respectively.

IQ AS A POSSIBLE MODERATOR
OF IN-TEXT INSTRUCTION EFFECTIVENESS

In this chapter, we are interested not only in the efficacy of in-text instruction on declarative knowledge and vocabulary acquisition but also whether child-level attributes moderate the effect of instruction. Baron and Kenny (1986) define a moderator variable as a "quantitative variable that affects the direction and/or strength of the relation between an independent or predictor variable and a dependent or criterion variable" (p. 1174). A moderator variable pinpoints the conditions under which an independent variable exerts its effects on a dependent variable. We focus on intelligence, assessed using a measure of Full-Scale IQ (FSIQ), as an important child-level predictor of response to in-text instruction. Multiple reviews of the literature have shown IQ to be highly predictive of concurrent and future reading comprehension skill (Gajria, Jitendra, Sood, & Sacks, 2007; Schatschneider, Harrell, & Buck, 2007). Furthermore, a review of the literature by Fuchs and Young (2006) and a treatment study by Berninger, Abbott, Vermeulen, and Fulton (2006) have identified intelligence as a significant predictor of children's response to intervention when the outcome measure of interest is reading comprehension.

OVERVIEW OF STUDIES

In this chapter, we present initial efficacy data from two studies evaluating the effects of a multicomponent instructional program for students in grades 3 to 5 who are struggling readers. In developing the instructional components and procedures, we recognize, and worked to exploit, the enormous potential of text to increase the vocabulary and declarative knowledge base of struggling readers. However, we also recognize that reading text without effective strategies for deriving and retaining vocabulary and knowledge is an ineffective means of instruction for struggling readers. Therefore, our primary objective in this study was to develop instructional dialogues, strategies, and materials that increased the probability that struggling readers would derive and retain vocabulary and declarative knowledge while reading text. To aid in generalization and transfer of these skills to the general education curriculum, the instructional program provided experience in applying the target skills in science and social studies texts. In addition, we examined possible treatment by FSIQ interactions as predictors of posttest knowledge and vocabulary skill. Significant interactions between treatment type and FSIQ would signal differences in response to treatment as a function of FSIQ.

In Study 1, we isolated the effects of metacognitive instruction on the retention of declarative knowledge in struggling readers. Specifically, we examined whether the use of reciprocal teaching (RT) practices, with its heavy emphasis on metacognition, during in-text reading would improve the reading comprehension skills of struggling readers. Studies have identified various obstacles encountered when using RT with struggling readers. For instance, it has been suggested that struggling students are unwilling or lack enough prior knowledge to lead productive RT sessions and that these students often modeled incorrect strategy usage and rarely provided the elaborations and inferences necessary for supporting understanding. For this reason, Hacker and Tenent (2002) have proposed that "having this process guided by experts (i.e., the teachers) rather than novices (i.e., the students) may have stronger impacts on learning" (p. 713). However, previous studies have suffered from inadequate experimental designs to isolate the effects of metacognition above and beyond strategy instruction in struggling readers. Furthermore, previous studies have not examined the possibility of individual differences explaining how children respond to RT instruction. It may be that some students make exceptional gains, while others attain modest or no gains. We examined whether there were benefits to including a metacognitive component to comprehension instruction on the retention of declarative knowledge in third- and fourth-grade children who were identified by their teachers as struggling readers. In addition, we examined whether FSIQ moderated the effects of metacognitive instruction among the struggling readers.

In Study 2, we examined the effects of text-level instructional programs designed to increase vocabulary and declarative knowledge acquisition during reading in expository text. This was a clinical trial involving struggling readers in grades 3 to 6. To our knowledge, no study has expressly contrasted the effects of two in-text training programs that share the same basic instructional procedures but vary in targeted knowledge acquisition. Specifically, we were interested in whether there were trade-offs between vocabulary learning and declarative knowledge acquisition based on the type of text-level instruction provided in expository text. Again, we examined whether FSIQ moderated the effects of instruction among the struggling readers.

ANALYTIC APPROACH TO ANALYZING CHILD × INSTRUCTIONAL RELATIONS

In both studies we used a randomized cluster design to evaluate the effects of in-text instruction and to examine possible moderating effects of FSIQ on struggling readers. Randomized cluster designs rely on the random assignment of clusters to treatment and control. This type of design allows causal relationships associated with treatment to be explored. In both studies small groups of struggling readers (i.e., clusters) were formed and randomly assigned to treatment conditions. Within a hierarchical linear modeling (HLM) framework, randomized clusters can be conceptualized as a two-level design, with students nested within treatment (Raudenbush & Bryk, 2002). Here, students are the Level 1 units and treatment clusters are the Level 2 units. The treatment contrast is defined at Level 2. In HLM, a one-way analysis of variance with random effects was used to estimate the proportion of within- and between-cluster variance on the outcome measures (i.e., intraclass correlation). In Study 1, 6% of the total variance on the knowledge measure resided at the level of the cluster. In Study 2, 15% of the variance in the knowledge measure and 11% of the variance in the vocabulary measure existed at the cluster level. Given the existence of significant variance at the level of the cluster, we used a two-level HLM.

In both studies we contrasted performance across three groups (two treatments and one control). We used dummy coding to examine treatment versus control (D_1 coded as 0.5, 0.5, and -1) and treatment 1 versus treatment 2 (D_2 coded as 1, -1, and 0). We controlled for pretest skill on the outcome measures of declarative knowledge and vocabulary and examined FSIQ as a moderator effect. The models for Study 1 and Study 2 are provided next:

Study 1

$$\text{Posttest Knowledge}_{ij} = \beta_{0j} + \gamma_{1j}(\text{Pretest Knowledge})_{ij} + \beta_{2j}(\text{FSIQ})_{ij} + r_{ij}$$
$$\beta_{0j} = \gamma_{00} + \gamma_{01}(D_1)_j + \gamma_{02}(D_2)_j + u_{0j}$$
$$\beta_{1j} = \gamma_{10}$$
$$\beta_{2j} = \gamma_{20} + \gamma_{21}(D_1)_j + \gamma_{22}(D_2)_j + u_{2j}$$

Study 2

$$\text{Posttest Knowledge}_{ij} = \beta_{0j} + \beta_{1j}(\text{Pretest Knowledge})_{ij} + \beta_{2j}(\text{FSIQ})_{ij} + r_{ij}$$
$$\beta_{0j} = \gamma_{00} + \gamma_{01}(D_1)_j + \gamma_{02}(D_2)_j + u_{0j}$$
$$\beta_{1j} = \gamma_{10}$$
$$\beta_{2j} = \gamma_{20} + \gamma_{21}(D_1)_j + \gamma_{22}(D_2)_j + u_{2j}$$

$$\text{Posttest Vocabulary}_{ij} = \beta_{0j} + \beta_{1j}(\text{Pretest Vocabulary})_{ij} + \beta_{2j}(\text{FSIQ})_{ij} + r_{ij}$$
$$\beta_{0j} = \gamma_{00} + \gamma_{01}(D_1)_j + \gamma_{02}(D_2)_j + u_{0j}$$
$$\beta_{1j} = \gamma_{10}$$
$$\beta_{2j} = \gamma_{20} + \gamma_{21}(D_1)_j + \gamma_{22}(D_2)_j + u_{2j}$$

At level 1 we examine the main effects of pretest knowledge and FSIQ on posttest performance. At level 2 we examine the main effects of treatment (D_1 and D_2) on posttest performance. Finally, we examine the cross-level interaction between child-level FSIQ and cluster-level treatment.

Study 1: Isolating the Effects of Metacognitive Instruction on the Retention of Declarative Knowledge

In Study 1 we assessed the additive affect of metacognitive instruction above and beyond strategy instruction. To accomplish this, 57 teacher-identified struggling readers in third and fourth grade were assigned to 25 different clusters. To be eligible for the study, children had to read at a rate of 40 words/min with accuracy of at least 75% in third-grade text. This ensured that children would be able to read in the science and social studies texts used in the study. Clusters were then randomly assigned to one of three conditions: (1) decoding only (DEC), (2) decoding + traditional strategy comprehension (TRAD), or (3) decoding + reciprocal teaching (RT). The DEC condition served as the control by providing children with decoding and fluency skill instruction without text reading. Clusters consisted of two to three children and each received either 30 min of instruction (DEC) or 60 min of instruction (TRAD or RT) three to four times per week for approximately 10 weeks for a total of 25 lessons. Instruction was provided outside the general education classroom by trained research assistants.

The DEC condition provided students with approximately 25 min of decoding and 5 min of fluency instruction. The decoding instruction incorporated practice with blending phonemes and application of three strategies from Word Identification Strategy Training, including compare and contrast, peeling-off affixes, and vowel variation (Gaskin, Downer, & Gaskins, 1986; Lovett, Lacerenza, & Borden, 2000). The compare and contrast strategy teaches children word identification by analogy (e.g., using a familiar word such as *rain* to identify an unfamiliar word with the same spelling pattern, such as *plain*) using a corpus of 120 key words that represent high-frequency English spelling patterns. In the peeling off strategy, children are taught 40 prefixes and suffixes (e.g., *un-, pre-, -ment, -tion*) and how to identify and segment affixes in multisyllabic words (e.g., *pre-/ven/-tion*). The vowel variation strategy teaches children to try different vowel pronunciations in an unknown word until a successful result is obtained. For example, when attempting to read the word *pint*, children try both the short- and long-vowel sound of *i* and then decide which vowel pronunciation yields a known word. Children were taught vowel sounds as well as vowel combinations with multiple pronunciations (e.g., *ea, ow, oo*). In addition to these strategies, children were taught an organizational structure for effective strategy application and evaluation known as the Game Plan (see Lovett et al., 2000). At the end of each decoding session, children received reading fluency instruction in short expository texts from the QuickReads series (Hiebert, 2003).

Students in the RT condition received 30 min of decoding and fluency instruction per session as described previously, as well as 30 min of comprehension instruction using the four RT strategies (questioning, summarizing, clarifying, and predicting). Students read three expository texts: *Young Pioneers* (Hamilton, 2001), *Chasing Tornadoes* (Gold, 1999), and *Secrets of the Rain Forests* (Meyers, 1999). In each text, students took turns reading a passage orally while the other students followed along in the book. After each passage, the students were first encouraged to clarify any idea or word that did not make sense in the passage. Students then generated questions pertaining to the main idea of the passage. Next, students created summaries that focused on the main idea of the passage but did not include details. Finally, students made predictions using clues (e.g., pictures, bold words, information in the previous paragraph) to guess what the next passage would be about. After each strategy, the group was encouraged to evaluate and extend each other's responses. Over the course of the program, the teacher modeled each of the four strategies, scaffolded instruction for each student, and slowly turned over responsibility of teaching the group to the students as they became more competent with the strategies.

Students in the TRAD condition also received an hour of instruction, including decoding, fluency instruction, and comprehension. Students in this condition read the same texts and learned the same RT comprehension strategies. This group, however, received the comprehension instruction without the metacognitive components. The teacher guided the group through answering questions, clarifying, summarizing, and predicting. In contrast to the RT condition, the teacher did not prompt the other students to evaluate or elaborate on answers, and the teacher maintained the leadership role throughout the program.

Students were given a pre- and posttreatment assessment on knowledge items that were presented in the texts. A total of 30 multiple-choice items made up the assessment. Twenty questions were generated directly from *Young Pioneers, Chasing Tornadoes,* and *Secrets of the Rain Forests*. Ten additional items were generated from books in the series that were not read as part of the study. This will allow us in the future to contrast items that children were exposed to versus those they were not. To control for reading ability, all items were read to the children at pre- and posttest. In addition, at the beginning of the study, each child was administered the four subtests of the Wechsler Abbreviated Scale of Intelligence (WASI; Wechsler, 1999), which is linked to the Wechsler Intelligence Scale for Children. The subtests comprise Vocabulary, Similarities, Matrix Reasoning, and Block Design and allow an estimate of a child's FSIQ. To better quantify the reading skills of the sample, we also individually administered the two subtests of the Test of Word Reading Efficiency (TOWRE; Torgesen, Wagner, & Rashotte, 1997): Sight Word Efficiency (SWE) and Decoding Efficiency (DE); the Passage Comprehension (PC) subtest of the Woodcock Reading Mastery Test (WRMT; Woodcock, 1998); and the Gray Oral Reading Test (GORT-4; Weiderhold & Bryant, 2004). Table 3.1 provides pretest means, standard deviations, and range of scores for the three treatment groups. At pretest the treatment groups answered on average about 13 questions correctly on the knowledge measure. The average standard score for the sample was 88 on FSIQ, 86 on TOWRE, 91 on PC, and 83 on GORT-4. There were no statistically significant group differences at pretest on any of the measures.

TABLE 3.1. Pretest Means, Standard Deviations, and Ranges on the Pretest Knowledge Measure and FSIQ as a Function of Condition: Study 1

	Measure	
	Pretest knowledge	FSIQ
DEC		
M	13.20	87.30
SD	3.14	12.33
Range	8–21	73–110
TRAD		
M	13.28	90.64
SD	3.43	13.85
Range	7–20	69–114
RT		
M	12.76	85.53
SD	3.66	10.52
Range	4–20	70–107

Note. FSIQ = Full-Scale IQ; DEC = decoding-only condition; TRAD = decoding + traditional strategy comprehension condition; RT = decoding + reciprocal teaching condition.

Table 3.2 presents the parameter estimates for the two-level HLM model. Controlling for pretest knowledge and FSIQ, children on average answered 16.31 questions correctly (γ_{00}) on the posttest knowledge measure. Children in the treatment conditions answered 2.72 more questions correctly compared with the control children (D_1, γ_{01}), and children in the RT condition answered on average 1.5 more questions correctly compared to children in the TRAD condition (D_2, γ_{02}). There was a main effect of pretest knowledge (γ_{10}) and FSIQ (γ_{20}) on posttest knowledge performance; high pretest knowledge and FSIQ were associated with higher posttest knowledge scores. In addition, a significant cross-level interaction between treatment (D_2) and FSIQ was detected (γ_{22}). This moderator relationship is depicted in Figure 3.1. For children with lower FSIQ scores, there is little difference between RT and TRAD in supporting declarative knowledge retention during in-text reading. However, as child FSIQ increases, there is a clear advantage of RT over TRAD on posttest declarative knowledge, even after controlling for pretest knowledge.

Results from Study 1 suggest that even though RT is more effective than TRAD, these effects are being carried by children with higher FSIQs, therefore, we must qualify for whom RT is most effective. At present, we do not have a definitive answer as to why FSIQ plays such an important role in children's ability to benefit from RT. An important element of RT is that children must internalize the four strategies to be able to monitor their strategy use and become better self-regulators of

TABLE 3.2. Prediction of Posttest Declarative Knowledge Using Treatment Condition, Pretest Declarative Knowledge, and FSIQ: Study 1

Fixed effects	γ	SE	p
β_0 intercept posttest knowledge			
γ_{00} mean	16.31	0.40	.000
γ_{01} treatment versus control (D_1)	2.72	0.55	.000
γ_{02} RT versus TRAD (D_2)	1.53	0.47	.004
β_1 pretest knowledge			
γ_{10} mean	0.34	0.16	.034
β_2 FSIQ			
γ_{20} mean	0.13	0.04	.005
γ_{21} treatment versus control (D_1)	0.08	0.05	.125
γ_{22} RT versus TRAD (D_2)	0.10	0.04	.021

Note. FSIQ = Full-Scale IQ; RT = decoding + reciprocal teaching condition; TRAD = decoding + traditional strategy comprehension condition.

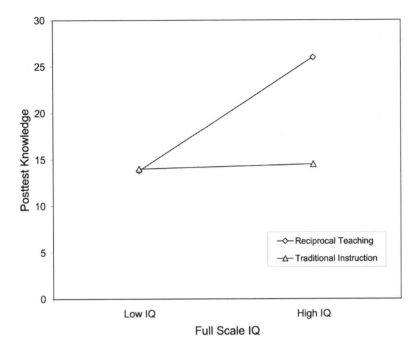

FIGURE 3.1. Moderating effects of Full-Scale IQ on posttest knowledge performance in the reciprocal teaching and traditional instruction groups: Study 1.

their own reading comprehension. We wonder whether the monitoring and self-regulatory aspects of RT place too high a cognitive demand on struggling readers with lower FSIQs. Additional work is needed before we conclude that the beneficial effects of RT should be reserved for struggling readers with elevated FSIQs.

Study 2: Facilitating Struggling Readers' Acquisition of Declarative Knowledge and Vocabulary Learning during Reading

In Study 2 we were interested in developing and evaluating the effects of an in-text vocabulary strategy program that borrowed techniques from the RT program. We were also interested in whether trade-offs may exist between vocabulary learning and declarative knowledge acquisition based on the type of text-level instruction provided to children during reading in expository text. For instance, we wondered whether children who focus on vocabulary learning during text reading would learn and retain less declarative knowledge compared with children who focused on knowledge building during text reading and vice versa. To accomplish this, 96 readers, in second to fifth grades were assigned to 28 different clusters, which were randomly assigned to three different conditions. Struggling readers were defined as children scoring below the 25th percentile on a standardized measure of reading comprehension (GORT-4) but able to read at least 40 words/min in third-grade text. Again, this allowed children to read the science and social studies texts used in the study. Clusters of two to four children received 90 min of instruction two times per week for 24 lessons (i.e., 36 hr of instruction). Instruction was provided at Vanderbilt University after school hours by trained research assistants. Clusters were randomly assigned to: (1) traditional comprehension instruction (COMP), (2) reciprocal teaching (KNOW), or (3) vocabulary instruction (VOC) conditions. All conditions were matched on instructional time. Students in all three conditions received the decoding and fluency instruction described in Study 1 for approximately 35 min per session. For the remainder of each session, students received comprehension instruction using the expository texts described in Study 1: *Young Pioneers, Chasing Tornadoes*, and *Secrets of the Rain Forests*. The COMP condition served as the control by providing children with the same program components but no strategy instruction during text reading. It was designed to mirror what we considered typical classroom practice in reading comprehension instruction. Students in this condition took turns reading the text without stopping to use a strategy or answer questions. At the end of the assigned reading for the session, students completed two to three worksheets. These worksheets consisted of drawing pictures, creating compare and contrast charts, matching terms, and answering cloze and multiple-choice questions about the text.

The KNOW condition was the same as the RT condition in Study 1. We rename it KNOW to represent training focused on promoting declarative knowledge learning. The VOC condition was created to parallel the KNOW condition in the amount of metacognition, dialogue, and gradual release of responsibility of teaching. In contrast to the KNOW condition, instruction in the vocabulary condition focused on the use of vocabulary strategies. We selected 80 target words across the three texts that were unlikely to be known to students, important to understanding the text, and likely to be found in other texts (high utility). In this condition, each student took turns reading a passage with identified target words and worked through four vocabulary strategies: (1) determining the part of speech (noun, verb, adjective), (2) using word analysis strategies (e.g., replacing *-un* with *not* to figure out that *unclear* means *not clear*), (3) using context clues, including signal words or phrases (e.g., *or, like, is known as*), or information in the text to infer meaning, and (4) a look-up strategy. A glossary was created for each target word and reviewed for the look-up strategy. The glossary contained a semantic map of antonyms and synonyms for each word as well as a short definition, part of speech, examples, nonexamples, and a sample sentence containing the target word. After working through each strategy, the students considered whether they had enough information to make sense of the text or needed to continue to the next strategy. The look-up strategy was always used last and only after the other strategies were exhausted.

Students were given a pre- and posttreatment assessment on knowledge and vocabulary items that were presented in the texts. The knowledge test was the same used in Study 1. A total of 40 multiple-choice items made up the vocabulary assessment. Thirty questions were generated directly from *Young Pioneers, Chasing Tornadoes,* and *Secrets of the Rain Forests.* Ten additional vocabulary items were generated from books in the series that were not read as part of the study. This will allow us in the future to contrast items that children were exposed to versus those they were not. To control for reading ability, all items were read to the children at pre- and posttest. In addition, at the beginning of the study, each child was administered the four subtests of the WASI (Wechsler, 1999). To better quantify the reading skills of the sample, we also individually administered the two subtests of the TOWRE (Torgesen et al., 1997)—SWE and DE—and the GORT-4 (Weiderhold & Bryant, 2004). Table 3.3 provides pretest means, standard deviations, and range of scores for the three treatment groups. At pretest the treatment groups answered on average about 13 knowledge questions and 14 vocabulary questions correctly. The average standard scores for the sample were 89 on the FSIQ, 90 on the TOWRE, and 82 on the GORT-4. There were no statistically significant group differences at pretest on any of the measures.

Table 3.4 presents the parameter estimates for the two-level HLM model of knowledge learning. Controlling for pretest knowledge and FSIQ, children on average answered 16.36 questions correctly (γ_{00}) on the posttest knowledge measure. Children in the treatment conditions (KNOW + VOC) answered only 0.21 more questions correctly compared with the control children (D_1, γ_{01}), and children in the KNOW condition answered on average 0.19 more questions correctly compared with chil-

TABLE 3.3. Pretest Means, Standard Deviations, and Ranges on the Pretest Knowledge Measure, Vocabulary Measure, and FSIQ as a Function of Condition: Study 2

	Measure		
	Pretest knowledge	Pretest vocabulary	FSIQ
COMP			
M	13.10	14.34	89.55
SD	3.17	5.15	13.00
Range	5–18	6–29	60–125
KNOW			
M	12.64	15.61	90.55
SD	3.52	5.12	14.61
Range	6–21	7–26	65–132
VOC			
M	13.42	13.42	87.81
SD	3.39	4.28	13.21
Range	6–23	5–29	64–128

Note. FSIQ = Full-Scale IQ; COMP = traditional comprehension instruction; KNOW = reciprocal teaching; VOC = vocabulary instruction.

dren in the VOC condition (D_2, γ_{02}). Results suggest that the type of in-text instruction (KNOW, VOC) had little additive effect over COMP on knowledge learning during reading. Importantly, though, there was no loss in declarative knowledge learning for children focusing on learning new vocabulary while reading.

There was a main effect of pretest knowledge (γ_{10}) and FSIQ (γ_{20}) on posttest knowledge performance: Higher pretest knowledge and FSIQ were associated with higher posttest knowledge scores. In addition, a significant cross-level interaction between treatment (D_1) and FSIQ was detected (γ_{21}). This moderator relationship is depicted in Figure 3.2. For children with lower FSIQ scores, there was an advantage for the in-text strategies (KNOW + VOC) over COMP in supporting declarative knowledge retention during in-text reading. However, as FSIQ increased, there was a clear advantage of COMP over the in-text strategy conditions. This suggests that a lack of some type of in-text instruction was detrimental to children with lower cognitive skills but advantageous for children of higher cognitive ability.

Table 3.5 presents the parameter estimates for the two-level HLM model of vocabulary learning. Controlling for pretest vocabulary and FSIQ, children on average answered 18.82 questions correctly (γ_{00}) on the posttest vocabulary measure. Children in the treatment conditions

TABLE 3.4. Prediction of Posttest Declarative Knowledge Using Treatment Condition, Pretest Declarative Knowledge, and FSIQ: Study 2

Fixed effects	γ	SE	p
β_0 intercept posttest knowledge			
γ_{00} mean	16.36	0.45	.000
γ_{01} treatment versus control (D_1)	0.21	0.69	.766
γ_{02} KNOW versus VOC (D_2)	0.19	0.48	.694
β_1 pretest knowledge			
γ_{10} mean	0.65	0.12	.000
β_2 FSIQ			
γ_{20} mean	0.15	0.03	.000
γ_{21} treatment versus control (D_1)	−0.11	0.03	.005
γ_{22} KNOW versus VOC (D_2)	0.02	0.03	.574

Note. FSIQ = Full-Scale IQ; KNOW = reciprocal teaching; VOC = vocabulary instruction.

(VOC + KNOW) answered 0.85 more vocabulary questions correctly compared with the control children (D_1, γ_{01}); this difference was not statistically significant. However, children in the VOC condition answered on average 1.95 more questions correctly compared with those in the KNOW condition (D_2, γ_{02}). There was a main effect of pretest vocabulary (γ_{10}) and FSIQ (γ_{20}) on posttest knowledge performance, with high pretest vocabulary and FSIQ being associated with higher posttest vocabulary scores. In addition, two significant cross-level interactions were identified between: treatment (D_1) and FSIQ (γ_{21}) and treatment (D_2) and FSIQ (γ_{22}). The moderator relationship between D_1 and FSIQ is depicted in Figure 3.3. For children with lower FSIQ scores, there was little difference between COMP and the in-text strategies (KNOW + VOC); however, at higher FSIQ, children in the in-text strategy condition outperformed those using the in-text strategies. Contrasting the two in-text strategies (see Figure 3.4), children with lower FSIQ showed similar performance across the VOC and KNOW conditions; however, as FSIQ increased, there was an advantage of the VOC over the KNOW condition, suggesting that much of the VOC effect was being driven by higher FSIQ children. Results suggest that the type of in-text instruction had a significant effect on vocabulary learning during reading, particularly in children with higher FSIQ. To achieve significant vocabulary gains, it is important that the in-text instruction focus on new vocabulary. It was also notable that vocabulary gains in the VOC condition did not come at the expense of knowledge gains.

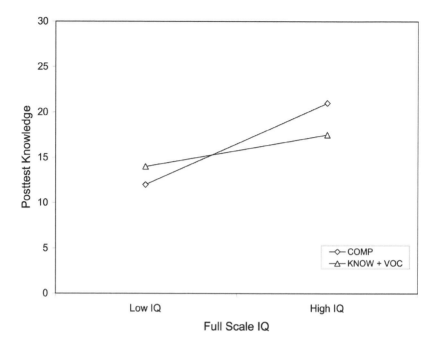

FIGURE 3.2. Moderating effects of Full-Scale IQ on posttest knowledge performance in the comprehension (COMP) and combined knowledge and vocabulary (KNOW + VOC) groups: Study 2.

TABLE 3.5. Prediction of Posttest Vocabulary Knowledge Using Treatment Condition, Pretest Vocabulary Knowledge, and FSIQ: Study 2

Fixed effects	γ	SE	p
β_0 intercept posttest vocabulary			
γ_{00} mean	18.82	0.65	.000
γ_{01} treatment versus control (D_1)	0.85	0.90	.360
γ_{02} VOC versus KNOW (D_2)	1.95	0.80	.030
β_1 pretest vocabulary			
γ_{10} mean	0.72	0.12	.000
β_2 FSIQ			
γ_{20} mean	0.15	0.02	.000
γ_{21} treatment versus control (D_1)	0.10	0.03	.004
γ_{22} KNOW versus VOC (D_2)	0.08	0.02	.032

Note. FSIQ = Full-Scale IQ; KNOW = reciprocal teaching; VOC = vocabulary instruction.

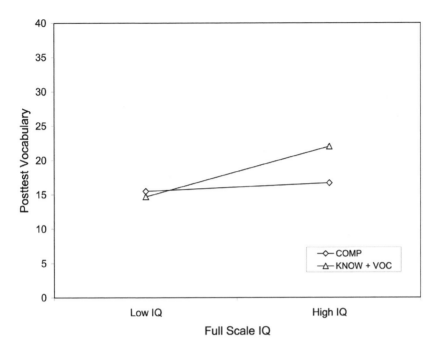

FIGURE 3.3. Moderating effects of Full-Scale IQ on posttest vocabulary performance in the comprehension (COMP) and combined knowledge and vocabulary (KNOW + VOC) groups.

CONCLUSIONS

Results from the two studies seem to converge in several important ways. In both studies we found significant treatment effects associated with in-text strategy use. In Study 1 we found that adding a metacognitive component to strategy training improved children's ability to retain declarative knowledge encountered in text. In Study 2 a vocabulary strategy improved children's ability to derive the meaning of unfamiliar words while not affecting the ability to retain declarative knowledge. However, in both studies, these treatment effects were moderated by child-level FSIQ. In addition, the moderating effect of FSIQ tended to favor children with higher FSIQ. We speculate that cognitive demands of our interventions may be too high for struggling readers with lower FSIQs to easily implement and automatize. Further, we wonder whether providing greater practice with each of the strate-

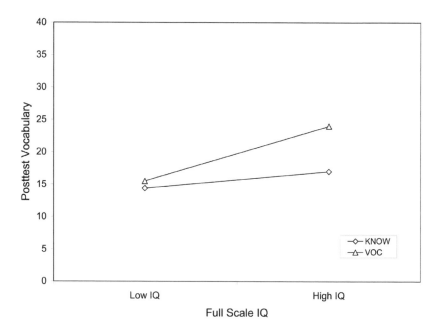

FIGURE 3.4. Moderating effects of Full-Scale IQ on posttest vocabulary performance in the vocabulary (VOC) and knowledge (KNOW) groups.

gies and longer periods of scaffolding might lessen the overall cognitive demands of the interventions and reduce the effects of FSIQ as a moderator of effectiveness. Additional work is needed before we conclude that the beneficial effects of the interventions should be reserved for struggling readers with elevated FSIQs. We encourage further research examining the role of IQ in moderating struggling readers' response to in-text strategy use.

ACKNOWLEDGMENTS

This research was supported in part by Grant No. H324D0100003 from the U.S. Department of Education, Office of Special Education Programs; Grant No. R305G050101 from the U.S. Department of Education, Institute of Education Sciences; and Core Grant No. HD15052 from the National Institute of Child Health and Human Development to Vanderbilt University. Statements do not reflect the position or policy of these agencies, and no official endorsement by them should be inferred.

REFERENCES

Adams, M. J. (1990). *Beginning to read: Thinking and learning about print*. Cambridge, MA: MIT Press.

Anderson, R. C., & Freebody, P. (1985). Vocabulary development. In H. Singer & R. B. Rudell (Eds.), *Theoretical models and processes of reading* (pp. 343–371). Newark, DE: IDA.

Anderson, R. C., & Pearson, P. D. (1984). A schemata–theoretic view of basic processes in reading. In P. D. Pearson, R. Barr, M. L. Kamil, & P. Mosenthal (Eds.), *Handbook of reading research* (pp. 255–291). New York: Longman.

Anderson, R. C., Reynolds, R. E., Schallert, D. L., & Goetz, E. T. (1977). Frameworks for comprehending discourse. *American Educational Research Journal, 14*, 367–381.

Anderson, R. C., Spiro, R. J., & Anderson, M. C. (1978). Schemata as scaffolding for the representation of information in connected discourse. *American Educational Research Journal, 15*, 433–440.

Baker, L. (1979). Comprehension monitoring: Identifying and coping with test confusion. *Journal of Reading Behavior, 11*, 365–374.

Baker, L., & Anderson, R. I. (1982). Effects of inconsistent information on text processing: Evidence for comprehension monitoring. *Reading Research Quarterly, 22*, 281–294.

Baker, L., & Brown, A. L. (1984). Metacognitive skills and reading. In P. D. Pearson, R. Barr, M. L. Kamil, & P. Mosenthal (Eds.), *Handbook of reading research* (pp. 353–394). New York: Longman.

Baker, S. K., Simmons, D. C., & Kame'enui, E. J. (1995). *Vocabulary acquisition: Curriculum and instructional implications for diverse learners* (Technical Report No. 14). Eugene: University of Oregon, National Center to Improve the Tools of Educators.

Baron, R. M., & Kenny, D. A. (1986). The moderator–mediator variable distinction in social psychological research: Conceptual, strategic, and statistical considerations. *Journal of Personality and Social Psychology, 51*, 1173–1182.

Baumann, J. F., & Kame'enui, E. J. (1991). Research on vocabulary instruction: Ode to Voltaire. In J. Flood, J. J. D. Lapp, & J. R. Squire (Eds.), *Handbook of research on teaching the English language arts* (pp. 604–632). New York: Macmillan.

Beck, I. L., McKeown, M. G., & Kucan, L. (2002). *Bringing words to life: Robust vocabulary instruction*. New York: Guilford Press.

Beck, I. L., Perfetti, C. A., & McKeown, M. G. (1982). The effects of long-term vocabulary instruction on lexical access and reading comprehension. *Journal of Educational Psychology, 74*, 506–521.

Berninger, V. W., Abbott, R. D., Vermeulen, K., & Fulton, C. M. (2006). Paths to reading comprehension in at-risk second-grade readers. *Journal of Learning Disabilities, 39*, 334–351.

Blachowicz, C. L., & Fisher, P. (2000). Vocabulary instruction. In M. L. Kamil, P. B. Mosenthal, P. D. Pearson, & R. Barr (Eds.), *Handbook of reading research: Vol. III* (pp. 503–524). Mahwah, NJ: Erlbaum.

Bransford, J. D., Stein, B. S., Shelton, T. S., & Owings, R. A. (1981). Cognition and adaptation: The importance of learning to learn. In J. Harvey (Ed.), *Cognition, social behavior, and the environment* (pp. 92–110). Hillsdale, NJ: Erlbaum.

Cain, K., & Oakhill, J. (1999). Inference making ability and its relation to comprehension failure in young children. *Reading and Writing, 11,* 489–503.

Carnine, D. W., Silbert, J., & Kameenui, E. J. (1997). *Direct instruction in reading.* Columbus, OH: Merrill.

Chiesi, H. L., Spilich, G. J., & Voss, J. F. (1979). Acquisition of domain-related information in relation to high and low domain knowledge. *Journal of Verbal Learning and Verbal Behavior, 18,* 257–274.

Cunningham, A. E., & Stanovich, K. E. (1991). Tracking the unique effects of print exposure in children: Associations with vocabulary, general knowledge, and spelling. *Journal of Educational Psychology, 83,* 264–274.

Cunningham, A. E., & Stanovich, K. E. (1998, Spring/Summer). What reading does for the mind. *American Educator,* pp. 8–15.

Deshler, D. D., Ellis, E. S., & Lenz, B. K. (1996). *Teaching adolescents with learning disabilities: Strategies and methods* (2nd ed.). Denver, CO: Love.

Dole, J. A., Valencia, S. W., Greer, E. A., & Wardrop, J. L. (1991). Effects of two types of prereading instruction on the comprehension of narrative and expository text. *Reading Research Quarterly, 26,* 142–159.

Fuchs, D., & Young, C. L. (2006). On the irrelevance of intelligence in predicting responsiveness to reading instruction. *Exceptional Children, 73,* 8–30.

Gajria, M., Jitendra, A. K., Sood, S., & Sacks, G. (2007). Improving comprehension of expository text in students with LD: A research synthesis. *Journal of Learning Disabilities, 40,* 210–225.

Garner, R. (1987). *Metacognition and reading comprehension.* Norwood, NJ: Ablex.

Gaskins, I. W., Downer, M. A., & Gaskins, R. W. (1986). *Introduction to the Benchmark School Word Identification/Vocabulary Development Program.* Media, PA: Benchmark School.

Gold, B. (1999). *Chasing tornadoes.* Tucson, AZ: Good Year Books.

Gough, P. B. (1996). How children learn to read and why they fail. *Annals of Dyslexia, 46,* 3–20.

Gough, P. B., & Tunmer, W. E. (1986). Decoding, reading, and reading disability. *Remedial and Special Education, 7,* 6–10.

Graves, M. F., Cooke, C. L., & LaBerge, C. L. (1983). Effects of previewing short stories. *Reading Research Quarterly, 18,* 262–276.

Hacker, D. J., & Tenent, A. (2002). Implementing reciprocal teaching in the classroom: Overcoming obstacles and making modifications. *Journal of Educational Psychology, 94,* 699–718.

Hamilton, T. (2001). *Young pioneers.* Lebanon, IN: Modern Curriculum Press.

Hayes, D. P., & Ahrens, M. (1988). Vocabulary simplification for children: A special case of "motherese"? *Journal of Child Language, 15,* 395–410.

Hiebert, E. H. (2003). *QuickReads: A research-based fluency program.* Parsippany, NJ: Modern Curriculum Press.

Jenkins, J. R., Matlock, B., & Slocum, T. A. (1989). Two approaches to vocabulary instruction: The teaching of individual word meanings and practice in deriving word meaning from context. *Reading Research Quarterly, 24,* 216–235.

Kamil, M. L. (2004). Vocabulary and comprehension instruction: Summary and implications of the National Reading Panel findings. In P. McCardle & V. Chhabra (Eds.), *The voice of evidence in reading research* (pp. 213–234). Baltimore, MD: Brookes.

Kintsch, W. (1998). *Comprehension: A paradigm for cognition.* Cambridge, UK: Cambridge University Press.

Landauer, T. K., & Dumais, S. T. (1996). How come you know so much? From practical problems to new memory theory. In D. J. Herrmann, C. McEvoy, C. Hertzog, P. Hertel, & M. K. Johnson (Eds.), *Basic and applied memory research theory in context, volume 1* (pp. 105–126). Mahwah, NJ: Erlbaum.

Langer, J. (1984). Examining background knowledge and text comprehension. *Reading Research Quarterly, 19,* 469–481.

Langer, J., & Nicolich, M. (1981). Prior knowledge and its relationship to comprehension. *Journal of Reading Behavior, 13,* 373–379.

Leach, J. M., Scarborough, H. S., & Rescorla, L. (2003). Late-emerging reading disabilities. *Journal of Educational Psychology, 95,* 211–224.

Lovett, M. W., Lacerenza, L., & Borden, S. (2000). Putting struggling readers on the PHAST track: A program to integrate phonological and strategy-based remedial reading instruction and maximize outcomes. *Journal of Learning Disabilities, 33,* 458–476.

Mastropieri, M. A., & Scruggs, T. E. (1997). Best practices in promoting reading comprehension in students with learning disabilities 1976 to 1996. *Remedial and Special Education, 18,* 197–213.

McCormick, S. (1989). Effects of previews on more skilled and skilled readers' comprehension of informational text. *Journal of Reading Behavior, 21,* 219–239.

Meyers, E. (1999). *Secrets of the rain forest.* Parsippany, NJ: Modern Curriculum Press.

Nagy, W., Anderson, R., & Herman, P. (1987). Learning word meanings from context during normal reading. *American Educational Research Journal, 24,* 237–270.

National Center for Learning Disabilities. (1999). *Two decades of research in learning disabilities: Reading comprehension, expressive writing, problem solving, self-concept keys to successful learning. A National Summit on Research in Learning Disabilities.* New York: Author.

Neuman, S. B. (1988). Enhancing children's comprehension through previewing. *National Reading Conference Yearbook, 37,* 219–224.

National Institute of Child Health and Human Development. (2000). *Report of the National Reading Panel* (NIH Publication No. 00-4754). Washington, DC: U.S. Government Printing Office.

Oakhill, J. (1984). Inferential and memory skills in children's comprehension of stories. *British Journal of Educational Psychology, 54,* 31–39.

Oakhill, J., Cain, K., & Yuill, N. (1998). Individual differences in children's comprehension skill: Toward an integrative model. In C. Hulme & R. M. Joshi

(Eds.), *Reading and spelling: Development and disorders* (pp. 343–368). Mahwah, NJ: Erlbaum.

Palincsar, A. S., & Brown, A. L. (1984). Reciprocal teaching of comprehension-foster and comprehension-monitoring activities. *Cognition and Instruction, 1,* 117–175.

Paris, S. G., & Oka, E. R. (1989). Strategies for comprehending text and coping with reading difficulties. *Learning Disability Quarterly, 12,* 32–42.

Pazzaglia, F., Cornoldi, C., & DeBeni, R. (1995). Knowledge about reading and self-evaluation in reading disabled children. In T. E. Scruggs & M. A. Mastropieri (Eds.), *Advances in learning and behavioral disabilities* (Vol. 9, pp. 91–118). Greenwich, CT: JAI Press.

Pearson, P. D., Hanson, J., & Gordon, C. (1979). The effect of background knowledge on young children's comprehension of explicit and implicit information. *Journal of Reading Behavior, 9,* 201–209.

Perfetti, C. A., Marron, M. A., & Foltz, P. W. (1996). Sources of comprehension failure: Theoretical perspectives and case studies. In C. Cornoldi & J. Oakhill (Eds.), *Reading comprehension difficulties: Processes and interventions* (pp. 137–165). Mahwah, NJ: Erlbaum.

Pressley, M. (2000). What should comprehension instruction be the instruction of? In M. L. Kamil, P. B. Mosenthal, P. D. Pearson, & R. Barr (Eds.), *Handbook of reading research: Vol. III* (pp. 545–562). Mahwah, NJ: Erlbaum.

RAND Reading Study Group. (2002). *Reading for understanding: Toward a R&D program in reading comprehension.* Santa Monica, CA: RAND Corporation.

Raudenbush, S. W., & Bryk, A. S. (2002). *Hierarchical linear models: Applications and data analysis methods.* London: Sage.

Recht, D. R., & Leslie, L. (1988). Effect of prior knowledge on good and poor readers memory of text. *Journal of Educational Psychology, 80,* 16–20.

Schatschneider, C., Harrell, E. R., & Buck, J. (2007). An individual-differences approach to the study of reading comprehension. In K. R. Tannenbaum, R. K. Wagner, & A. E. Muse (Eds.), *Vocabulary acquisition: Implications for reading comprehension* (pp. 249–275). New York: Guilford Press.

Smith, M. K. (1941). Measurement of the size of general English vocabulary through the elementary grades and high school. *Genetic Psychological Monographs, 24,* 311–345.

Snow, C. E., Burns, M. S., & Griffin, P. (1998). *Preventing reading difficulties in young children.* Washington, DC: National Academic Press.

Spilich, G. J., Vesonder, G. T., Chiesi, H. L., & Voss, J. F. (1979). Text processing of domain related information for individuals with high and low domain knowledge. *Journal of Verbal Learning and Verbal Behavior, 18,* 275–290.

Stanovich, K. E. (1986). Matthew effects in reading: Some consequences of individual differences in the acquisition of literacy. *Reading Research Quarterly, 21,* 360–406.

Stanovich, K. E. (2000). *Progress in understanding reading.* New York: Guilford Press.

Stanovich, K. E., & Cunningham, A. E. (1993). Where does knowledge come from? Specific associations between print exposure and information acquisition. *Journal of Educational Psychology, 85,* 211–229.

Stanovich, K. E., Cunningham, A. E., & West, R. F. (1998). Literacy experiences and the shaping of cognition. In S. Paris & H. Wellman (Eds.), *Global prospects of education: Development, culture, and schooling* (pp. 253–288). Washington, DC: American Psychological Association.

Stanovich, K. E., & West, R. F. (1989). Exposure to print and orthographic processing. *Reading Research Quarterly, 24*, 402–433.

Stanovich, K. E., West, R. F., Cunningham, A. E., Cipielewski, J., & Siddiqui, S. (1996). The role of inadequate print exposure as a determinant of reading comprehension problems. In C. Cornoldi & J. Oakhill (Eds.), *Reading comprehension difficulties: Processes and interventions* (pp. 15–68). Mahwah, NJ: Erlbaum.

Sternberg, R. J. (1985). *Beyond IQ: A triarchic theory of human intelligence.* Cambridge, UK: Cambridge University Press.

Sternberg, R. J. (1987). Most vocabulary is learned from context. In M. G. McKeown & M. E. Curtis (Eds.), *The nature of vocabulary acquisition* (pp. 89–105). Hillsdale, NJ: Erlbaum.

Swanborn, M. S. L., & de Glopper, K. (1999). Incidental word learning while reading: A meta-analysis. *Review of Educational Research, 69*, 261–285.

Tomesen, M., & Aarnoutse, C. (1998). The effects of an instructional program for deriving word meanings. *Educational Studies, 24*, 107–128.

Torgesen, J. K. (1998, Spring/Summer). Catch them before they fall: Identification and assessment to prevent reading failure in young children. *American Educator*, pp. 32–40.

Torgesen, J. K., Wagner, R. K., & Rashotte, C. A. (1997). *Test of word reading efficiency.* Austin, TX: PRO-ED.

Weiderhold, J. L., & Bryant, B. R. (2004). *Gray Oral Reading Test—Fourth edition (GORT-4).* San Antonio, TX: Pearson.

Weschler, D. (1999). *Wechsler Abbreviated Scale of Intelligence.* San Antonio, TX: Psychological Corporation.

West, R. F., Stanovich, K. E., & Mitchell, H. R. (1993). Reading in the real world and its correlates. *Reading Research Quarterly, 28*, 34–50.

White, T. G., Graves, M. F., & Slater, W. H. (1990). Growth of reading vocabulary in diverse elementary schools: Decoding and word meaning. *Journal of Educational Psychology, 82*, 281–290.

Woodcock, R.W. (1998). *Woodcock Reading Mastery Test—Revised/normative update.* Circle Pines, MN: American Guidance Service.

Yuill, N., & Oakhill, J. (1991). *Children's problems in text comprehension.* Cambridge, UK: Cambridge University Press.

PART II

DEVELOPMENTAL APPROACHES

4

How Children Read for Comprehension

Eye Movements in Developing Readers

Ralph Radach, Christiane Schmitten,
Lisa Glover, *and* Lynn Huestegge

The use of eye movements to study reading dates back to the very beginning of psychology as an experimental science. In fact, many of the early discoveries about the very nature of eye movements were made in the context of reading (Wade, Tatler, & Heller, 2003). A textbook on reading that made frequent reference to eye movement data appeared as early as the beginning of the 20th century (Huey, 1908). Building on this tradition, the analysis of eye movements has become one of the most successful methodologies in the ongoing quest to understand the dynamics of normal and impaired reading (see Radach & Kennedy, 2004, for a recent introduction and Rayner, 1998, for a seminal review).

Much of the progress in this rapidly developing area of research is owed to advancements in recording technology. Current eye-tracking configurations allow monitoring of ongoing reading behavior with letter-level precision at high temporal resolution while preserving a relatively natural reading situation. From oculomotor data the nature and time line of ongoing visual and linguistic processing can be inferred either for the purpose of testing specific psycholinguistic hypotheses or as a base for developing models of reading. In recent years, this productive tradition of research on information processing in normal reading has entered a new stage. A number of computational models have been developed that aim to simulate and explain key aspects of the reading process (e.g., Engbert, Nuthmann, Richter, & Kliegl, 2005; McDonald, Carpenter, & Shillcock, 2005; Reichle, Rayner, & Pollatsek, 2003; Reilly & Radach, 2006). The existing models have proven quite successful in accounting for a large number of empirical observations in normal reading (Radach, Reilly, & Inhoff, 2007), but to date no such modeling approach has been adapted to accommodate characteristics of developing readers. Therefore, one of the goals of the present chapter is to provide a review on the state of empirical work in the area as a step toward extending contemporary models of dynamic reading into the developmental domain.

Looking at the vast number of publications using eye tracking to study reading, it is quite striking how little attention has been paid to developmental research in this context. This lack of work is rather surprising given the basic fact that normal reading development is a prerequisite of adequately developed literacy skills, which, in turn, are a necessary condition for leading a successful life in our society. As a consequence, considerable investment is being made to foster research into the search for causes and remedies for reading impairments. Although recent advances in this area of research have been impressive, no consistent causal explanation of developmental dyslexia has so far emerged (see Vellutino, Fletcher, Snowling, & Scanlon, 2004; Ramus et al., 2003, for discussions of competing accounts).

In our view, one reason for this problematic state of affairs is that the massive investment in work on developmental reading disabilities has not been backed by a thorough study of the development of normal reading during the first school years. We are convinced that knowing how successful reading evolves is a necessary precondition to a causal understanding of developmental delays and disabilities. This chapter first reviews studies that used oculomotor analyses to study reading development in general. We then examine in detail some important similarities and differences between silent and oral reading. Based on data recently collected in our group, a cross-linguistic perspective to this discussion is added that may help to illuminate how the context of a particular language codetermines the task of becoming a skilled reader.

Although our discussion focuses on eye movement data, we are aware that other important approaches to the study of reading development and its underlying mechanisms exist. There is a strong and successful tradition of psychometric assessments, using performance measures to examine the development of reading fluency and comprehension. Similarly, tasks that are considered component skills of reading are frequently examined to uncover cognitive mechanisms underlying normal and abnormal reading development. Both of these approaches are represented in this volume with chapters written by leading experts in the field. Looking at reading more from a basic science angle, vibrant fields of experimental research use single-word paradigms (now often combined with brain imaging techniques) to study word processing, asking in many cases questions that parallel those raised in oculomotor studies (e.g., Coltheart, Rastle, Perry, Langdon, & Ziegler, 2001; Jacobs & Grainger, 1994). At this point in the history of our field, these different theoretical traditions and methodological approaches are still largely in a state of friendly coexistence. We hope that the present volume will serve to help unite the field and that our chapter can make a contribution in this direction.

DEVELOPMENTAL STUDIES OF EYE MOVEMENTS IN READING

Important early studies of eye movements during reading were done with longitudinal designs by Buswell (1922) and Taylor, Frackenpohl, and Petee (1960). The Taylor et al. study is especially noteworthy, because it included more than 12,000 students from all grades, from elementary to high school, reading short passages of text. Despite the limitations of the recording techniques available to these authors, they were able to report consistent developmental trajectories with regard to a number of key oculomotor measures. These include a marked reduction of mean fixation duration and number of fixations during reading over the first 6 years in school. Interestingly, in all studies the developmental trend did not include leftward eye movements back to previously viewed text (regressions), which accounted for between 20 and 25% of all saccades until the sixth grade (see later discussion and Inhoff, Weger, & Radach, 2005, for a discussion). A serious technical limitation of these early studies is that, because of the insensitivity of recording, many small saccades were presumably overlooked, making the average values of both fixation durations and saccade amplitudes questionable.

More recent work using improved methodology and technology of data collection replicated these early results (see Rayner, 1985, for a discussion) but also advanced the field substantially by addressing more specific research questions. One central issue concerns the perceptual span in reading, the area around the current fixation position within which linguistic information of a certain kind (e.g., letter discrimination) can be acquired during a single fixation (e.g., Underwood & Zola, 1986). Rayner (1986) reported the span to be smaller for developing readers than for adults, but the typical asymmetry with more parafoveal processing occurring to the right of fixation was already present in very young readers. Very similar results were obtained in a recent follow up study by Haikio, Bertram, Hyona, and Niemi (2009), using a sample of Finnish readers. The letter identity span was found to be smaller than the span for identifying letter features. In addition, the letter identity span of slower readers turned out to be smaller than the one found for faster readers, suggesting that slower readers cannot allocate as much of their processing resources to words beyond the current fixation.

The first and so far only extensive longitudinal eye movement study of normal reading with letter-level accuracy of measurement was published by McConkie et al. (1991). They collected data from initially more than 200 children from the end of first to fifth grade. This study provided the first realistic estimation of what should be considered "normal" variability within a sample of readers performing within 1 year of grade level. These analyses indicated that, as could be expected, variability is much larger compared with adults and gradually reduces as young readers progress in their development. Another intriguing finding was that young children made many more small saccadic movements. As an example, 9% of all eye movements made by first graders were less then two characters in length. In contrast, students in fifth grade made such small saccades only 4% of the time. This striking difference is likely to reflect an emphasis on sublexical processing units in younger children, possibly related to mental effort in grapheme-to-phoneme conversion. Also interesting is that there is a much larger proportion of very short fixation durations—less than 120 ms—which are unlikely to be controlled directly by information acquired during the current fixation. The reason for this finding remains unclear.

Importantly, McConkie et al. closely investigated saccade landing positions within words and found that students at the end of first grade already show typical characteristics of adult saccade metrics. A Gaussian distribution of incoming saccade landing positions, commonly referred to as the preferred viewing position phenomenon (Rayner,

1979), strongly supported the word-based nature of saccade control. The standard deviations of landing site distributions were not larger then those for adults, suggesting that the basic oculomotor targeting mechanism is well in place in normally developing readers by the end of first grade. Another interesting finding was a sharp reduction of the frequency with which a currently fixated word was immediately refixated, suggesting a greater automaticity of word recognition as development progresses. As an example, first graders refixated five letter words 57% of the time compared with 15% in a sample of adult readers (McConkie, Kerr, Reddix, Zola, & Jacobs, 1989). Part of this difference is due to the fact the landing positions of incoming initial saccades are further to the left in younger children, leading to refixations, because landing on word initial-letter positions is less optimal for word processing (see Radach & McConkie, 1998, for a detailed discussion). However, even when this source of variance was controlled, the difference in refixation rate remained strong.

Overall, analyses of local saccade fixation patterns in the McConkie et al. study marked a new chapter in the history of oculomotor research with children. In prior research, interpretation of data was compromised by averaging over indicators reflecting qualitatively different mental processes. As one important example, the word-based analyses by McConkie et al. helped solve the mystery as to why the rate of regressions apparently stays more or less constant over the first 6 years of school. They reported that with progressing development of reading skill intraword regressions (regressive refixations) become less frequent while the percentage of interword regressions (saccades going back to the left of the current word) actually increases. The decrease in the number of regressive refixations reflects the overall tendency of reduced refixations, which tend to follow leftward within word saccades when the initial landing position was to the right of the word center (McConkie et al., 1989; O'Regan, 1990). Radach and McConkie (1998) and Inhoff, Weger, and Radach (2005) have demonstrated that interword regressions represent a distinct class of saccades based on different mechanisms of visuomotor control. Short-distance regressions back to the last one or two words may serve to catch up on missed lexical access or an ambiguous semantic role, whereas long-range regressions may be used to repair comprehension problems on the sentence and text levels. The fact that these operations become *more* frequent in older students may very well reflect an important (and so far overlooked) aspect of successful reading development.

Looking at fixation durations, it is important to note that the first and second of two fixations made within a word are actually of shorter duration than a single fixation would be on the same word (Kliegl, Olson, & Davidson, 1983). As increases in cognitive workload during reading often lead to more refixations, reporting *average* fixation durations may obscure important differences in local text difficulty or reading ability (Inhoff & Radach, 1998). However, a difficulty in the interpretation of the McConkie et al. data arises, especially with respect to the more cognitively driven temporal measures such as fixation and gaze durations. Over several time points of assessment from first to fifth grades each student was asked to read "age-appropriate" texts, which are likely to differ on several levels, including vocabulary, syntactic complexity, and text coherence. Therefore, changes in the eye movement records are not clearly attributable to developmental factors but may also derive from differences in properties of texts.

Hyönä and Olson (1995) collected the first accurate oculomotor data while children were reading aloud and found that normally developing fourth graders exhibited typical word frequency and word length effects: They spent more time on infrequent compared with frequent words and on long compared with shorter words. However, these findings were based on a post hoc classification of words into frequency band that did not control for potentially confounding variables, especially the local visual configuration and the relevant linguistic context for the selected target words.

This problem was addressed more appropriately in a sentence-reading study by Huestegge, Radach, Corbic, and Huestegge (2009), who varied word frequency and length in a well-controlled two-factorial design. Eye movement data were collected during oral reading in 21 normally developing children during their second and fourth grades at a school in Aachen, Germany. The Huestegge et al. study is also unique in that it combined oculomotor methodology with the measurement of word-naming latencies. Word- and picture-naming performance was examined using the same items that served as target words in the reading experiment. This allowed the examination of performance in the processing of identical words outside the context of the dynamic reading situation. Huestegge et al. used identical sentence materials at second and fourth grades, thus avoiding the potential confounds with "age-appropriate" text. Comparing verbal responses with the respective pictures and words in the naming task allowed them to verify explicitly that participants at the second grade understood and adequately responded to all stimuli. In addition to the sentence-reading and naming tasks, psychometric tests were used that are relevant for the assessment of reading development and may help to specify its underlying mechanisms. These included the Coloured Progressive Matrices (CPM; Raven, Raven, & Court, 1998) as a test of general cognitive abilities and several reading ability tests for German that are based on different methodological approaches, namely the Salzburger Lese-Rechtschreibtest (SLRT; Landerl, Wimmer, & Moser, 2001), the Würzberger Leise Lase Probe (WLLP; Küspert & Schneider, 1998), and the Salzburger Lese Screening (SLS; Mayringer & Wimmer, 2003). In the fourth grade, measures of rapid automatized naming (RAN) and phonological awareness were also added.

Results from the sentence-reading task indicate that reading rate rose from 66 words/min (SD = 28.08) at the end of the second grade to 103 words/min (SD = 16.92) at the end of fourth grade, which represents an increase of about 36%. Interestingly, comprehension (as assessed using questions on sentence-level semantic relations) remained unchanged, suggesting that readers attempted to adjust the fluency of reading for a satisfactory level of comprehension. A second important observation is that variability between participants is much lower at fourth grade with respect to reading rate, gaze durations, and total reading times. This confirms similar observations by McConkie et al. (1991) and likely reflects the fact that individual reading skills substantially differ among younger children.

Looking at local word-based fixation patterns, as also found by McConkie et al., there was a marked decrease in the number of immediate refixations on the target words. A further interesting observation was that at second grade, readers did not send their eyes as far into target words. The difference in mean initial landing position amounted to 0.3, which may not appear large but the effect is very significant and in the order of what can be observed when comparing saccades into words with highly redundant versus irregular initial letter clusters (Hyönä & Olson, 1995; Radach, Heller, & Inhoff, 2002). Additional analyses indicated that the landing position effect held for a range of saccade launch distances to the left of the target word. This is quite remarkable because, everything else being equal, the inflated number of refixations on the word before the target (an adjective of controlled length) should actually have pushed the initial saccade landing position to the right (Radach & Kempe, 1993; Radach & McConkie, 1998). Perhaps the best explanation for this pattern of results is in terms of a more conservative or "careful" reading strategy (O'Regan, 1992) at second grade. Two components—shorter saccades into the next word and more refixations at any given resulting landing position—serve to provide optimal visual input for spatially distributed processing of sublexical and lexical information.

This kind of strategic difference is a top-down adjustment that, together with changes in local word-processing load, produces the observable developmental change in oculomotor reading behavior.

Figure 4.1 presents viewing duration data for all cells of the design at second and fourth grades. Word-viewing time measures decreased quite dramatically during 2 years of reading development. Apparent are the classic word length and frequency effects on gaze durations and total reading times (Rayner, 1998), while initial fixation durations were not affected by frequency. Effect sizes for gaze duration and total reading time were reduced at fourth grade, which may be explained in terms of a more automatic lexical access in more advanced readers where less familiar words no longer lead to excessive viewing durations. Note that the infrequent words were well known to the second graders, as suggested by low error rates of about 1% in the picture- and words-naming tasks. The decrease of word-viewing time from second to fourth grade was reflected in initial fixation durations, refixation time (additional fixations during the first pass over a word), and rereading time (fixations during later passes after first leaving the word). This strongly suggests that performance is enhanced across all word-processing stages, including decoding and contextual integration. In the naming task, a decrease in latency of about 9% for pictures and 15% for words from second to fourth grade was found. As in the reading task, word length and frequency effects were less pronounced at fourth grade.

A comparison of single-word naming and target word reading in the reading task indicated that naming times were generally longer than total reading times on the same items. In addition to the natural (and perhaps relatively constant) eye–voice lag, this may also be related to the dynamic nature of sentence reading, where the eyes do not have to remain on a word until it is fully processed (see, e.g., Kliegl, Nuthmann, & Engbert, 2006; Reichle et al., 2003). Subject-based correlations between word-naming latencies and total reading times were moderate: $.57 < r < .90$ for second graders and $.26 < r < .60$ for fourth graders (see Schilling, Rayner, & Chumbley, 1998, for data on adult readers). However, an analysis of item-based correlations of word-naming latencies with gaze durations and total reading times indicated that these correlations were significant at second grade but not fourth grade. Apparently, for a more developed reader, single word-naming latencies do not reliably predict the speed of word processing in normal reading. During the second grade, the common variance may reflect grapheme–phoneme conversion processes, whereas in the fourth grade this ability is already highly automatic, so that both tasks share fewer common components.

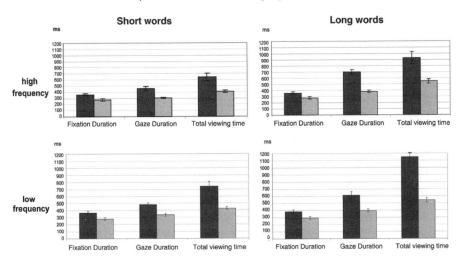

FIGURE 4.1. Word-viewing duration measures for sentence reading in children in second grade (dark gray) and fourth grade (light gray). Data are based on a longitudinal design with identical reading materials. Panels show effects on target words of varying word length (4–5 vs. 7–8 letters) and word frequency.

Saccade latencies for pro- and antisaccades and the amount of erroneous prosaccades in the antisaccade task decreased from second to fourth grade (see, e.g., Klein, 2001, for normative developmental data on these tasks). However, none of the oculomotor variables in the pro- and antisaccade tasks correlated significantly with any oculomotor measure of reading, including mean and initial fixation durations, for both second and fourth grade data. A regression analysis used a composite measure of oculomotor speed (mean latencies over several conditions in the pro- and antisaccade tasks), the number of erroneous prosaccades, and single word-naming latencies in second grade for the prediction of total reading times in fourth grade. Only naming latencies turned out to be a significant predictor, suggesting that linguistic, not oculomotor, skills were the driving force behind the acquisition of oral reading ability. Most likely, the limiting factor in the development of reading skills is the process of linguistic word decoding and integration and not any aspect of basic oculomotor development. The lack of any significant correlation between nonreading saccade parameters and reading performance appears quite discouraging for the view that simple saccade tasks remote from reading may contribute to a better understanding of developmental reading problems (see Biscaldi, Fishcer, & Hartnegg, 2000; see the more detailed discussion later in this chapter).

The additional assessments used at fourth grade revealed that phonological awareness measures correlated highly with measures related to the reading of single words (e.g., word naming) but not with measures reflecting the dynamic reading of words in the context of meaningful sentences like gaze durations and total reading times. In contrast, performance in a letter RAN task correlated highly with gaze durations and total reading times (see also Holland, McIntosh, & Huffman, 2004). In line with Neuhaus and Swank (2002), this corroborates the claim that the letter version of the RAN forms a basic reading test, comprising processes of phonological encoding, orthographic recognition, and articulation, all of which are fundamental prerequisites of normal oral reading.

COMPARING SILENT AND ORAL READING

Reading performance of children at the elementary level is usually assessed via oral reading. Reading aloud appears to provide an easy way to track errors, and many teachers generalize oral reading performance to provide a valid and reliable assessment for the general reading ability of a child. It is thus not surprising that oral reading fluency serves as a major benchmark in reading instruction and corresponding diagnostic assessments. However, in our opinion, it is rather unclear to what extent the ubiquitous extrapolation from oral to silent reading is really justified. Surprisingly little is known at this point about the precise nature of differences between reading aloud versus silently and their developmental dynamics. In the previous section, two oculomotor studies of reading development—McConkie et al. (silent) and Huestegge et al. (oral)—suggested that a number of similar developmental tendencies in silent and oral reading exist on a general level. In this section, we provide a more direct comparison after briefly addressing some relevant theoretical issues.

It is obvious that, for both the silent and oral mode, text comprehension is the eventual goal of the reading process (Anderson & Swanson, 1937; Karp, 1943; van Bon & Libert, 1997). However, beyond this basic commonality, the fundamental difference is that oral reading, via articulation and intonation, adds a language production component to the process. From this, fascinating issues arise regarding the degree to which this is merely an *addition* to the machinery of information processing active in silent reading and whether and how it also changes operations within levels and modules of processing that are not obviously related to the sounding out of words. In the following discussion, we explore the commonalities and differences of both reading modes with respect to four key aspects: phonological recoding and "inner speech," reading speed, comprehension, and eye movements.

The first, and seemingly trivial, observation that can be made when comparing silent and oral reading is the slower speed in the oral mode. Buswell (1922) reported a speed of 250 words/min during reading aloud compared with up to 600 words during silent reading (see Juel & Holmes, 1981; Salasoo, 1986; and Sovik, Arntzen, & Samuelstuen, 2000, for more recent, similar estimates). Presumably, the major speed-limiting factors in oral reading in adults are the inherent physiological constraints. The pronunciation of words is only possible during exhalation and is also limited by the time course of the speech production system. On the other hand, it also makes sense to see the problem from the perspective of the recipient of the spoken language stream. As the ultimate goal in oral reading is the communication to a listener, the capacity of speech perception on the part of the listener is clearly a limiting factor, and in most situations there is no need to speed up the process beyond the pace of a convenient conversation.

However, the picture may be quite different in beginning and developing readers. As illustrated later, during the initial years of reading development the speed of reading aloud is much less different from silent reading. This is in line with the observation that inner speech or subarticulation is more salient in beginning readers, pointing to the possibility that speech production-related factors may impose limitations for oral reading speed in early readers (Aaronson & Ferres, 1986; Abramson & Goldinger, 1997). In the following sections, we briefly discuss the role of phonological recoding and inner speech in reading aloud and explore some relation between reading mode and comprehension. We then return to the issue of speed in more detail when considering eye movement analyses of dynamic reading in both silent and oral reading.

Phonological Recoding and Inner Speech

Early reading researchers made the observation that silent reading appears to include subarticulation. It appeared that silent reading is not possible without at least weak movements of tongue, vocal musculature, and lips (Pinter, 1913; Reed, 1916). This led to the assumption that some kind of "inner speech" is prominent, especially in early readers, and becomes less salient and noticeable in more skilled readers (Huey, 1908). Modern reading research has produced solid evidence that processing operations related to sound properties of text are active in various ways during silent reading (see van Orden & Kloos, 2004, for a review).

1. It has been demonstrated that phonological properties of words play a substantial role in word recognition, even in very early phases long before any articulation-related processing could occur. Perhaps the most fascinating of these demonstrations have been made using eye movement-contingent display changes during silent sentence reading. Pollatsek, Lesch, Morris, and Rayner (1992) used the boundary technique (see Rayner & Slattery, Chapter 2, this volume) such that when their eyes crossed an invisible boundary, a preview word changed to the target word. As an example, this preview string can be (1) identical to the target word (*beach* used as a preview for *beach*), (2) a homophone of the target word (*beech* used as a preview for *beach*), (3) an orthographic control word (*bench* as a preview for *beach*), or (4) a completely unrelated consonant string (*jfzrp* as a preview for *beach*). Using this method, Pollatsek et al. demonstrated that a homophone of a target word, when presented as a preview in the parafovea, facilitated processing of the target word seen on the next fixation more than a preview of a word matched with the homophone in visual similarity to the target word (see Miellet & Sparrow, 2004, for converging evidence).

The related "fast priming paradigm" uses phonological priming during the first approximately 30 ms of target word-viewing time, using display changes during the first fixation on the target word (Lee, Binder, Kim, Pollatsek, & Rayner, 1999). Taken together, both techniques provided unequivocal evidence that knowledge about phonological word properties is activated extremely quickly in the time course of word recognition. From this and similar lines of work, it can be concluded that such fast sound processing may, in fact, be part and parcel of every act of word recognition. It is interesting to note that Chace, Rayner, and Well (2005) showed that the phonological preview benefit obtained using the boundary paradigm was present only in skilled readers, suggesting that less skilled readers may not be able to use this kind of sound code early during the time line of word recognition.

2. It is beyond doubt that in normal reading a division of labor exists between a direct route of word processing and an indirect route-based phonological recoding. Tracing the literature on phonological recoding during reading for meaning is far beyond the scope of this chapter (e.g.,

Coltheart, Laxon, Rickard, & Elton, 1988). The most prominent theoretical expression of this research tradition is the family of dual-route models of reading (Coltheart, Curtis, Atkins, & Haller, 1993; Coltheart et al., 2001; see Coltheart, 2000, for a brief overview). A beautiful demonstration of the interplay between these complementary sides of reading is a study by Coltheart and Doctor (1980), in which children misjudged the meaning of senseless sentences far more often if they were phonologically correct. It is quite clear that the phonological route of word recognition during reading is more important in young readers, because their knowledge of words and the automaticity of word processing are less developed. To our knowledge, there is no evidence on whether and how the balance between direct and indirect word processing differs between silent and oral reading.

3. A solid case can be made for effects of vocal length on word processing in silent reading (Abramson & Goldinger, 1997). To provide only a few examples, vocal length has an impact on response times in lexical decision tasks even if articulation is not necessary, and tongue twisters, appearing in sentences, increase semantic judgment times (Perfetti, 1982). Similar results have been reported by Ashby, Treiman, Kessler, and Rayner (2006) for gaze durations during sentence reading. These findings suggest that speech-like properties of phonological representation substantially modulate word processing during silent reading.

4. It has been shown in various ways that phonological working memory supports reading. To examine the time course of this type of working memory, Inhoff, Connine, and Radach (2002) developed the saccade contingent eye–speech paradigm. In this technique, a companion word is presented acoustically after the eye crosses an invisible boundary just before moving into a target word. Gaze duration on the target word increased drastically for all types of acoustic stimulation, including identical and dissimilar words. Critically, this increase persisted for gaze durations beyond the target word when the companion word was phonologically similar, indicating interference and thus reflecting the decay time of the memory trace (Inhoff, Connie, Eiter, Radach, & Heller, 2004). When Inhoff et al. (2001) partitioned their data between readers with longer versus shorter gaze durations, the effect was attenuated in less fluent readers, suggesting that a functioning phonological working memory is an essential component of efficient reading. Together with other data, these findings indicate that during silent reading for comprehension, phonological representations are activated at several stages during the time line of word processing. Moreover, at

least one of these forms of representation stays active for some time in the phonological compartment of working memory. These representations, in turn, help to store information for sentence processing and text comprehension (Baddeley, Thomson, & Buchanan, 1975).

Reading Comprehension

A review of the existing literature does not allow one to draw a clear conclusion regarding the influence of reading mode on comprehension. Some studies report better comprehension during oral reading (Collins, 1961; Schroiff, 1984), whereas others favor silent mode (Judd & Buswell, 1922; Poulton & Brown, 1967). To make the inconclusive picture complete, there are also quite a few studies that fail to find significant differences (Swalm, 1973; Juel & Holmes, 1981; Salasoo, 1986). The inconclusive findings of prior studies can perhaps partly be explained by methodological differences, such as the use of different age groups and inadequate specification of reading ability. As one important example, in the studies mentioned previously, the assessment approaches used to examine comprehension varied on a continuum between simple word verification to complex reasoning tasks (see Radach, Huestegge, & Reilly, 2008, for a recent discussion of task effects).

On a more theoretical level, there could be several reasons why one or the other reading mode might produce better comprehension. It is feasible to assume that oral reading supports comprehension because the reader benefits from the additional auditive input via "listening" to the ongoing speech production. Also, the conversion of graphemes into phonemic output is likely to demand more attention toward sublexical units of processing, which may benefit word recognition and comprehension (Swalm, 1973; Miller & Smith, 1990; Prior & Welling, 2001). Both arguments can be combined into the idea of a fundamental "mental economy," so that if a string of words is processed for a longer time in any part of the language-processing system, the build-up of a mental text representation should profit.

On the other hand, the possibility can be considered that in oral reading processing of a word may stop after its pronunciation and that the focus on the grapheme-to-sound route of reading may actually hamper assess to more direct lexical and/or semantic information (Juel & Holmes, 1981). On a meta-level of cognitive control, it can also be argued that in the dual-task situation of (silently) reading for comprehension plus oral production (including speech planning and articulation), the oral production stream of processing occupies shared resources that would otherwise be available for postlexical processing toward comprehension. A prima faci argument in favor of this view is familiar to every adult student of a foreign language: The actual task of reading aloud does not require the slightest bit of comprehension.

The situation has been clarified to a certain extent by Juel and Holmes (1981), who reported a longitudinal study on silent versus oral reading that attempted to take control for several potentially confounding factors. They concluded that beginning and especially struggling early readers show better achievement during oral reading, whereas third and fourth graders do not differ and skilled readers show better results during silent reading. A more detailed analysis of the third and fourth graders demonstrated that the reading comprehension of the more skilled readers among them were higher during silent reading. It is tempting to conclude from these results that the degree to which reading becomes more automatic and relies more on direct lexical access determines the relative advantage of silent versus oral reading for comprehension.

A related issue is whether factors can be specified that may help improve comprehension in either silent or oral reading. A conclusion that can be drawn from the prior discussion is that beginning and poor reader's comprehension should benefit more from oral reading, whereas more skilled readers may profit more from silent reading. It remains a challenge for future research to determine the turning point at which training in the silent reading mode becomes more effective. One important premise for this transition is apparently the internalization of the reading process (Kragler, 1995; Prior & Welling, 2001). Prior and Welling (2001) argue that "when reading is internalized, it is modified and constructed to serve a self-regulatory and self-guiding purpose. It is not simply a copy of the previous social reading now going on in the reader's head. It is transformed, and this change may explain why comprehension is typically superior after silent reading for advanced readers" (Prior & Welling, 2001, p. 4). Given that there was an obvious difference between third and fourth graders in the Juel and Holmes (1981) study, it is conceivable that this period describes the time window within which the hypothesized transformation process occurs for a majority of developing readers.

Eye Movements

As discussed, research on eye movements in reading can be divided into an early phase, during which summary measures are reported, and a contemporary phase, which is dominated by precise analyses of word-based local fixation patterns (see Rayner, 1998, for a more elaborate discussion of the history of the field). In early research, it was found that oral reading is associated with a substantially larger number of fixations that are also of longer duration. The higher number of fixations while reading aloud has been assumed to be based on a higher probability to fixate every word. Judd (1918) and Buswell (1922) both suggested that in order to read aloud it is necessary to pay attention to every single word, while it is perfectly possible to skip words during silent reading and nevertheless comprehend the text. However, it was not known where these extra fixations are placed and which spatial and temporal parameter adjustments are made in the control system to implement the change from a silent to an oral mode of reading.

In addition to a higher number of fixations per line of text, Sovik, Arntzen, and Samuelstuen (2000) also found more regressions during oral reading. They suggested that more regressions may be needed to understand the main ideas of the text because oral reading is generally slower. It has also been suggested that the higher regression rate during oral reading is related to the complexity of text material. If the material is of high complexity (e.g., consisting of passive sentences), the oral–silent difference in the amount of regressions is elevated (Wanat, 1971, cited in Levin, 1979). The number of fixations and regressive saccades correlate with total reading speed ($r = .84$; Sovik et al., 2000). This correlation appears to support the assumption that these phenomena are related to the same source of variance in reading speed. As discussed previously, however, this type of account suffers from an inability to distinguish between regressive refixations and interword regressions and should, therefore, be seen with caution.

It is possible that reading mode also has an effect on the perceptual span in reading. In early research, it was often assumed that the perceptual span can be approximated based on the spatial distribution of fixations over a line of text. This indirect expression of the perceptual span, often referred to as the "recognition span," was believed to reflect the number of processed words during a fixation. As an example, Sovik et al. (2000) computed recognition span as the average number of words per fixation for a sample of 12-year-old readers and found a rather nonsurprising correlation to reading speed. Concluding from this correlation that *recognition span* predicts the fluency of reading may be tempting, but it invites a rather serious lapse of reasoning. From a theoretical point of view, the logic behind the concept is flawed as long as it is unknown to what extent successive fixations reflect processing of different versus identical words.[1] If in the absence of direct measurement of the perceptual span an approximation in terms of recognition span is taken to be valid, the data obviously suggest that the span is smaller for oral reading. However, this argument is again close to circular, because an increased number of fixations is usually assumed to be a consequence of the smaller span, which, in turn, is determined on the basis of the same increased fixation frequency.

To our knowledge, a study recently completed in our laboratory represents the first attempt to compare silent and oral reading using a methodology that includes analyses of word-based fixation patterns (Radach, Schmitten, Glover, & Vorstius, 2009). In this study, 20 fourth-grade elementary school students (age range, 9–10 years) were asked to read sentences for comprehension either silently or aloud. All students were reading at or near grade level, had English as their first language, and had normal or corrected-to-normal visual acuity. Materials included 120 relatively simple declarative sentences with recurring actors and recipients. To ensure reading for comprehension, 40 of the sentences were followed by comprehension questions targeting either simple (actor, object, location) or more complex (condition, causality) semantic relations. To allow for an orthogonal comparison of word length and word frequency, each experimental sentence contained either a low- or high-frequency target word of a short (four or five letters) or long (six or seven letters) length, respectively. In addition, the word familiarity was controlled using the *The Educators Word Frequency Guide* (Zeno, Ivens, Millard, & Duvvuri, 1995) to make sure that the determination of word frequency was adequate for children too.

Results indicated that in oral reading, not surprisingly, substantially more fixations are being made and interword saccades are of markedly smaller amplitudes. The size of word frequency effects on viewing duration measures remained appoximately the same, even though gaze durations and total word-reading times were much longer in oral compared with silent reading. Here, in addition to sublexial and lexical word processing, these measures presumably also reflect post-word recognition speech planning and articulation processes, as found in research on delayed naming (e.g., Coltheart & Doctor, 1980; Inhoff & Topolski, 1994). It is interesting that, at least for good readers, such production-related components of oral reading appear equally sensitive to a word frequency manipulation as reflected in temporal eye movement parameters.

Figure 4.2 presents a comparison of viewing duration data for both silent and oral reading using a decomposition into initial fixation dura-

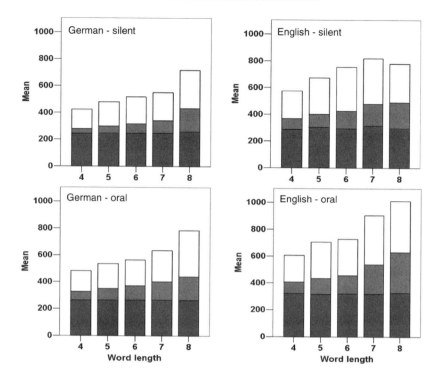

FIGURE 4.2. Decomposition of word-viewing durations into initial fixation durations (black), refixation time (gray), and rereading time (white). Panels represent data (in milliseconds) for words four to eight letters in length collected while U.S. versus German fourth-grade students were reading structurally identical sentences silently versus aloud.

tions, time for additional fixations during first-pass reading (refixations time), and time spent during later passes over the same word (rereading time; see also "Adding a Cross-Linguistic Perspective" for more details). Because fixation durations were only slightly longer, many of the observed prolonged word-viewing times when reading aloud were due to more refixations made within the same word. These extra refixations originate from two sources, with relative importance of both factors varying between individual readers. One source is a fixation position-independent increase in refixation frequency that manifests itself in a simple elevation of the u-shaped refixations curve describing the frequency of refixating the same word as a function of initial saccade landing position (McConkie et al., 1989). The second contributing factor is a launch site-independent leftward shift of these incoming progressive interword saccade landing positions. This is a remarkable local adjustment, because the higher frequency of refixating the prior word causes a shortening of saccade launch distance, which, in turn, should have led to a rightward shift of subsequent saccade landing positions (Radach & McConkie, 1998). In sum, these patterns of intraword and interword saccades indicate how a global change in reading behavior is implemented in specific adjustments of local word fixation patterns.

ADDING A CROSS-LINGUISTIC PERSPECTIVE

Most research on reading development is conducted in English, and, as is the case in many other areas of cognitive and educational research, findings of these studies are often generalized to other languages. In doing so, it is (often implicitly) assumed that basic reading processes, at least in alphabetic writing systems using Roman script, are universal; therefore, studies in English are sufficient to provide an understanding of reading in general. However, investigations in languages other than English have shown that the linguistic environment and the writing system of a reader have a substantial impact on reading behavior (e.g., Frost, 1994; Hutzler & Wimmer, 2004; Aro & Wimmer, 2003; Caravolas, Volin, & Hulme, 2005; Eme & Golder, 2005).

Orthographies using Roman script vary widely in the consistency of their grapheme–phoneme and phoneme–grapheme correspondences. In consideration of this fact, languages can be placed on a continuum of consistency and transparency. The transparent (shallow) orthographies have consistent grapheme–phoneme mappings as, for example, in Italian, German, Spanish, and Serbo-Croatian. In contrast, in intransparent (deep) orthographies, like English, the same letter can represent different phonemes depending on its surrounding letters, and, vice versa, the same phoneme can be represented by different letters (Frost, Katz, & Bentin, 1987; Frost, 1994; Eme & Golder, 2005). Overall, the location of a language on that consistency continuum depends on the amount of grapheme–phoneme correspondence rules, which are necessary to read correctly. "The degree of irregularity is (then) defined as the percentage of words for which the rule pronunciation disagrees with the lexical pronunciation" (Ziegler, Perry, & Coltheart, 2000, p. 415).

Computational linguistic analysis of spelling body–rime correspondences showed that, for the English language, 31% of all monosyllabic words are feed-forward inconsistent, which means in the direction of spelling to pronunciation, and 72% are inconsistent backward, from phonology to spelling. In German, the corresponding feed-forward inconsistency in monosyllabic words is only 16% and the backward inconsistency, 53%; for French, the forward inconsistency is 12% (Ziegler, Jacobs, & Stone, 1996; Wimmer & Mayringer, 2002). Within- and across-language research has shown that the consistency of orthography has substantial impact on the reading behavior in general and reading development in particular (e.g., Frost et al., 1987; Frost, 1994; Wimmer & Goswami, 1994; Aro & Wimmer, 2003; Ziegler & Goswami, 2005; Eme & Golder, 2005; Caravolas, Volin, & Hulme, 2005). When discussing results of such comparisons, some caution is warranted because there may be sources of variance that are very difficult to control, among them school systems, teacher quality, methods of reading instructions, amount of reading instruction within curricula, and demographic and socioeconomic characteristics.

With respect to the process of learning to read, a straightforward prediction can be derived from the prior discussion. Learning should be easier if the relationship between visual symbols (graphemes) and the corresponding sounds (phonemes) is more systematic. One important aspect of this general rule concerns the context sensitivity of pronunciation. As an example, in German the letter *a* is always pronounced /a/ like in *hand*, *garten*, or *ball*, whereas it is pronounced different in the English equivalents *hand*, *garden*, and *ball* (Hutzler & Wimmer, 2004). There is indeed substantial evidence indicating that children who learn to read in more consistent orthographies make faster progress in phoneme awareness, word recognition speed, spelling accuracy, and phonological recoding during the first years of schooling (e.g., Seymour, Aro, & Erskine, 2003; Wimmer & Goswami, 1994). In an attempt to quantify such differences, Ziegler and Goswami (2005) looked at the number of errors made when reading words or nonwords in various European languages. Whereas Italian second-grade students achieved an accuracy score of 94% in word reading and 82% in nonword reading, British children had scores of 70% and 45%, respectively. A cross-linguistic study in 14 European countries (Seymour et al., 2003) confirmed the advantage in learning to read in languages with more transparent orthographies. The development of grapheme–phoneme recoding skills took longer in less transparent languages, like English. Also, it appeared that the reading ability of English children depends less on phonological recoding because of the opaque relationship between graphemes and phonemes. Therefore, they have to learn more explicit rules, like reading new words via analogy to already known spelling patterns, during the process of reading acquisition instead of grapheme–

phoneme conversation rules (Wimmer & Goswami, 1994; Aro & Wimmer, 2003).

Converging evidence concerns the different types of reading errors made by German and English beginning readers. Misreading observed in German children most frequently involves nonsense words, whereas errors among the English readers primarily involve false real words. The nonsense word errors presumably occur because German children's reading depends on assembled pronunciation. In contrast, the English children use apparently direct access to the word, which results then in word errors (Wimmer & Hummer, 1990; Wimmer & Goswami, 1994). All these findings support the idea that, in languages with "shallow" orthography, the reader uses smaller chunks for computing phonology than in "deeper" orthographies. These smaller chunks are more regular and easier to learn; thus, the readers make fewer errors in nonword reading (Frost, 1994; Ziegler et al., 2000).

The findings discussed previously are based on research using single-word processing paradigms, like naming, lexical decision, and semantic priming. To our knowledge, there have been so far no studies directly comparing different languages with respect to corresponding dynamic reading situations in normal children. We recently completed a study including structurally similar sentences in English and German with fourth-grade readers. Most of the sentences were generated by directly translating from German into English (see "Comparing Silent and Oral Reading" for some aspects of methodology). Figure 4.2 presents a decomposition of total word-viewing time into three components: time spent during the initial fixation on the word, time used for immediate refixations within the first reading pass (refixation time), and time for reinspections of the same word during later passes (rereading time). This more compact way of reporting data was chosen here over directly plotting initial fixation durations, gaze durations, and total viewing times, as done in Figure 4.1, because it allows presenting more conditions in one figure.

Looking at Figure 4.2, it is apparent that there is not much difference between U.S. and German fourth-grade readers in the duration of initial fixations made on words during the reading of equivalent sentences. In contrast, the second component of word-viewing time, refixation duration, is strikingly longer among readers of English. This increased amount of time spend refixating is likely to reflect a higher mental effort necessary to achieve lexical access. In the absence of any traceable difference in target word frequency, this difference is presumably based on the intransparent nature of grapheme–phoneme correspondence in English, as discussed previously for other methodologies. It is well known that increased difficulty in word processing on the lexical level translates primarily into an increase in the number of refixations (rather than inflating the initial fixation). As first shown by Kliegl, Olson, and Davidson (1983), the first of two fixations tends to be shorter than a single fixation, which means that the decision to refixate must be based on a fast educated guess about the to-be-expected mental effort associated with the processing of the current word.

The hypothesis of increased difficulty in lexical access works well in explaining the difference in refixation time. However, this is not the case for the second large difference apparent in Figure 4.2: a much higher rereading time in English. One could argue that English readers leave the target word more often prematurely and then have to return immediately for a completion of lexical processing. Even assuming that such a pattern of lexical spillover into subsequent fixations exists and is sometimes associated with returns to the target (Rayner & Duffy, 1986; Kliegl et al., 2006), a suboptimal processing strategy like this is unlikely in normal fourth-grade readers and can hardly account for the size of the observed difference. Moreover, syntactic processing difficulty can also be ruled out as the reason for the observed difference, because sentence structure was carefully held constant between the English and German versions of the sentence.

Our best candidate for an explanation of the increase in rereading time is a factor that, in our view, has not received enough attention in the existing literature on developing readers. Consider an English word like *exit*, which without context can be interpreted as a verb, noun, or adjective. There are also multiple ways to use it in compounds or equivalent phrases, such as "emergency exit" or "exit strategy." Virtually all of these possibilities are explicitly coded in German via inflection or productive compounding of nouns (Inhoff, Radach, & Heller, 2000), so that contextual processing is usually not needed to fully process the words meaning. Of course, the obvious advantage of explicit coding is partly offset by the fact that in many cases (but not in the study discussed here) words become longer or phases have to include more words to convey the same message.[2] The resolution of lexical ambiguities during sentence reading in English is an established topic of experimental research (see Mason & Just, 2007: Sereno, O'Donnell, & Rayner, 2006, for recent examples).

From the prior discussions of significant differences between written languages like English and German, it should follow that the pattern of difficulties observed in struggling readers should also be language dependent. Indeed, Hutzler and Wimmer (2004), in their (monolingual) study, suggested that the eye movement patterns of German students with developmental dyslexia differ from their counterparts in English. Common observations in English are frequent misreading of words when reading aloud, more regressions, and more and longer fixations compared with students reading at grade level. In contrast, German dyslexics make only slightly more fixations and shorter saccades regressions but show a larger effect of word length on viewing duration parameters. It appears that the key difference, more regressions, is in line with the increased rereading times for English in our direct cross-linguistic comparison. The larger impact of word length in German may reflect a greater reliance on phonological recoding in a more regular orthography (see De Luca, Di Pace, Judica, Spinelli, & Zoccoletti, 1999; De Luca, Borrelli, Judica, Spinelli, & Zoccolotti, 2002, for converging evidence on Italian readers with developmental dyslexia).

CONCLUSION

The present chapter attempted to sketch the state of the art in the area of developmental reading research based on analyses of oculomotor data. We have argued that this research is needed both as a contribution toward a better understanding of an important aspect of mental development in general but also as a baseline to evaluate performance in struggling or specifically impaired readers. After a brief introduction, we summarized basic developmental trends and then broadened the discussion to include comparisons between silent and oral reading with regard to several aspects of processing. Finally, a cross-linguistic perspective was introduced to illuminate the impact of language differences on how students master the task of reading. As we have seen, there are many interesting pieces of evidence addressing different angles of the problem. However, we are still lacking a comprehensive picture of the directions and determinants of development in dynamic reading and, to name just one major deficit, of the range of normal variability within such development.

The best way of addressing these complex and challenging issues will be in terms of well-controlled and comprehensive longitudinal research. The work by McConkie et al. (1991) has provided a promising first step in this direction, establishing the analysis of word-based saccade fixation patterns as the methodological standard in the field. As our own data have shown, advances in recoding technology now permit precise measurement of eye movements during oral reading. Future research should aim to provide individual developmental trajectories for both silent and oral reading well into middle or even high school level. One important insight that such comparisons can deliver is to determine at which point in reading development (and why) silent reading becomes substantially more effective in terms of speed and comprehension. A related key question is which early indicators can predict specific aspects of success in silent and oral reading and to what extent growth in both modes of reading is interrelated.

This research will also have to address the tricky issue of age-appropriate reading materials. It is, of course, inadequate to ask students from first to fifth grade to reread identical materials throughout the course of a longitudinal project. However, using educational text materials that are at the "appropriate grade level" may introduce multiple combined changes in terms of vocabulary, sentence complexity, or even text coherence that are every experimenter's nightmare. Up to a certain point of proficiency, a developing reader can be matched at every grade level with more difficult text so that, at least on a global level of fluency, developmental changes are almost completely offset. Perhaps the best possible solution to this conundrum would be a careful combination of well-defined aspects of text difficulty that change from one point of measurement to the next, while other attributes or types of reading materials are held constant as a baseline throughout the entire time line of a longitudinal project.

Another key aspect of future research should be the combination of dynamic reading with psychometric assessments of reading ability and measures of component skills. From a cognitive science point of view, there are a number of good candidates for basic skills that may determine performance and developmental growth in reading such as working memory, phonological processing skills, word knowledge, attentional and visuomotor abilities, and general mental speed. In this context, it appears essential to prefer measures that do not themselves have a history of complex interrelation with multiple facets of performance. A good example would be RAN tasks, which have a well-established predictive utility, while the underlying cognitive processes are still quite controversial (see Wagner, Torgesen, & Rashotte, 1994; Vukovic & Siegel, 2006, for discussions).

For many potential component skills, a selection of valid and reliable measures has already been established. Interestingly, this is not the case for visuomotor abilities, so that it is currently difficult to substantiate the common anecdotic reports of reading problems related to attention or spatial navigation. We are skeptical of attempts to capture such potential visuomotor problems in reading development with laboratory tasks that are remote from reading. Consequently, we are now developing a reading-like scanning task that incorporates much of the visuomotor dynamics of normal reading without imposing linguistic processing demands (Radach, Vorstius, & Günther, 2008). More generally, we strongly advocate the combination of experimental eye movement research with more psychometric and data analytic approaches as described in several chapters of the present volume. This will serve to broaden the scope of knowledge gained on both sides of the methodological spectrum. Moreover, combining the strengths of both approaches may also help eye movement-based developmental reading research establishing the educational credibility that is necessary to make an impact toward improving instructional practice and intervention for struggling readers.

NOTES

1. This discussion touches on the issue of sequential versus parallel word processing in reading. Positions on this issue range from strictly sequential word processing to limited parallel word processing within the limits of the perceptual span. It should be noted that the parallel position, although advocating temporal overlap in the processing of spatially adjacent words, is not necessarily in harmony with the idea of extrapolating a "recognition span" from the number of fixations on a line of text.

2. Looking at the problem more generally, there are several types of ambiguities on the lexical level that also exist in German but appear more frequent in English. Very common are homonyms, in which words have the same spelling but two or more meanings. An example is the word *mean*, which can describe an unkind person, an average, or the definition of a word. Another kind of lexical ambiguity is the heteronym, in which words are spelled the same but have different meanings and pronunciations. An example of this is *dove*, which can refer to a type of bird or can describe the action of jumping. The less frequent case of contronyms includes words that are spelled the same and pronounced the same but have two completely opposite meanings: for example, *Anxious*, where a person can be excited and eagerly looking forward to an event or might experience mental distress because of a perceived danger or misfortune. An experienced native reader of English may take all these decisions for granted but students in fourth grade might not be quite as efficient. Importantly, even a skilled reader is likely to spend more time with processing on a contextual level than is the case in a language that is less packed with lexical ambiguities (*www. tesolcourse. com/tesol-course-articles/common-linguistic/article-01-mg.php*; see

also Zhang, 2007, for a more detailed discussion from the perspective of foreign learners of English).

REFERENCES

Aaronson, D., & Ferres, S. (1986). Reading strategies for children and adults: A quantitative model. *Psychological Review, 93*, 89–112.

Abramson, M., & Goldinger, S. D. (1997). What the reader´s eye tells the mind´s ear: Silent reading activates inner speech. *Perception and Psychophysics, 59*, 1059–1068.

Anderson, I. H., & Swanson, D. E. (1937). Common factors in eye movements in silent and oral reading. *Psychological Monographs, 48*, 61–69.

Aro, M., & Wimmer, H. (2003). Learning to read: English in comparison to six more regular orthographies. *Applied Psycholinguistics, 24*, 621–635.

Ashby, J., Treiman, R., Kessler, B., & Rayner, K. (2006). Vowel processing during silent reading: Evidence from eye movements. *Journal of Experimental Psychology: Learning, Memory, and Cognition, 32*, 416–424.

Baddeley, A. D., Thomson, N., & Buchanan, M. (1975). Word length and the structure of short-term memory. *Journal of Verbal Learning and Verbal Behavior, 14*, 575–589.

Biscaldi, M., Fischer, B., & Hartnegg, K. (2000). Voluntary saccade control in dyslexia. *Perception, 29*, 509–521.

Bon, W. H. J. van, & Libert, J. E. A. (1997). Oral reading and silent reading compared. Evidence for a subtype of poor readers. *Polish Psychological Bulletin, 28*, 5–70.

Buswell, G. T. (1922). *Fundamental reading habits, a study of their development*. Chicago: Chicago University Press.

Caravolas, M., Volin, J., & Hulme, C. (2005). Phoneme awareness is a key component of alphabetic literacy skills in consistent and inconsistent orthographies: Evidence from Czech and English children. *Journal of Experimental Child Psychology, 92*, 107–139.

Chace, K. H., Rayner, K., & Well, A. D. (2005). Eye movements and phonological preview benefit: Effects of reading skill. *Canadian Journal of Experimental Psychology, 59*, 209–217.

Collins, R. (1961). The comprehension of prose materials by college freshmen when read silently and when read aloud. *The Journal of Educational Research, 55*, 79–83.

Coltheart, M. (2000). Dual routes from print to speech and dual routes from print to meaning. In A. Kennedy, R. Radach, D. Heller, & J. Pynte (Eds.), *Reading as a perceptual process* (pp. 475–490). Elsevier: Amsterdam.

Coltheart, M., Curtis, B., Atkins, P., & Haller, M. (1993). Models of reading aloud: Dual route and parallel-distributed-processing approaches. *Psychological Review, 100*, 589–608.

Coltheart, M., & Doctor, E. A. (1980). Children´s use of phonological encoding when reading for meaning. *Memory & Cognition, 8*, 195–209.

Coltheart, M., Laxon, V., Rickard, M., & Elton, C. (1988). Phonological recoding in reading for meaning by adults and children. *Journal of Experimental Psychology: Learning, Memory, and Cognition, 14*, 387–397.

Coltheart, M., Rastle, K., Perry, P., Langdon, R., & Ziegler, J. (2001). DRC: A dual route cascaded model of visual word recognition and reading aloud. *Psychological Review, 108*, 204–256.

De Luca, M., Borrelli, M., Judica, A., Spinelli, D., & Zoccolotti, P. (2002). Reading words and pseudowords: An eye movement study of developmental dyslexia. *Brain and Language, 80(3)*, 617–626.

De Luca, M., Di Pace, E., Judica, A., Spinelli, D., & Zoccoletti, P. (1999). Eye movement patterns in linguistic and non-linguistic tasks in developmental surface dyslexia. *Neuropsychologica, 37*, 1407–1420.

Eme, E., & Golder, C. (2005). Word-reading and word-spelling styles of French beginners: Do all children learn to read and spell in the same way? *Reading and Writing, 18*, 157–188.

Engbert, R., Nuthmann, A., Richter, E. M., & Kliegl, R. (2005). SWIFT: A dynamical model of saccade generation during reading. *Psychological Review, 112*, 777–813.

Frost, R. (1994). Prelexical and postlexical strategies in reading: Evidence from a deep and a shallow orthography. *Journal of Experimental Psychology: Learning, Memory, and Cognition, 20*, 116–129.

Frost, R., Katz, L., & Bentin, S. (1987). Strategies for visual word recognition and orthographical depth: A multilingual comparison. *Journal of Experimental Psychology: Human Perception and Performance, 13*, 104–115.

Haikio, T., Bertram, R., Hyona, J., & Niemi, P. (2009). Development of the letter identity span in reading: Evidence from the eye movement moving window paradigm. *Journal of Experimental Child Psychology, 102*, 167–181.

Holland, J., McIntosh, D. E., & Huffman, L. (2004). The role of phonological awareness, rapid automatized naming, and orthographic processing in word reading. *Journal of Psychoeducational Assessment, 22*, 233–260.

Huestegge, L., Radach, R., Corbic, D., & Huestegge, S. M. (2009). *Oculomotor and linguistic determinants of reading development: A longitudinal study.* Manuscript under review.

Huey, E. B. (1908). *The psychology and pedagogy of reading.* Cambridge, MA: MIT Press.

Hutzler, F., & Wimmer, H. (2004). Eye movements of dyslexic children when reading in a regular orthography. *Brain and Language 89(1)*, 235–242.

Hyönä, J., & Olson, R. K. (1995). Eye fixation patterns among dyslexic and normal readers: Effects of word length and word frequency. *Journal of Experimental Psychology: Learning, Memory, and Cognition, 6*, 1430–1440.

Inhoff, A. W., Connine, C., Eiter, B., Radach, R., & Heller, D. (2004). Phonological representations of words in working memory during sentence reading. *Psychonomic Bulletin & Review, 11*, 320–325.

Inhoff, A. W., Connine, C. & Radach, R. (2002). A contingent speech technique in eye movement research on reading. *Behavior Research Methods, Instruments, & Computers, 34*, 471–480.

Inhoff, A. W., Radach, R., & Heller, D. (2000). Complex compounds in German:

Interword spaces facilitate segmentation but hinder assignment of meaning. *Journal of Memory and Language, 42,* 23–50.

Inhoff, A. W., & Topolski, R. (1994). Use of phonological codes during eye fixations in reading and on-line delayed naming tasks. *Journal of Memory and Language, 33,* 689–713.

Inhoff, A. W., Weger, U. W., & Radach, R. (2005). Sources of information for the programming of short- and long-range regressions during reading. In G. Underwood (Ed.), *Cognitive processes in eye guidance.* New York: Oxford University Press.

Jacobs, A. M., & Grainger, J. (1994). Models of visual word recognition: Sampling the state of the art. *Journal of Experimental Psychology: Human Perception and Performance, 20,* 1311–1334.

Judd, C. H. (1918). *Reading: Its nature and development* [Educational Monograph no. 10]. Chicago, University of Chicago.

Judd, C. H., & Buswell, G. T. (1922). Silent reading: A study of various types. *Supplementary Educational Monographs, 23.*

Juel, C., & Holmes, B. (1981). Oral and silent reading of sentences. *Reading Research Quarterly, 4,* 545–568.

Karp, M. (1943). Silent before oral reading. *The Elementary School Journal, 44,* 102–104.

Klein, C. (2001). Development of prosaccade and antisaccade task performance in participants aged 6 to 26 years. *Psychophysiology, 38,* 179–189.

Kliegl, R., Nuthmann, A., & Engbert, R. (2006). Tracking the mind during reading: The influence of past, present, and future words on fixation durations. *Journal of Experimental Psychology: General, 135,* 12–35.

Kliegl, R., Olson, R. K., & Davidson, B. J. (1983). On problems of unconfounding perceptual and language processes. In K. Rayner (Ed.), *Eye movements in reading and perceptual and language processes* (pp. 333–343). New York: Academic Press.

Kragler, S. (1995). The transition from oral to silent reading. *Reading Psychology, 16*(4), 395–408.

Küspert, P., & Schneider, W. (1998). *Würzburger Leise Leseprobe (WLLP). Handanweisung* [Würzburg test of silent reading: Test Manual]. Göttingen, Germany: Hogrefe.

Landerl, K., Wimmer, H., & Moser, E. (2001). *SLRT. Salzburger Lese- und Rechtschreibtest. Verfahren zur Differentialdiagnose von Störungen des Lesens und Schreibens für die 1. bis 4. Schulstufe Handbuch* [Salzburg Reading and Spelling Test: An approach to the differential diagnoses of reading and writing problems in grades 1 to 4. Manual]. Bern, Germany: Hans Huber.

Lee, Y., Binder, K., Kim, J., Pollatsek, A., & Rayner, K. (1999). Activation of phonological codes during eye fixations in reading. *Journal of Experimental Psychology: Human Perception and Performance, 25,* 948–964.

Levin, H. (1979). *The eye–voice span.* Cambridge, MA: MIT Press.

Mason, R. A., & Just, M. A. (2007). Lexical ambiguity in sentence comprehension. *Brain Research, 1146,* 115–127.

Mayringer, H., & Wimmer, H. (2003). *SLS 1–4. Salzburger Lese-Screening für die*

Klassenstufen 1–4. Manual [Salzburg reading screening for grades 1–4]. Bern, Germany: Hans Huber.

McConkie, G. W., Kerr, P. W., Reddix, M. D., Zola, D., & Jacobs, A. M. (1989). Eye movement control during reading: II. Frequency of refixating a word. *Perception & Psychophysics, 46,* 245–253.

McConkie, G. W., Zola, D., Grimes, J., Kerr, P. W., Bryant, N. R., & Wolff, P. M. (1991). Children's eye movements during reading. In J. F. Stein (Ed.), *Vision and visual dyslexia* (pp. 251–262). London: Macmillan Press.

McDonald, S. A., Carpenter, R. H., & Shillcock, R. C. (2005). An anatomically constrained, stochastic model of eye movement control in reading. *Psychological Review, 112,* 814–840.

Miellet, S., & Sparrow, L. (2004). Phonological codes are assembled before word fixation: Evidence from boundary paradigm in sentence reading. *Brain and Language, 90,* 299–310.

Miller, S. D., & Smith, D. E. (1990). Relations among oral reading, silent reading and listening comprehension of students at differing competency levels. *Reading Research and Instruction, 29,* 73–84.

Neuhaus, G. F., & Swank, P. R. (2002). Understanding the relations between RAN letter subtest components and word reading in first-grade students. *Journal of Learning Disabilities, 35,* 158–174.

Orden, G. C. van, & Kloos, H. (2004). The question of phonology and reading. In M. Snowling, C. Hulme, & M. Seidenberg (Eds.), *The science of reading: A handbook* (pp. 61–78). Oxford, UK: Blackwell.

O'Regan, J. K. (1990). Eye movements and reading. In E. Kowler (Ed.), *Eye movements and their role in visual and cognitive processes* (pp. 395–453). Amsterdam: Elsevier.

O'Regan, J. K. (1992). Optimal viewing position in words and the strategy-tactics theory of eye movements in reading. In K. Rayner (Ed.), *Eye movements and visual cognition: Scene perception and reading* (pp. 333–354). New York: Springer.

Perfetti, C. A. (1982). Dyslexia: From dysverbia to dramamine. *PsycCRITIQUES, 27*(2), 104–105.

Pinter, R. (1913). Oral and silent reading of fourth grade pupils. *Journal of Educational Psychology, 4,* 333–337.

Pollatsek, A., Lesch, M., Morris, R. K., & Rayner, K. (1992). Phonological codes are used in integrating information across saccades in word identification and reading. *Journal of Experimental Psychology: Human Perception and Performance, 18,* 148–162.

Poulton, E. C., & Brown, C. H. (1967). Memory after reading aloud and reading silently. *The British Journal of Psychology, 58,* 219–222.

Prior, S. M., & Welling, K. A. (2001). A Vygotskian analysis of the transition from oral and silent reading. *Reading Psychology, 22,* 1–15.

Radach, R., Huestegge, L., & Reilly, R. (2008). The role of global top-down factors in local eye movement control in reading. *Psychological Research, 72,* 675–688.

Radach, R., Inhoff, A. W., & Heller, D. (2002). The role of attention and spatial selection in fluent reading. In E. Witruk, A. Friederici, & T. Lachmann

(Eds.), *Basic functions of language, reading and reading disability* (pp. 137–154). Dordrecht, the Netherlands: Kluwer.

Radach, R., & Kempe, V. (1993). An individual analysis of initial fixation positions in reading. In G. d'Ydewalle & J. Van Rensbergen (Eds.), *Perception and cognition: Advances in eye research* (pp. 213–226). Amsterdam: North-Holland.

Radach, R., & Kennedy, A. (2004). Theoretical perspectives on eye movements in reading: Past controversies, current deficits and an agenda for future research. *European Journal of Cognitive Psychology, 16*, 3–26.

Radach, R., & McConkie, G. W. (1998). Determinants of fixation positions in words during reading. In G. Underwood (Ed.), *Eye guidance in reading and scene perception* (pp. 77–100). Oxford, UK: Elsevier.

Radach, R., Reilly, R., & Inhoff, A. W. (2007). Models of oculomotor control in reading: Towards a theoretical foundation of current debates. In R. van Gompel, M. Fischer, W. Murray, & R. Hill (Eds.), *Eye movements: A window on mind and brain* (pp. 237–269). Oxford, UK: Elsevier.

Radach, R., Schmitten, C., Glover, L., & Vorstius, C. (2009). *Word processing and oculomotor control during oral and silent reading in elementary school students.* Manuscript in preparation.

Radach, R., Vorstius, C., & Günther, T. (2008). *Tracking non-linguistic visual processing demands critical for early reading.* Paper presented at the XXIX International Congress of Psychology, Berlin.

Ramus, F., Rosen, S., Dakin, S. C., Day, B. L., Castellote, J. M., White, S., & Frith, U. (2003). Theories of developmental dyslexia: Insights from a multiple case study of dyslexic adults. *Brain, 126*, 841–865.

Raven, J. C., Raven, J., & Court, J. H. (1998). *Raven's Progressive Matrices und Vocabulary Scales.* Frankfurt, Germany: Swets & Zeitlinger.

Rayner, K. (1979). Eye guidance in reading: Fixation locations within words. *Perception, 8*, 21–30.

Rayner, K. (1985). The role of eye movements in learning to read and reading disability. *Remedial and Special Education, 6*, 53–60.

Rayner, K. (1986). Eye movements and the perceptual span in beginning and skilled readers. *Journal of Experimental Child Psychology, 41*, 211–236.

Rayner, K. (1998). Eye mevements in reading and information processing: 20 years of research. *Psychological Bulletin, 124*, 372–422.

Rayner, K., & Duffy, S. D. (1986). Lexical complexity and fixation times in reading: Effects of word frequency, verb complexity and lexical ambiguity. *Memory & Cognition, 14*, 191–201.

Reed, H. B. (1916). The existence and function of inner speech in thought processes. *Journal of Experimental Psychology, 1*, 365–392.

Reichle, E. D., Rayner, K., & Pollatsek, A. (2003). The E–Z Reader model of eye movement control in reading: Comparisons to other models. *Behavioral and Brain Sciences, 26*, 445–476.

Reilly, R., & Radach, R. (2006). Some empirical tests of an interactive activation model of eye movement control in reading. *Cognitive Systems Research, 7*, 34–55.

Salasoo, A. (1986). Cognitive processing in oral and silent reading comprehension. *Reading Research Quarterly, 21*, 59–69.

Schilling, H. E. H., Rayner, K., & Chumbley, J. I. (1998). Comparing naming, lexical decision, and eye fixation times: Word frequency effects and individual differences. *Memory & Cognition, 26,* 1270–1281.

Schroiff, H. W. (1984). Secondary task effects on oculomotor behaviour in reading. In A. G. Gale & F. Johnson (Eds.), *Theoretical and applied aspects of eye movement research* (pp. 241–250). Amsterdam: North Holland/Elsevier Science.

Sereno, S. S., O'Donnell, P. J., & Rayner, K. (2006). Eye movements and lexical ambiguity resolution: Investigating the subordinate-bias effect. *Journal of Experimental Psychology: Human Perception and Performance, 32,* 335–350.

Seymour, P. H. K., Aro, M., & Erskine, J. M. (2003). Foundation literacy acquisition in European orthographies. *British Journal of Psychology, 94,* 143–174.

Sovik, N., Arntzen, O., & Samuelstuen, M. (2000). Eye-movement parameters and reading speed. *Reading and Writing, 13,* 237–255.

Swalm, J. E. (1973). A comparison of oral reading, silent reading and listening comprehension. *Education, 92,* 111–115.

Taylor, S. E., Frackenpohl, H., & Petee, J. L. (1960). Grade level norms for the components of the fundamental reading skill. E.D.L. In *Research and Information Bulletin, vol. 3.* Huntington, NY: Educational Developmental Labs.

Underwood, N. R., & Zola, D. (1986). The span of letter recognition of good and poor readers. *Reading Research Quarterly, 21,* 6–19.

Vellutino, F. R., Fletcher, J. M., Snowling, M. J., & Scanlon, D. M. (2004). Specific reading disability (dyslexia): What have we learned in the past four decades? *Journal of Child Psychology and Psychiatry, 45,* 2–40.

Vukovic, R. K., & Siegel, L. S. (2006). The double deficit hypothesis: A comprehensive review of the evidence. *Journal of Learning Disabilities, 39,* 25–47.

Wade, N. J., Tatler, B. W., & Heller, D. (2003). Dodge-ing the issue: Dodge, javal, hering, and the measurement of saccades in eye-movement research. *Perception, 32(7),* 793–804.

Wagner, R. K., Torgesen, J. K., & Rashotte, C. A. (1994). Development of reading related phonological processing abilities: New evidence of bidirectional causality from a latent variable longitudinal study. *Developmental Psychology, 30,* 4–31.

Wimmer, H., & Goswami, U. (1994). The influence of orthographic consistency on reading development: Word recognition in English and German children. *Cognition, 51,* 91–103.

Wimmer, H., & Hummer, P. (1990). How German speaking first graders read and spell: Doubts on the importance of the logographic stage. *Applied Psycholinguistics, 11,* 349–368.

Wimmer, H., & Mayringer, H. (2002). Dysfluent reading in the absence of spelling difficulties: A specific disability in regular orthographies. *Journal of Educational Psychology, 94,* 272–277.

Zeno, S. M., Ivens, S. H., Millard, R. T., & Duvvuri, R. (1995). *The Educator's Word Frequency Guide.* Brewster, NY: Touchstone Applied Science Associates (TASA) Inc.

Zhang, Q.-L. (2007). A discussion of ambiguity in English. *US–China Foreign Language, 5,* 1–5.

Ziegler, J. C. & Goswami, U. (2005). Reading acquisition developmental dyslexia, and skilled reading across languages: A psycholinguistic grain size
theory. *Psychological Bulletin, 131*, 3–29.

Ziegler, J. C., Jacobs, A. M., & Stone, G. O. (1996). Statistical analysis of the bidirectional inconsistency of spelling and sound in French. *Behavior Research
Methods, Instruments, & Computers, 28*, 504–515.

Ziegler, J. C., Perry, C., & Coltheart, M. (2000). The DRC model of visual word
recognition and reading aloud: An extension to German. *European Journal
of Cognitive Psychology, 12*, 413–430.

5

Reading between the Lines

Developmental and Individual Differences in Cognitive Processes in Reading Comprehension

Paul van den Broek, Mary Jane White,
Panayiota Kendeou, *and* Sarah Carlson

Reading comprehension is an essential component of lifelong learning. Individuals who experience difficulties reading and understanding information presented to them tend to suffer from problems in school, in the workplace, and in their communities (National Center for Education Statistics, 2002; National Reading Panel, 2000). Not only is formal education difficult for these individuals, but the opportunities to reflect, share ideas, and reason effectively are hindered in all aspects of their lives. Thus, it is essential that we understand the processes that lead to successful reading comprehension and the ways in which these processes can fail. Such understanding can have far-reaching implications for educational practice, specifically with respect to assessment, diagnosis, and intervention for both good and struggling readers.

In this chapter, we discuss the cognitive processes underlying reading comprehension and the development of these processes. The chapter consists of three major sections. The first section provides a general overview of cognitive processes in reading comprehension drawing on recent cognitive theories. The second section summarizes the development of reading comprehension and difficulties experienced by struggling readers in the context of findings from two large-scale studies. In the third and final section, we discuss theoretical and practical implications derived from the results of this research.

COGNITIVE PROCESSES IN READING COMPREHENSION

Extensive research has examined the cognitive processes of reading comprehension (e.g., Gernsbacher, 1990; Graesser, Singer, & Trabasso, 1994; Kintsch & van Dijk, 1978; Trabasso & van den Broek, 1985; van den Broek, 1994; Wagner, Piasta, & Torgesen, 2006; Whitehurst & Lonigan, 1998; Zwaan & Rapp, 2006). A common theme that has emerged is that to comprehend a text, it is essential that a reader is able to translate written code into meaningful language units and to combine these units into a coherent mental representation of the text. This representation can be accessed by the reader for different purposes after reading is completed: to recall information from the text, to answer questions, to apply the knowledge obtained from the text, to draw parallels to other texts, and so on. Thus, it is the quality of the reader's final representation of a text that determines the ultimate success of his or her comprehension of that text.

Investigations of the construction of coherent representations focus on both the cognitive processes involved during reading comprehension itself, as they occur moment by moment when the reader proceeds through a text (*online*), and the properties of the resulting representations once reading has been completed (*offline*). These online processes and offline representations are causally related: The processes that unfold during moment-by-moment reading comprehension provide the basis for the construction of the offline text representation in the reader's mind. If the online processes fail, so does the final representation.

Comprehension Processes during Reading (Online)

The online construction of a coherent mental representation of the text involves a complex set of processes that involve connecting and integrating the text information that the reader currently is reading with information that occurred earlier in the text as well as with information from background knowledge. Some of these processes are quick, automatic, and relatively effortless, whereas others are slow, strategic, and relatively effortful. The mix of automatic and strategic processes differs among individual readers and, indeed, for a particular reader across reading situations (e.g., as a function of fatigue, text difficulty, or reading purpose).

The process of interconnecting and integrating information is constrained, on the one hand, by the limitations of human attentional capacity and short-term memory and, on the other hand, by the *standards of coherence* that a reader attempts to maintain in a particular reading situation (e.g., as a function of motivation or goal for reading, the nature of the reading task; see van den Broek, Risden, & Husebye-Hartmann, 1995; van de Velde, 1989). Readers can use a wide range of standards to maintain coherence, but two types of standards, causal coherence and referential coherence, are prevalent in virtually all reading situations and are particularly important for the construction of coherent representations (e.g., Graesser & Clark, 1985; Kintsch, 1988; O'Brien & Myers, 1987; Trabasso & Sperry, 1985). Consider, for example, the sentence pair:

John dropped the banana peel on the floor. Mary fell on her back.

Most readers infer that the information in these two sentences is causally connected, often without realizing that a causal inference has been made. The fact that John dropped the banana peel on the floor is not sufficient to explain why Mary fell unless the reader infers that banana peels are slippery, and when slippery things are stepped upon a person may fall (van den Broek, 1990). Causal coherence, therefore, is attained when there is sufficient information provided by the text or by the background knowledge of the reader to explain the nature of the events.

In addition, referential coherence occurs when the reader connects objects, characters, and other entities across sentences in the text. Consider, for example, the sentence pair:

The lady gave the waiter $10. He returned to give her the change.

For this pair of sentences, most readers establish referential coherence by inferring that "he" in the second sentence refers to the "waiter" in the first sentence and that "her" refers to the "lady," again usually without even becoming aware of making such inferences. Interestingly, readers also tend to infer a causal relation, based on their script knowledge of waiters (and restaurants), people paying waiters, and so on.

Thus, as the reader progresses through a text, he or she attempts to maintain coherence by gathering information from the currently read sentence while integrating this information with previously read text and background knowledge. The reader does this by attempting to identify causal, referential, and other relations. Any such attempt, though, needs to take place within rather severe limitations of a person's working memory or attentional limitations; a reader is unable to simply accumulate every piece of information provided or activated by the text but instead is subject to a continuous waxing and waning of available information.

A useful way to conceptualize this process is as an unfolding landscape in which individual pieces of information constantly fluctuate in their levels of activation over time (for a review, see the landscape model by van den Broek, Risden, Fletcher, & Thurlow, 1996; see also Goldman & Varma, 1995). Only pieces of information that are activated simultaneously can be connected by the comprehender. As a result, if to-be-connected pieces of information are readily available at the same time (e.g., if they are presented close in time or are available close in the text), comprehension is an effortless, automatic process. If to-be-connected pieces of information are not readily available, the execution of strategic processes is required, resulting in more effortful reading or even failure to comprehend altogether. There are considerable individual and developmental differences in the effectiveness and efficiency of the various processes that result in the landscape of activations (reflecting differences in, e.g., background knowledge, working memory, experience, motivation, knowledge of strategies).

The Mental Representation of Texts (Offline)

A memory representation of the text and relevant background knowledge emerges from the dynamically fluctuating landscape of activation, processes, and strategies. This representation is coherent to the extent that it forms a *network* of relations (Graesser & Clark, 1985; O'Brien & Myers, 1987; Trabasso & van den Broek, 1985). An example of a causal network is presented in Figure 5.1. The numbered nodes in this network refer to unique ideas from the beginning of a narrative story, listed in Figure 5.2. The story is about Lenore, a young princess who becomes sick. In the network in Figure 5.1, the *arrows* between the nodes represent the causal connections between the corresponding text units. For example, Lenore's illness (unit/node 3) causes the King to become concerned about his daughter (unit/node 10), which, in turn, causes the King to ask if his daughter needs anything (unit/node 13).

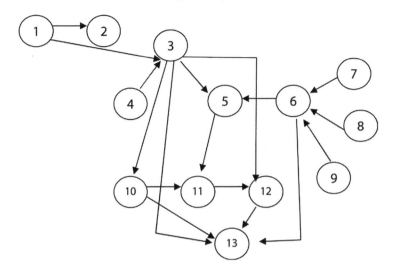

FIGURE 5.1. Causal network representation of *Many Moons* excerpt.

For accurate comprehension to occur, it is necessary that one's mental representation reflects such a network representation. This representation includes both *quantitative* and *qualitative* aspects of the representation. Therefore, assessment of comprehension needs to involve both aspects. For example, measurements of children's memory for a text should not only provide an index of *how much* they recall (the quantitative aspect) but also *what* is recalled (the qualitative aspect): Ideas that

1. Once upon a time, there lived a Princess named Lenore
2. who was ten years old.
3. One day, Lenore became ill
4. from eating too many chocolate-raspberry tarts.
5. The royal physician was called to come
6. to make Lenore feel better.
7. He took her temperature,
8. felt her pulse,
9. and made her stick out her tongue.
10. Knowing that the King was concerned,
11. the physician brought him in after he was finished with the examination.
12. When the King saw his daughter lying there,
13. he asked if there was anything she wanted.

FIGURE 5.2. Excerpt from *Many Moons*, written text used for narrative comprehension task.

have many connections play a more central role in the causal network structure than do ideas with few connections. Indeed, skilled comprehenders recall highly connected ideas more often than they recall ideas with few connections (e.g., Graesser & Clark, 1985; Trabasso, Secco, & van den Broek, 1984; Trabasso & Sperry, 1985; van den Broek & Lorch, 1993). For example, for the story in Figures 5.1 and 5.2, skilled readers are more likely to recall that Lenore became ill (unit/node 3, with six connections) than to recall that the princess was 10 years old (unit/node 2, with one connection). The quality of recall is more indicative of good comprehension than the quantity, for adults as well as children (e.g., Casteel, 1993; Goldman & Varnhagen, 1986; Trabasso et al., 1984).

DEVELOPMENT OF
READING COMPREHENSION

For skilled adult readers, the construction of a coherent, meaningful representation most of the time is rather effortless. For beginning or struggling readers, however, constructing this representation often requires considerable effort, drawing on comprehension skills such as monitoring and inference generation as well as developing literacy skills related to the written code (e.g., phonemic awareness, letter and word identification) and oral language skills (e.g., vocabulary knowledge; Cain, Oakhill, & Bryant, 2004; Gough & Tunmer, 1986; Oakhill & Cain, 2007; Oakhill, Cain, & Bryant, 2003; Paris & Paris, 2003; Storch & Whitehurst, 2002; Whitehurst & Lonigan, 1998).

Investigations of children's memory for narratives show that children, too, are sensitive to the causal and referential structure of the events they encounter. Even children as young as 4 years tend to remember ideas with many meaningful connections more often than ideas with few connections. However, systematic age differences also emerge. For instance, older children are more sensitive to the causal structure of a story than are younger children (and adults are even more sensitive). In addition, younger children tend to focus on recalling causal relations that occur within a particular episode of a story, whereas older children are better able to identify causal relations that span across multiple episodes and events in a story. Identifying causal relations across multiple episodes of a story leads to a broader, more complex understanding of abstract components, such as a story's overall theme. Younger children also tend to emphasize relations between the concrete events in a story, whereas older children are able to notice relations involving more abstract components, such as underlying intentions and goals of characters (van den Broek, 1997; Williams, 1993)

Early Contributions to the Development of Reading Comprehension

The fact that even preschool children engage in extensive coherence building raises the following questions: (1) How do code-related and oral comprehension skills develop? (2) How do these two sets of skills combine—or not combine—to support the development of reading comprehension skills? To address these questions, we tested two groups of preschool and kindergarten children (at the ages of 4 and 6 years, respectively) and monitored them as they transitioned from prereaders into beginning readers, testing them again after 2 years (at the ages of 6 and 8, respectively).

At each testing time, oral comprehension skills—the ability to extract meaning about events and facts and identify semantic relations between those events and facts—and code-related literacy skills—the ability to translate written symbols into meaningful words—were assessed. At each age, video and audio narratives were used to assess oral comprehension skills, in addition to receptive vocabulary as measured by the Peabody Picture Vocabulary Test-III (Dunn & Dunn, 1997). For the 8-year-old children, a written narrative was included to assess reading comprehension. All narratives were age appropriate (based on Flesch-Kincaid scores) and were analyzed in accordance with the principles described in the previous section to determine their causal structures. Outcome variables for the comprehension measures were the total amounts of recall of idea units that were causally central to the causal network structure (i.e., with many connections), representing a combination of quantitative and qualitative aspects of the child's representation of each narrative. Code-related skills were examined using measures of phonemic awareness and letter and word identification (Storch & Whitehurst, 2002).

Oral comprehension and code-related skills emerged as unique and interrelated factors that contribute to overall reading comprehension. With regard to the development of these skills, oral comprehension skills at one age uniquely predicted oral comprehension skills 2 years later (i.e., from age 4 to age 6 and from age 6 to age 8). Similarly, a child's code-related skills at one age predicted that child's code-related skills 2 years later. These two unique sets of skills were also interrelated, particularly at the youngest age. For preschool children (age 4), oral comprehension skills strongly predicted code-related skills. As children developed, the predictive relation became weaker, suggesting that these two types of skills gradually separate as a child develops.

With regard to later reading skills, oral comprehension and code-related skills in early elementary school each independently predicted reading comprehension (i.e., at age 8). Thus, oral comprehension and code-related skills jointly contribute to reading comprehension skills in a child's early elementary school years.

In summary, well before children learn to read, oral comprehension and code-related skills are present as separate yet interrelated sets of skills. Each of these sets of skills follows its own developmental trajectory, with the skills at one age predicting the same skills 2 years later. When the child eventually reads texts for comprehension, in the early elementary school grades, each of these two sets of skills independently contributes to reading success.

Traditionally, the emphasis in preschool education has been on developing code-related skills as a means to improve later reading comprehension. Our findings support that practice, but they suggest that oral comprehension, in addition to code-related literacy skills, also should be emphasized during early instruction if reading comprehension skills are to develop by the time a child is in early elementary school. This is particularly important because after these early school years, texts increasingly become the means for conveying content and, hence, a lack of skills that are prerequisite to comprehension likely results in a cascade of academic failures. Thus, comprehension skills, such as inference generation and comprehension monitoring, developed in the early grades become more and more important for academic success in the higher grades. Yet as national reports continue to show, large numbers of students in later elementary school and in high school struggle to adequately comprehend what they read in school or at home, even when decoding skills have been mastered. To help struggling readers in the later grades, it is important to gain insight into the kinds of difficulties that they experience. In doing so, it is important to consider the processes *during* reading, because that is when the majority of problems originate.

Later Contributions to the Development of Reading Comprehension

We investigated how struggling and proficient readers differ as they integrate and connect information during reading by observing data from eye movements and think-aloud protocols. These methodologies were chosen because they provided both quantitative and qualitative aspects of online comprehension processes, parallel to our analysis of comprehension processes in the resulting representation (offline) from our study of young readers.

Struggling, average, and proficient readers from fourth-, seventh-, and ninth-grade classes participated in this study. Levels of reading comprehension ability were assessed by means of the Maze Test of Curriculum Based Measurement (CBM-Maze; Deno, 1985; Espin & Foegen, 1996). Students in each grade were divided into equal subgroups based on the distribution of Maze scores; those in the lower 20% of the distribution were identified as struggling readers and those between 40 and 60% and over 80% of the distribution as average and proficient readers, respectively. The validity of the identified subgroups was tested by comparing their scores on the standardized Gates-MacGinitie Reading Comprehension Test (MacGinitie, MacGinitie, Maria, & Dreyer, 2000). Comprehension scores of the subgroups as assessed by the Gates-MacGinitie test differed significantly, and the differences were consistent with the CBM-Maze test results.

All students read a variety of (age-appropriate) texts in both eye-tracking and think-aloud tasks. The eye-tracking methodology reveals the number, duration, and type of eye movements that occur when reading a text, thus capturing quantitative and qualitative aspects of online comprehension processes. Hence, it allows one to determine how many fixations and how much time a reader devotes to a particular area in the text as well as whether the reader returned to that area of the text after having continued reading (i.e., looking back at prior text). The think-aloud methodology reveals the inferential and noninferential processes executed by students as they proceed through a text, thus capturing quantitative and qualitative aspects of online comprehension processes in a manner complementary to that by eye tracking. The types of processes revealed during think-aloud procedures range from readers repeating text in their own words (i.e., paraphrasing) to making specific predictions about an event that will occur later in the text (i.e., predictive inference).

The eye-tracking results were remarkably consistent across the three grades. At each grade level, struggling readers proceeded through the texts with the same number of fixations as average and proficient readers, but fixation times were longer for struggling readers than for their more proficient peers. In addition, struggling, average, and proficient readers looked back to the previous text with equal frequency, but struggling readers were less systematic than more proficient readers with respect to *what* information they reread. For example, struggling readers returned to reread parts of the text as often as did the other readers, but instead of reading specific, informative segments, as proficient readers did, the struggling readers reread entire sections of the text—and often uninformative sections at that—before returning to their starting point.

The cognitive processes identified in the think-aloud protocols revealed two distinct subgroups of struggling readers, each displaying a unique pattern of comprehension processes. Each subgroup produced less-than-optimal mental representations of the texts they read, as evidenced by poor memory for the texts. With regard to the online processes during reading, one subgroup of struggling readers was more inclined than the other to engage in the generation of elaborative inferences, inferences that draw on the reader's background knowledge. Indeed, they did so as frequently as did more proficient readers; however, unlike the more proficient readers, this subgroup of struggling readers frequently produced elaborative inferences that were invalid in the context of the text. The second subgroup of struggling readers was more inclined to depend on the text. Unlike the other group of struggling readers (and unlike proficient readers), this subgroup of struggling readers restricted its inferential activities mostly to the textual information itself, paraphrasing or repeating the text and generating few elaborative inferences.

Interestingly, as a group, struggling readers did not exhibit cognitive processes that were dramatically different from average and good readers. In fact, struggling readers proceeded through the text in similar fashion as more proficient readers, generating inferential and non-inferential processes that could, in principle, help them integrate information into a coherent representation of the text. However, it was the relatively ineffectual and time-consuming manner in which struggling readers made their way through the text that distinguished them from the more proficient readers (cf. Long, Oppy, & Sealy, 1994). In addition, struggling and proficient readers differed in the strategies used during reading, with struggling readers overemphasizing either generating elaborative inferences or paraphrasing the text. Thus, struggling readers appear to comprise at least two distinct subgroups, with one subgroup going *beyond* the text to try and establish a coherent representation (but doing so ineffectively) and another staying *within* the text to try and establish a coherent representation, thereby limiting their ability to recognize important relations. These distinct subgroups of struggling readers can perhaps be described as explorers and plodders, respectively, in analogy to subgroups of dyslexic readers in the context of word processing (Olson, Kliegl, Davidson, & Foltz, 1985). Other subgroups may exist as well. Unfortunately, neither of these patterns of processes help struggling readers achieve success in their effort to accurately comprehend what they are reading.

DISCUSSION

The described research results contribute to our understanding of the development of reading comprehension and to efforts to prevent, diagnose, and remedy reading comprehension problems across the school years.

Theoretical Implications

Examining the types and quality of cognitive processes that occur during reading (online) and the properties of the textual representation once reading is completed (offline) across different age groups and different ability levels expands our understanding of reading comprehension. The results of the first study reported here indicate that, already in the preschool years, two distinct clusters of skills relevant to later reading comprehension exist: those involving the translation of the written code (letter, words) into concepts and meaningful language and those involving the identification of meaningful relations and the construction of coherence among the facts, events, and other concepts conveyed by the language. These clusters show remarkable stability as children mature and, importantly, make strong, independent contributions to reading comprehension by the time children begin to read. It appears that both sets of skills are necessary for reading comprehension.

Although for many children the necessary skills have developed when they are ready to read texts for learning and comprehension, many others struggle, even into higher elementary and high school grades. The results of the second study indicate that struggling readers tend to generate inaccurate and incomplete representations during reading. When we considered their online processes, it appeared that the struggling readers did not differ from more proficient readers in the types of cognitive processes in which they engaged per se but that they did differ with respect to the effectiveness and efficiency of those processes. Moreover, the results suggest that struggling readers comprise different subgroups. In our study, two such subgroups were identified consistently for each of the three grades that were investigated (4th, 7th, and 9th). One subgroup of struggling readers drew extensively on background knowledge to infer connections between text units and between text units and their prior knowledge; unfortunately, the activated background knowledge frequently was irrelevant or incorrect in the context of the text. The second subgroup of struggling readers tended to limit their processing to the text itself, frequently rereading or otherwise reprocessing text units, without bringing in relevant background knowledge.

It is important to note that these subgroups were indistinguishable with respect to their performance once reading was completed. For example, both subgroups differed from more proficient readers in terms of memory for the texts to the same degree. It is only when online processes during reading were considered that the subgroups emerged. In this study, two subgroups were identified. Future research may identify additional subgroups or be able to make finer grained distinctions within the subgroups that we identified.

Practical Implications

The finding that two distinct clusters of skills—associated with translating the written code and with comprehension, respectively—come together in early elementary school-age children's reading comprehension and, moreover, that these clusters of skills already are present and developing in the preschool years has implications for instructional practice. First, although the importance of providing preschool children with the opportunity to learn and practice code-related skills, such as phonemic awareness and word decoding, is generally recognized, the current results point to the importance of including comprehension skills in instruction as well. These skills can be introduced and practiced in nonreading contexts such as television viewing or listening (cf. van den Broek, Lorch, & Thurlow, 1996) and should be aimed at developing children's ability to create coherence. This includes awareness of coherence as well as specific strategies for constructing coherence. Causal coherence and referential coherence are good starting points because they tend to be amply present in the narrative materials to which preschool children typically are exposed and because these types of coherence also are central to other types of information, including the expository texts used in later school years. It is important to note that, although these skills can be introduced as strategies, the goal should be that they eventually become internalized and automatized so that they can be applied without consuming excessive attentional resources (Laberge & Samuels, 1974).

Second, early identification of potential problems in comprehension ability may open the door for interventions that ensure that children have the comprehension skills necessary for reading comprehension once they enter elementary school. To identify potential problems and to assess the effectiveness of interventions, proper comprehension assessment tools need to be developed.

This leads to a third implication of our results: The goal of comprehension assessment is to determine whether a reader is able to generate a coherent and accurate representation of the presented information. Such assessment should include both the quantity and quality of a student's representation, focusing on the constructed (causal) network (Kendeou, van den Broek, White, & Lynch, 2007; van den Broek et al., 2005). Most traditional assessments are limited to measuring quantity (e.g., the amount of information a child recalls). At least as important is the quality of the representation. In the current studies, we present one example of assessment of quality: gauging the extent to which a child's recall is sensitive to the centrality of information (i.e., the extent to which he or she remembers highly connected information). Other ways could easily be developed: for example, asking coherence building questions aimed at different levels of inference making and using item–response-type techniques to scale the questions—and the skills they gauge—on qualitatively different dimensions.

The results regarding struggling readers highlight a fourth implication for educational practice: Diagnosis of reading problems and intervention in struggling readers benefit from consideration of the actual processes in which these readers engage as they proceed through a text. Struggling readers may appear similar in terms of the product of their comprehension yet differ when their cognitive processes are considered. Moreover, it is the online processes that provide the foundation for successful—and failed—coherence building, so interventions and useful diagnosis are most likely to be effective when applied to the reader's activities *during* reading and when they are based on an understanding of which processes are being executed properly and which are not. Indeed, many strategy interventions in the literature address potential causes of reading difficulties by methods that implicitly are assumed to improve the effectiveness of processing, although such processing is not directly assessed (e.g., Dole, Duffy, Roehler, & Pearson, 1991; Fuchs,

Fuchs, Mathes, & Simmons, 1997; Palincsar & Brown, 1984; Pressley, 1998, 2000; Yuill & Oakhill, 1988). Our results suggest that explicit focus on processing, both in attempts to understand the origin of (reading) comprehension problems and the development of interventions, is essential. This, in turn, has a further implication for assessment, besides the quantity–quality distinction, namely that assessment tools should include process measures as well.

In conclusion, successful reading comprehension depends on the development of different skills, ranging from skills particular to translating the textual code into meaningful concepts to skills particular to combining units of information into a coherent whole. All of these skills begin their developmental trajectory well before the school years. Indeed, the processes and skills in preschool children described here themselves likely have precursors, at even earlier ages (see van den Broek, Bauer, & Bourg, 1997). Although in education comprehension usually is conceptualized as a *product*, it is as much a *process*. Educational practice is likely to benefit greatly in diagnosis and intervention by explicitly considering the cognitive processes that lead readers to success or failure.

ACKNOWLEDGMENTS

This research was supported by grants from the Center for Cognitive Sciences and the Department of Educational Psychology (both University of Minnesota), from the Center for the Improvement of Early Reading Achievement, and by a Reading Scale-up grant (CFDA 84.305) from the U.S. Institute of Education Sciences. Paul van den Broek received support through the Guy Bond Endowment for Reading Research, University of Minnesota. Panayiota Kendeou received support through a McGill University Researcher Fund.

REFERENCES

Cain, K., Oakhill, J., & Bryant, P. E. (2004). Children's reading comprehension ability: Concurrent prediction by working memory, verbal ability, and component skills. *Journal of Educational Psychology, 96,* 31–42.

Casteel, M. A. (1993). Effects of inference necessity and reading goal on children's inferential generation. *Developmental Psychology, 29,* 346–357.

Deno, S. L. (1985). Curriculum-based measurement: The emerging alternative. *Exceptional Children, 52,* 219–232.

Dole, J. A., Duffy, G. G., Roehler, L. R., & Pearson, P. D. (1991). Moving from the old to the new: Research on reading comprehension instruction. *Review of Educational Research, 61,* 239–264.

Dunn, L. M., & Dunn, L. M. (1997). *Peabody Picture Vocabulary Test—3rd edition (PPVT-III)*. Circle Pines, MN: American Guidance Services.

Espin, C. A., & Foegen, A. (1996). Validity of general outcome measures for predicting secondary students' performance on content-area tasks. *Exceptional Children, 62,* 497–514.

Fuchs, D., Fuchs, L. S., Mathes, P. G., & Simmons, D. C. (1997). Peer-assisted learning strategies: Making classrooms more responsive to diversity. *American Educational Research Journal, 34,* 174–206.

Gernsbacher, M. A. (1990). *Language comprehension as structure building*. Hillsdale, NJ: Erlbaum.

Goldman, S. R., & Varma, S. (1995). CAPping the construction-integration model of discourse comprehension. In C. A. Weaver, S. Mannes, & C. R. Fletcher (Eds.), *Discourse comprehension: Essays in honor of Walter Kintsch* (pp. 337–358). Mahwah, NJ: Erlbaum.

Goldman, S. R., & Varnhagen, C. K. (1986). Memory for embedded and sequential story structures. *Journal of Memory and Language, 25,* 401–418.

Gough, P. B., & Tunmer, W. E. (1986). Decoding, reading, and reading disability. *Remedial and Special Education, 7,* 6–10.

Graesser, A. C., & Clark, L. F. (1985). *Structures and procedures of implicit knowledge*. Norwood, NJ: Ablex.

Graesser, A. C., Singer, M., & Trabasso, T. (1994). Constructing inferences during narrative comprehension. *Psychological Review, 101,* 371–395.

Kendeou, P., van den Broek, P., White, M. J., & Lynch, J. (2007). Comprehension in preschool and early elementary children: Skill development and strategy interventions. In D. S. McNamara (Ed.), *Reading comprehension strategies: Theories, interventions, and technologies* (pp. 27–45). New York: Erlbaum.

Kintsch, W. (1988). The use of knowledge in discourse processing: A construction-integration model. *Psychological Review, 95,* 163–182.

Kintsch, W., & van Dijk, T. A. (1978). Toward a model of text comprehension and production. *Psychological Review, 85,* 363–394.

LaBerge, D., & Samuels, S. J. (1974). Toward a theory of automatic information processing in reading. *Cognitive Psychology, 6,* 293–323.

Long, D. L., Oppy, B. J., & Seely, M. R. (1994). Individual differences in the time course of inferential processing. *Journal of Experimental Psychology: Learning, Memory, and Cognition, 20,* 1456–1470.

MacGinitie, W. H., MacGinitie, R. K., Maria, K., & Dreyer, L. G. (2000). *The Gates-MacGinitie Reading Tests (GMRT)*. Itasca, IL: Riverside.

National Center for Education Statistics. (2002). National assessment of educational progress. Washington, DC: Author.

National Reading Panel. (2000). *Teaching children to read: An evidence-based assessment of the scientific research literature on reading and its implications for reading instruction: Reports of the subgroups.* (NIH Publication No. 00-4754). Washington, DC: U.S. Government Printing Office.

Oakhill, J., & Cain, K. (2007). Issues of causality in children's reading comprehension. In D. McNamara (Ed.), *Reading comprehension strategies: Theories, interventions, and technologies* (pp. 47–71). New York: Erlbaum.

Oakhill, J., Cain, K., & Bryant, P. E. (2003). The dissociation of word reading and text comprehension: Evidence from component skills. *Language and Cognitive Processes, 18*, 443–468.

O'Brien, E. J., & Myers, J. L. (1987). The role of causal connections in the retrieval of text. *Memory & Cognition, 15*, 419–427.

Olson, R. K., Kliegl, R., Davidson, B. J., & Foltz, G. (1985). Individual and developmental differences in reading disability. In G. E. MacKinnon & T. G. Waller (Eds.), *Reading research: Advances in theory and practice* (Vol. 4, pp. 1–64). New York: Academic Press.

Palincsar, A. S., & Brown, A. L. (1984). Reciprocal teaching of comprehension: Fostering and monitoring activities. *Cognition and Instruction, 1*, 117–175.

Paris, A. H., & Paris, S. G. (2003). Assessing narrative comprehension in young children. *Reading Research Quarterly, 38*, 36–76.

Pressley, M. (1998). Comprehension strategies instruction. In J. Osborn & F. Lehr (Eds.), *Literacy for all: Issues in teaching and learning* (pp. 113–133). New York: Guilford Press.

Pressley, M. (2000). What should comprehension instruction be the instruction of? In M. L. Kamil, P. B. Mosenthal, P. D. Pearson, & R. Barr (Eds.), *Handbook of reading research* (Vol. 3, pp. 545–586). Mahwah, NJ: Erlbaum.

Storch, S. A., & Whitehurst, G. J. (2002). Oral language and code-related precursors to reading: Evidence from a longitudinal structural model. *Developmental Psychology, 38*, 934–947.

Trabasso, T., Secco, T., & van den Broek, P. (1984). Causal cohesion and story coherence. In H. Mandl, N. L. Stein, & T. Trabasso (Eds.), *Learning and comprehension of text* (pp. 83–111). Mahwah, NJ: Erlbaum.

Trabasso, T., & Sperry, L. L. (1985). Causal relatedness and importance of story events. *Journal of Memory and Language, 24*, 595–611.

Trabasso, T., & van den Broek, P. (1985). Causal thinking and the representation of narrative events. *Journal of Memory and Language, 24*, 612–630.

van den Broek, P. (1990). The causal inference maker: Towards a process model of inference generation in text comprehension. In D. A. Balota, G. B. Flores d'Arcais, & K. Rayner (Eds.), *Comprehension processes in reading* (pp. 423–445). Hillsdale, NJ: Erlbaum.

van den Broek, P. (1994). Comprehension and memory of narrative texts. In M. A. Gernsbacher (Ed.), *Handbook of psycholinguistics* (pp. 539–588). London: Academic Press.

van den Broek, P. (1997). Discovering the cement of the universe: The development of event comprehension from childhood to adulthood. In P. van den Broek , P. J. Bauer, & T. Bourg (Eds.), *Developmental spans in event comprehension and representation* (pp. 321–342). Mahwah, NJ: Erlbaum.

van den Broek, P., Bauer, P. J., & Bourg, T. (Eds.). (1997). *Developmental spans in event comprehension and representation*. Mahwah, NJ: Erlbaum.

van den Broek, P., Kendeou, P., Kremer, K., Lynch, J. S., Butler, J., White, M. J., et al. (2005). Assessment of comprehension abilities in young children. In S. Paris & S. Stahl (Eds.), *New directions in assessment of reading comprehension* (pp. 107–130). Mahwah, NJ: Erlbaum.

van den Broek, P., & Lorch, R. F., Jr. (1993). Network representation of causal relations in memory for narrative texts: Evidence from primed recognition. *Discourse Processes, 16,* 75–98.

van den Broek, P., Lorch, E. P., & Thurlow, R. (1996). Children's and adults' memory for television stories: The role of causal factors, story-grammar categories, and hierarchical level. *Child Development, 67,* 3010–3028.

van den Broek, P., Risden, K., Fletcher, C. R., & Thurlow, R. (1996). A "landscape" view of reading: Fluctuating patterns of activation and the construction of a stable memory representation. In B. K. Britton & A. C. Graesser (Eds.), *Models of understanding text* (pp. 165–187). Mahwah, NJ: Erlbaum.

van den Broek, P., Risden, K., & Husebye-Hartmann, E. (1995). The role of readers' standards for coherence in the generation of inferences during reading. In R. F. Lorch & E. J. O'Brien (Eds.), *Sources of coherence in reading* (pp. 353–373). Hillsdale, NJ: Erlbaum.

van de Velde, R. G. (1989). Man, verbal text, inferencing, and coherence. In W. Heydrich, F. Neubauer, J. S. Petofi, & E. Sozer (Eds.), *Connexity and coherence: Analysis of text and discourse* (pp. 174–217). New York: Walter de Gruyter.

Wagner, R. K., Piasta, S. B., & Torgesen, J. K. (2006). Learning to read. In M. J. Traxler & M. A. Gernsbacher (Eds.), *Handbook of psycholinguistics* (2nd ed., pp. 1111–1142). New York: Elsevier.

Whitehurst, G. J., & Lonigan, C. J. (1998). Child development and emergent literacy. *Child Development, 69,* 848–872.

Williams, J. P. (1993). Comprehension of students with and without learning disabilities: Identification of narrative themes and idiosyncratic text representations. *Journal of Special Education, 25,* 135–154.

Yuill, N., & Oakhill, J. (1988). Effects of inference awareness training on poor reading comprehension. *Applied Cognitive Psychology, 2,* 33–45.

Zwaan, R. A., & Rapp, D. N. (2006). Discourse comprehension. In M. J. Traxler & M. A. Gernsbacher (Eds.), *Handbook of psycholinguistics* (2nd ed., pp. 725–764). New York: Elsevier.

6

The Roles of Fluent Decoding and Vocabulary in the Development of Reading Comprehension

Kanu Priya *and* Richard K. Wagner

Reading comprehension is the process of simultaneously extracting and constructing meaning through interaction and involvement with written language (Snow, 2002). This process of interaction and involvement with the text is a function of both reader and text variables (Goldman, Saul, & Cote, 1995; Harp & Mayer, 1998; Miller, Stine-Morrow, Kirkorian, & Conroy, 2004; Rosa, 1994).

Comprehension of written text represents the successful orchestration of just about every process—from basic vision to complex linguistic reasoning—that has been studied by experimental, cognitive, and educational psychologists since the beginning of their respective fields (Crowder & Wagner, 1991; Graesser, Millis, & Zwaan, 1997; Rayner & Pollatsek, 1989). Furthermore, in addition to considering what goes on in the head of the reader (i.e., person variables), a comprehensive account of reading comprehension would require explaining how the reader, text, and purpose for reading interact within a sociocultural context (Gee, 2000; Goldman & Rakestraw, 2000; Snow, 2002).

Because the complexity of reading comprehension can be overwhelming, it is important to adopt criteria for focusing on key variables for study. Given a goal of understanding origins of individual

124

and developmental differences in reading comprehension, reasonable candidates for these criteria are to focus on variables that (1) account for appreciable variance in reading comprehension, (2) appear to causally influence individual and developmental differences in reading comprehension as opposed to being mere byproducts of these differences, and (3) have levels of performance that might be manipulated through instruction, given the need to improving the reading comprehension performance of a substantial number of readers. Two person variables that appear to meet these criteria are decoding fluency and vocabulary. Two task variables that appear to be important are type of text to be read and the nature of the questions that are used to assess comprehension. Finally, technological developments have resulted in new contexts for reading that need to be considered.

FLUENT DECODING
AND READING COMPREHENSION

For most poor readers, poor word-level decoding is considered to be the critical bottleneck that accounts for accompanying poor comprehension (Adams, 1990; Lyon, 1995; Metsala & Ehri, 1998). Interventions given to poor readers have been shown to be effective in improving decoding accuracy, yet comparable gains in comprehension have not routinely been obtained (e.g., Torgesen, Wagner, Rashotte, Rose, et al., 1999). One explanation is that interventions improve decoding accuracy more readily than fluency. For example, Torgesen et al. (2001) provided 67.5 hr of intensive intervention to 60 highly impaired readers. Performance on measures of decoding accuracy went from the 75th to the 90th percentile, whereas reading rate began and remained at roughly the 70th percentile.

According to the National Reading Panel report (2000), a fluent reader has well-developed word recognition skills and can read text with speed, accuracy, and proper expression. Measures of reading fluency typically involve time-based measures of accurate word reading, either for connected text (Jenkins, Fuchs, van den Broek, Espin, & Deno, 2003) or for lists of words or pseudowords (Torgesen, Wagner, & Rashotte, 1999). Fluency typically is quantified as number of words read correctly per minute or for some other time interval (Jenkins et al., 2003).

Fluency is widely regarded as being necessary for good reading comprehension (Fuchs, Fuchs, Hosp, & Jenkins, 2001; Jenkins et al., 2003; Kuhn & Stahl, 2003; National Reading Panel, 2000; Yovanoff, Duesbery,

Alonzo, & Tindal, 2005). Typical correlations between reading comprehension and fluency range from .42 to .68 (Fuchs et al., 2001; Mather, Hammill, Allen, & Roberts, 2004; Yovanoff et al., 2005). The National Center for Educational Statistics (Donahue et al., 1999; National Reading Panel, 2000) conducted the National Assessment of Educational Progress (NAEP) assessment of the status of fluency achievement in American education, and this study, too, found a moderately strong relation between fluency and reading comprehension (Donahue, Voelkl, Campbell, & Mazzeo, 1999; National Reading Panel, 2000).

An explanation for relations between fluency and reading comprehension is that fluent decoding frees up cognitive resources that can be used by higher level comprehension processes (National Reading Panel, 2000). Three influential theories of fluency have been applied to the case of oral reading: LaBerge and Samuels's automaticity theory (1974), Stanovich's interactive–compensatory model of reading (1980, 2000), and Posner and Snyders's (1975) theory of expectancy.

LaBerge and Samuels describe how the execution of a complex skill necessitates the coordination of many component processes within a short time frame. If each component within a skill requires attention, the performance of the skill would exceed attentional capacity and, therefore, be impossible to perform. If, however, enough of the component skills are executed automatically, then the attentional load would be within tolerable limits, allowing successful performance. This theory considers phonological coding as a target of automaticity. It is a "bottom-up" serial-stage model of reading and requires that higher level processes (e.g., comprehension) await the completion of lower ones (e.g., decoding).

The interactive–compensatory model of reading similarly posits that fast and automatic word recognition is an important determinant of fluent reading (Stanovich, 1980). This model of reading assumes that deficiencies at any level in the processing hierarchy can be compensated for by a greater use of information from other levels, and that this compensation takes place irrespective of the level of deficient process. In reading contexts, this means that under some circumstances the poor decoding skills of less skilled readers could lead them to rely more on contextual information (Stanovich, 2000).

The Posner and Snyder theory of expectancy illustrates how semantic context affects word recognition via two independently acting processes: the automatic-activation process and the conscious-attention mechanism. For good readers, rapid word recognition short-circuits the conscious-attention mechanism and the automatic component of contextual processing dominates. For poor readers, contextual facilitation results from the combined effects of the two processes whereby the reliance on the conscious-attention mechanism for word recognition leaves few resources left for comprehension (Fuchs et al., 2001).

These perspectives share the assumption that efficient low-level word recognition frees up capacity for higher level, integrative processing of text and thus assume a single resource pool available for word recognition and comprehension. A separate resource pool for the two processes of word recognition and comprehension would prove troublesome for these serial-stage or even compensatory models of reading. Whether different cognitive processes depend on a single resource pool or can take advantage of independent resource pools is a matter of debate in several domains (Barrouillet & Camos, 2001; Bayliss, Jarrold, Gunn, & Baddeley, 2003). Even though there may be differences of opinion within these theoretical frameworks over what reading fluency is and how individuals proceed toward comprehension, there is unanimous agreement that reading fluency is necessary for good reading comprehension (Fuchs et al., 2001; LaBerge & Samuels, 1974; Stanovich, 2000).

The development of oral reading fluency shows greatest growth in the primary grades, with a negatively accelerating curve through the intermediate grades and perhaps into junior high school (Fuchs et al., 2001). On the basis of studies comparing students from fourth through eighth grades, Yovanoff et al. (2005) suggest that both vocabulary and fluency are important predictors of reading comprehension at all grades; however, the role of vocabulary becomes more important and fluency less important as grade level increases (see also Jenkins & Jewell, 1993; Kuhn & Stahl, 2003; Sassenrath, 1972).

VOCABULARY AND READING COMPREHENSION

Vocabulary refers to the knowledge of lexical meanings of words and the concepts connected to these meanings (Aarnoutse, Van Leeuwe, Voeten, & Oud, 2001). Individual differences in vocabulary are related to reading comprehension (Joshi, 2005; Nagy & Herman, 1987; Stahl & Fairbanks, 1986), with correlations ranging from .48 to .66 (Muter, Hulme, Snowling, & Stevenson, 2004; Yovanoff et al., 2005).

Anderson and Freebody (1981) identified three alternative causal relations between vocabulary and reading comprehension (Nagy, 2007). The first alternative is that individual and developmental differences causally affect reading comprehension instrumentally because knowing the meanings of words is a prerequisite to comprehending the passage. The second alternative, referred to as the knowledge hypothesis, is that vocabulary represents conceptual knowledge, and it is conceptual knowledge that makes comprehension possible. The third alternative, the aptitude hypothesis, suggests that vocabulary and comprehension are not causally related but rather are both correlates of underlying cognitive ability. Training studies in which the effects of improving vocabulary on reading comprehension are examined could be useful in comparing alternative causal relations. Unfortunately, the effects of vocabulary instruction on reading comprehension have been inconsistent. There is some support for the view that extensive training that requires children to use the words in multiple contexts and occasions is associated with modest effects on comprehension, whereas rote learning of definitions is not (Beck & McKeown, 1991).

Reasonably well-developed vocabulary knowledge would seem to be essential for reading at any grade level (Joshi, 2005; Muter et al., 2004; National Institute of Child Health and Human Development, 2005; Yovanoff et al., 2005), and relations between vocabulary and reading comprehension are likely to be reciprocal. Individuals able to comprehend written texts successfully are motivated, in turn, to read more, and this leads to an increase in their vocabulary (Cain, Oakhill, & Elbro, 2003; Joshi, 2005; Nagy & Herman, 1987; National Reading Panel, 2000; Pulido, 2004).

NARRATIVE AND EXPOSITORY TEXT TYPES

One of the elements that seems to make a difference in reading comprehension studies is whether the text being read is narrative or expository. The features of any given text have a large impact on comprehension (Snow, 2002). Most studies utilize either narrative passages or expository material to elicit comprehension scores (Degand & Sanders, 2002; Rosa, 1994). Although work has been done (Scott & Windsor, 2000; Zabrucky & Moore, 1999) comparing narrative and expository texts, very little has addressed the question of whether vocabulary and fluency differentially predict comprehension of narrative and expository texts.

Narrative texts are easier to comprehend than expository texts, especially for children with learning disabilities (Scott & Windsor, 2000). One possible explanation may be familiarity with content, but that alone does not explain the full picture. Even bizarre events and fantastic literature can produce a reasonably high level of understanding on part of the reader (Graesser, Golding, & Long, 1991). Stories, it seems, are inherently easier to comprehend and to recall even if they have novel elements in them.

INFERENTIAL AND NONINFERENTIAL QUESTIONS

Comprehension questions can be broadly classified as inferential and noninferential. Although noninferential questions are easier to answer, the difference in performance is more pronounced in expository material (Wagner, Priya, & Rashotte, 2006). In contrast to narrative text, expository text is decontextualized and is written to inform readers of the new concepts, generic truths, and technical material (Graesser, Singer, & Trabasso, 1994). Readers do not have extensive background knowledge about the topics in expository texts to generate enough inferences during comprehension as opposed to the amount of inferences they can generate during comprehension of narrative texts. Background knowledge alone is not sufficient for making correct inferences, however (Cain & Oakhill, 1998, 1999; Cain, Oakhill, Barnes, & Bryant, 2001).

Inference-making ability requires the reader to connect different sentences and ideas within the text in order to build a fully integrated and coherent representation of the text (Cain & Oakhill, 1998). Inferred information thus is based on the text, but not stated explicitly, requiring readers to interpret the text through existing knowledge. Most inferential questions are more difficult for children than those requiring explicit text recall (Allen, 1985). With age, readers' inferential skills develop to a greater extent than general question answering ability. The difference between performance on types of questions accessing given information and those relying on inferences increases with the age (Cain & Oakhill, 1998). Adult readers thus show a difference in comprehension performance for inferential and noninferential questions. Do they also show a difference in performance on the type of text? What happens to performance on these two types of questions as an interaction with the text type?

TRADITIONAL VERSUS ELECTRONIC CONTEXTS

If you imagine a child reading, the image that is likely to come to mind is a child holding a book. However, much of the reading professionals do, and more of the reading that children are doing, is occurring in electronic contexts such as reading web pages, electronic books, or using computer-based educational programs. Reading in electronic contexts provides opportunities for providing assistance to readers, such as the pronunciation or meaning for unknown printed words. Determining what kinds of assistance to provide to whom is a potentially important purpose of assessment.

The National Research Council's *Knowing What Students Know: The Science and Design of Educational Assessments* (Pellegrino, Chudowsky, & Glaser, 2001) made two general recommendations for educational assessment. First, assessments should be grounded more fully in a model of cognition, learning, or development. Second, research should be directed toward assessments that have implications for the classroom—where teaching and learning occur—including technology-based instructional contexts. This second recommendation is a call for greater reliance on formative assessment.

Much of the reading that students do today occurs in electronic contexts such as web pages and electronic books, and these contexts provide new opportunities for formative assessment and assistance. For example, passage-specific assessment and assistance are possible, although our knowledge of how to do so effectively is in its infancy (Kamil, Intrator, & Kim, 2000).

One preliminary question that needs to be answered is, how important is passage-specific assessment information (Wagner et al., 2006)? Consider the case of decoding. It may be the case that with generic measures of decoding (e.g., Test of Word Reading Efficiency [TOWRE]) and information about the relative decoding difficulty of words in a passage, little additional information would be provided by passage-specific assessment. This outcome would be likely if decoding is regular and predictable in the sense that a generic measure of decoding was sufficient to accurately determine decoding skill and the relative difficulty of words was similar across individuals. One way of picturing this situation if you happen to know about item–response theory (IRT) modeling is that an IRT model that places individuals and items on the same scale would provide a good fit to the data. Alternatively, if it turned out that the relative decoding difficulty of words varied across individuals as a function of their reading experience and interests, it might be necessary to measure the decoding difficulty of the specific words in the passage. This would be necessary because a given word might be relatively easy for one reader and relatively difficult for another reader, even if both readers were identical in overall decoding skill. Returning to an IRT conceptualization, under these circumstances an IRT model that places individuals and items on the same scale would provide a poor fit to the data.

Whatever turns out to be the case for decoding, the situation for vocabulary might be different. Vocabulary knowledge might be more passage specific than decoding or, conversely, decoding might be more passage specific than vocabulary.

We have carried out several developmental studies of the effects of passage type and question type on reading comprehension performance and of the relative strength of generic and passage-specific measures of fluency and vocabulary as predictors of both comprehension and reading rate. The results of one recent study are highlighted.

Participants were randomly sampled second-grade and fourth-grade readers. The 181 second-grade students and 187 fourth-grade students read narrative and expository passages and were given two measures of vocabulary.

A sample fourth-grade narrative passage and passage questions are presented in Figure 6.1. The passage describes how Rita wrote an essay on how she spent her summer vacation when she returned to school in the fall. While her friends had visited exotic places, Rita had to stay at home to care for a visiting aunt who was recovering from surgery. After reading the passage, students were given noninferential questions about what one of Rita's friends saw in Mexico and who came to stay with Rita's family. Students also were given inferential questions that required them to infer that the reason the aunt came was because she was unable to care for herself and to make a reasonable inference about what Rita would write about in her essay given the title "The Silver Dollar." A sample fourth-grade expository passage and passage questions are presented in Figure 6.2. The topic of the passage is rainbows, and students are asked noninferential questions about where, in addition to the sky, rainbows occur and what colors are always present in rainbows. Inferential questions required the reader to infer how a prism operates and to determine whether it would be possible for rainbows to occur at night even if we could not see them.

The generic measure of vocabulary was the Vocabulary subtest on the Stanford–Binet Intelligence Scale, and a passage-specific vocabulary measure was created by using vocabulary from the passage itself. Two measures of decoding fluency also were given. The generic decoding fluency measure was the TOWRE. The passage-specific decoding fluency measure was a TOWRE-like test but with items from the passages to be read. Participants answered comprehension questions after

How I Spent My Summer Vacation

"How I spent my summer vacation" was the topic for Rita's first essay when school resumed. Her two best friends did exciting things during the summer. Shana went to Mexico. She had seen the Aztec pyramids, and she brought Rita a colorful woven change purse for a present. Juan went to Montana. He had gone fishing with his brother and hiked up hills. Since Rita didn't go anywhere, she thought that her vacation would sound dull. She thought about what she had done during the summer. During Rita's summer vacation, her Aunt Marta came to visit. Marta had just had surgery on her wrists. It took several weeks before Marta could even do simple jobs. Rita helped her aunt whenever she could. She opened doors and cut her food. She even held the phone for Aunt Marta when her cousin Alex called. When Aunt Marta left, she gave Rita a silver dollar for all her help. Rita put the silver dollar in the purse that Shana had brought from Mexico. Now Rita knew what she would write in her essay. She was going to title her essay "The Silver Dollar."

Noninferential Questions
- What did Shana see in Mexico?
- Who came to stay with Rita's family?

Inferential Questions
- Why do you think Aunt Marta came to stay with them?
- What did Rita write about in her essay "The Silver Dollar"?

FIGURE 6.1. Example of a fourth-grade narrative text and comprehension questions.

Rainbows

Have you ever seen a rainbow in the sky? Have you ever seen a rainbow in a puddle? You might have wondered why we see rainbows. The main reason we see a rainbow is that the light from the sun strikes water drops. The water drops could be rain, a puddle, spraying water, or even fog. The sun's light passes through the water drops. The drops act like a glass prism. The water drops break up the sunlight into all the different colors that are actually there. Do you know what colors you will always find in a rainbow? If you don't, just remember Roy G. Biv! **R**ed **O**range **Y**ellow **G**reen **B**lue **I**ndigo **V**iolet. The sun's light is made up of all these colors. You will always see the same colors in every rainbow. Rainbows can be seen only when the person is standing between the water and the sun's light. Even if rainbows don't end in a glorious pot of gold that is protected by a leprechaun, they are a beautiful sight to see. They always remind us of the splendor of nature.

Noninferential Questions
- What other places, besides the sky, can we see rainbows?
- What colors will you always find in a rainbow?

Inferential Questions
- What does a prism do?
- Could rainbows happen at night even if we can't see them? Why?

FIGURE 6.2. Example of a fourth-grade expository text and comprehension questions.

reading the passages that were either inferential or noninferential in nature.

A repeated measures Analysis of Variance was carried out to examine the effects of grade, passage type, and question type on reading comprehension performance. These results are presented in Table 6.1. The main effect of grade was significant, indicating that fourth-grade students outperformed second-grade students on the comprehension questions. This result is not directly of interest, however, in that different passages were given to the second-grade and fourth-grade participants. There was no main effect of passage type, meaning that the questions associated with the narrative passages were about as difficult overall as the questions associated with the expository passages. However, there was a significant interaction between grade and passage type. The fourth-grade expository passages were relatively harder than narrative passages compared with the second-grade passages. This probably reflects the more technical nature of the expository passages used in fourth grade compared with second grade. There was a main effect of question type, with inferential questions being more difficult that noninferential questions. Finally, there was an interaction between passage type and question type, with a greater difference in difficulty for inferential compared with noninferential questions for expository passages compared with narrative passages.

Doing comparable analyses but on reading rate rather than comprehension performance yielded a significant effect of grade on reading rate, $F(1, 364) = 23.2$, $p < .001$, with no other significant effects.

Results for predicting reading comprehension performance using generic and passage-specific measures are presented in Table 6.2. Vocabulary was a better predictor than fluency for reading compre-

TABLE 6.1. Repeated-Measures Analysis of Variance for Effect of Grade, Passage Type, and Question Type on Comprehension Performance

Source	SS	df	MS	F	p
Grade	7992.7	1	7992.7	3357.5	< .001
Passage type	0.5	1	0.5	0.6	.436
Passage type by grade	100.7	1	100.7	131.4	< .001
Question type	412.2	1	412.1	592.6	< .001
Question type by grade	0.6	1	0.6	0.8	.352
Passage type by question type	25.3	1	25.3	39.4	< .001
Passage type by question type by grade	0.5	1	0.5	.7	.405

TABLE 6.2. Generic and Passage-Specific Predictors of Reading Comprehension Performance

Dependent variable	Predictor	Grade 2 beta	r	Grade 4 beta	R
Narrative passages					
	Specific vocabulary	.171*	.455**	.289**	.459**
	Generic vocabulary	.342**	.571**	.146	.385**
	Specific fluency	.221	.502**	.222	.378**
	Generic fluency	.091	.479**	−.057	.324**
Expository passages					
	Specific vocabulary	.172*	.441**	.224**	.431**
	Generic vocabulary	.401**	.535**	.393**	.503**
	Specific fluency	.016	.307**	.049	.240**
	Generic fluency	.056	.302**	−.091	.230**

$*p < .05; **p < .01.$

hension. For both narrative and expository texts, both passage-specific vocabulary and generic vocabulary made independent contributions to prediction of reading comprehension.

Results for predicting reading rate using generic and passage-specific measures are presented in Table 6.3. For reading rate, fluency was a better predictor than vocabulary. Whether the generic or passage-specific measure was a better predictor varied across grade level.

In summary, the results suggest the value of both generic and passage-specific assessments. Both generic and passage-specific assessments of vocabulary made independent contributions to predicting performance on the reading comprehension questions. Generic and passage-specific assessments of decoding predicted reading rate differentially depending on grade level.

Understanding the development of reading comprehension requires considering person variables such as decoding fluency and vocabulary, text variables such as narrative versus expository text type, task variables such as inferential versus noninferential question type, and context. The results of the study reported also suggest that, in addition to expected main effects, interactions between variables are commonplace.

Making progress in further understanding a phenomenon as complex as the development of reading comprehension will require com-

TABLE 6.3. Generic and Passage-Specific Predictors of Reading Rate

Dependent variable	Predictor	Grade 2 beta	r	Grade 4 beta	R
Narrative passages					
	Specific vocabulary	.060	.105	−.047	.209**
	Generic vocabulary	−.048	.099	.132	.256**
	Specific fluency	−.228	.233	.457**	.402**
	Generic fluency	.514**	.304**	−.103	.325**
Expository passages					
	Specific vocabulary	−.099	.009	.021	.288**
	Generic vocabulary	.006	.062	.109	.310**
	Specific fluency	−.119	.217**	.273*	.471**
	Generic fluency	.402*	.258**	.163	.458**

$*p < .05; **p < .01.$

plex, multivariate designs that incorporate variables representing person, text, task, and context.

ACKNOWLEDGMENTS

Preparation of this chapter was supported by Grant No. P50 HD052120 from the National Institute of Child Health and Human Development and by Grant No. R305G030104 from the Institute of Education Sciences.

REFERENCES

Aarnoutse, C., Van Leeuwe, J., Voeten, M., & Oud, H. (2001). Development of decoding, reading comprehension, vocabulary and spelling during the elementary school years. *Reading and Writing, 14*(1), 61–89.

Adams, M. J. (1990). *Beginning to read: Thinking and learning abut print.* Cambridge, MA: MIT Press.

Allen, J. (1985). Inferential comprehension: The effects of text source, decoding ability, and mode. *Reading Research Quarterly, 20*(5), 603–615.

Anderson, R. C., & Freebody, P. (1981). Vocabulary knowledge. In J. Guthrie (Ed.), *Comprehension and teaching: Research reviews* (pp. 77–117). Newark, DE: International Reading Association.

Barrouillet, P., & Camos, V. (2001). Developmental increase in working memory span: Resource sharing or temporal decay? *Journal of Memory and Language, 45*(1), 1–20.

Bayliss, D. M., Jarrold, C., Gunn, D. M., & Baddeley, A. D. (2003). The complexities of complex span: Explaining individual differences in working memory in children and adults. *Journal of Experimental Psychology: General, 132*(1), 71–92.

Beck, I. L., & McKeown, M. G. (1991). Conditions of vocabulary acquisition. In R. Barr, M. L. Kamil, P. Mosenthal, & P. D. Pearson (Eds.), *Handbook of reading research* (Vol. 2, pp. 789–814). New York: Longman.

Cain, K., & Oakhill, J. (1998). Comprehension skill and inference-making ability: Issues of causality. In C. Hulme & R. M. Joshi (Eds.), *Reading and spelling* (pp. 329–342). Mahwah, NJ: Erlbaum.

Cain, K., & Oakhill, J. V. (1999). Inference making ability and its relation to comprehension failure in young children. *Reading and Writing, 11*(5–6), 489–503.

Cain, K., Oakhill, J. V., Barnes, M. A., & Bryant, P. E. (2001). Comprehension skill, inference-making ability, and the relation to knowledge. *Memory & Cognition, 29*(6), 850–859.

Cain, K., Oakhill, J. V., & Elbro, C. (2003). The ability to learn new word meanings from context by school-age children with and without language comprehension difficulties. *Journal of Child Language, 30*(3), 681–694.

Crowder, R. G., & Wagner, R. K. (1991). *The psychology of reading.* New York: Oxford University Press.

Gee, J. P. (2000). Discourse and sociocultural studies in reading. In M. L. Kamil, P. B. Mosenthal, P. D. Pearson, & R. Barr (Eds.), *Handbook of reading research, Vol. 3* (pp. 195–208). Mahwah, NJ: Erlbaum.

Graesser, A. C., Millis, K., & Zwaan, R. A. (1997). Discourse comprehension. *Annual Review of Psychology, 48*, 163–189.

Degand, L., & Sanders, T. (2002). The impact of relational markers on expository text comprehension in L1 and L2. *Reading and Writing, 15*(7–8), 739–757.

Donahue, P. L., Voelkl, K. E., Campbell, J. R., & Mazzeo, J. (1999). The NAEP 1998 reading report card for the nation and the states. *Education Statistics Quarterly, 1*(2), 21–27.

Fuchs, L. S., Fuchs, D., Hosp, M. K., & Jenkins, J. R. (2001). Oral reading fluency as an indicator of reading competence: A theoretical, empirical, and historical analysis. *Scientific Studies of Reading, 5*(3), 239–256.

Goldman, S. R., & Rakestraw, J. A. (2000). Structural aspects of constructing meaning from text. In M. L. Kamil, P. B. Mosenthal, P. D. Pearson, & R. Barr (Eds.), *Handbook of reading research, Vol. 3* (pp. 311–336). Mahwah, NJ: Erlbaum.

Goldman, S. R., Saul, E., & Cote, N. (1995). Paragraphing, reader, and task effects on discourse comprehension. *Discourse Processes, 20*(3), 273–305.

Graesser, A. C., Golding, J. M., & Long, D. L. (1991). Narrative representation and comprehension. In R. Barr, M. L. Kamil, P. B. Mosenthal, & P. D. Pearson (Eds.), *Handbook of reading research* (Vol. 2, pp. 171–205). Hillsdale, NJ: Erlbaum.

Graesser, A. C., Singer, M., & Trabasso, T. (1994). Constructing inferences during narrative text comprehension. *Psychological Review, 101*(3), 371–395.

Harp, S. F., & Mayer, R. E. (1998). How seductive details do their damage: A theory of cognitive interest in science learning. *Journal of Educational Psychology, 90*(3), 414–434.

Jenkins, J. R., Fuchs, L. S., van den Broek, P., Espin, C., & Deno, S. L. (2003). Sources of individual differences in reading comprehension and reading fluency. *Journal of Educational Psychology, 95*(4), 719–729.

Jenkins, J. R., & Jewell, M. (1993). Examining the validity of two measures for formative teaching: Reading aloud and maze. *Exceptional Children, 59*(5), 421–432.

Joshi, R. M. (2005). Vocabulary: A critical component of comprehension. *Reading & Writing Quarterly: Overcoming Learning Difficulties, 21*(3), 209–219.

Kamil, M. L., Intrator, S. M., & Kim, H. S. (2000). The effects of other technologies on literacy and literacy learning. In M. L. Kamil, P. B. Mosenthal, P. D. Pearson, & R. Barr (Eds.), *Handbook of reading research* (Vol. 3, pp. 771–790). Mahwah, NJ: Erlbaum.

Kuhn, M. R., & Stahl, S. A. (2003). Fluency: A review of developmental and remedial practices. *Journal of Educational Psychology, 95*(1), 3–21.

LaBerge, D., & Samuels, S. J. (1974). Toward a theory of automatic information processing in reading. *Cognitive Psychology, 6*(2), 293–323.

Lyon, G. R. (1995). Towards a definition of dyslexia. *Annals of Dyslexia, 45,* 3–27.

Mather, N., Hammill, D. D., Allen, E. A., & Roberts, R. (2004). *Test of Silent Word Reading Fluency—Examiner's Manual.* Austin, TX: PRO-ED.

Metsala, J., & Ehri, L. C. (1998). *Word recognition in beginning reading.* Hillsdale, NJ: Erlbaum.

Miller, L. M. S., Stine-Morrow, E. A. L., Kirkorian, H. L., & Conroy, M. L. (2004). Adult age differences in knowledge-driven reading. *Journal of Educational Psychology, 96*(4), 811–821.

Muter, V., Hulme, C., Snowling, M. J., & Stevenson, J. (2004). Phonemes, rimes, vocabulary, and grammatical skills as foundations of early reading development: Evidence from a longitudinal study. *Developmental Psychology, 40*(5), 665–681.

Nagy, W. E. (2007). Metalinguistic awareness and the vocabulary-comprehension connection. In R. K. Wagner, A. E. Muse, & K. R. Tannenbaum (Eds.), *Vocabulary acquisition: Implications for reading comprehension* (pp. 52–77). New York: Guilford Press.

Nagy, W. E., & Herman, P. A. (1987). Breadth and depth of vocabulary knowledge: Implications for acquisition and instruction. In M. G. McKeown & M. E. Curtis (Eds.), *The nature of vocabulary acquisition* (pp. 19–35). Hillsdale, NJ: Erlbaum.

National Institute of Child Health and Human Development. (2005). Pathways to reading: The role of oral language in the transition to reading. *Developmental Psychology, 41*(2), 428–442.

National Reading Panel. (2000). *Report of the national reading panel: Teaching children to read. Report of the subgroups* (NIH Publication No. 00-4754). Washington, DC: U.S. Department of Health and Human Services, National Institutes of Health.

National Reading Panel. (2000). *Report of the National Reading Panel: Teaching children to read. Report of the subgroups* (NIH Publication No. 00-4754). Washington, DC: U.S. Department of Health and Human Services, National Institutes of Health.

Pellegrino, J. W., Chudowsky, N., & Glaser, R. (Eds.). (2001). *Knowing what students know*. Washington, DC: National Academies Press.

Posner, M. I., & Snyder, C. R. R. (1975). Facilitation and inhibition in the processing of signals. In P. M. Rabbitt & S. Dornic (Eds.), *Attention and performance: Vol. 5* (pp. 669–682). San Diego, CA: Academic Press.

Pulido, D. (2004). The relationship between text comprehension and second language incidental vocabulary acquisition: A matter of topic familiarity? *Language Learning, 54*(3), 469–523.

Rayner, K., & Pollatsek, A. (1989). *The psychology of reading*. Englewood Cliffs, NJ: Prentice Hall.

Rosa, M. H. (1994). Relationships between cognitive styles and reading comprehension of expository text of African American males. *Journal of Negro Education, 63*(4), 546–555.

Sassenrath, J. M. (1972). Alpha factor analyses of reading measures at the elementary, secondary, and college levels. *Journal of Reading Behavior, 5*(4), 1972–1973.

Scott, C. M., & Windsor, J. (2000). General language performance measures in spoken and written narrative and expository discourse of school-age children with language learning disabilities. *Journal of Speech, Language, and Hearing Research, 43*(2), 324–339.

Snow, C. (2002). *Reading for understanding: Toward a research and development program in reading comprehension*. Arlington, VA: RAND.

Stahl, S. A., & Fairbanks, M. M. (1986). The effects of vocabulary instruction: A model-based meta-analysis. *Review of Educational Research, 56*(1), 72–110.

Stanovich, K. E. (1980). Toward an interactive–compensatory model of individual differences in the development of reading fluency. *Reading Research Quarterly, 16*(1), 32–71.

Stanovich, K. E. (2000). *Progress in understanding reading: Scientific foundations and new frontiers*. New York: Guilford Press.

Togresen, J. K., Alexander, A. W., Wagner, R. K., Rashotte, C. A., Voeller, K., Conway, T., & Rose, E. (2001). Intensive remedial instruction for children with severe reading disabilities: Immediate and long-term outcomes from two instructional approaches. *Journal of Learning Disabilities, 34*, 33–58.

Torgesen, J. K., Wagner, R. K., & Rashotte, C. A. (1999). *Test of Word Reading Efficiency—Examiner's manual*. Austin, TX: PRO-ED.

Torgesen, J. K., Wagner, R. K., Rashotte, C. A., Rose, E., Lindamood, P., Conway, T., et al. (1999). Preventing reading failure in young children with phonological processing disabilities: Group and individual responses to instruction. *Journal of Educational Psychology, 91*, 1–15.

Wagner, R. K., Priya, K., & Rashotte, C. A. (2006, April). *Formative and summative assessments of reading comprehension: Implications for reading in electronic con-*

texts. Paper presented at the annual meeting of the American Education Research Association, San Francisco.

Yovanoff, P., Duesbery, L., Alonzo, J., & Tindal, G. (2005). Grade-level invariance of a theoretical causal structure predicting reading comprehension with vocabulary and oral reading fluency. *Educational Measurement: Issues and Practice, 24*(3), 4–12.

Zabrucky, K. M., & Moore, D. (1999). Influence of text genre on adults' monitoring of understanding and recall. *Educational Gerontology, 25*(8), 691–710.

PART III

INDIVIDUAL-DIFFERENCES APPROACHES

7

Reading Comprehension Development from 8 to 14 Years

The Contribution of Component Skills and Processes

Kate Cain *and* Jane Oakhill

A long-term goal of research into reading comprehension must be to identify ways in which reading comprehension might be fostered in normal development and improved in those who have difficulties with it. Such a goal requires first that problems with reading comprehension be identified early, that appropriate skills and strategies are identified as candidates for training, and that effective training procedures are put in place. This chapter is primarily concerned with the second of these issues: deciding which skills to train. It is important to select those skills where there is evidence of a causal link to comprehension skill. Many studies have demonstrated that various skills and abilities are correlated with comprehension (for a review, see Cain & Oakhill, 2007), but there is obviously no point in training skills that result from being good at comprehension or those that are only incidentally related to it. Much of this chapter comprises a discussion of the methods by which causality might be investigated and the results we, and others, have obtained using such methods that are related to reading comprehension ability.

WHAT IS SUCCESSFUL
READING COMPREHENSION?

Reading and listening comprehension are complex skills. More accurately, successful reading comprehension requires the coordination and interaction of several skills, many of which are common to listening comprehension. To understand a text of several sentences, the reader must retrieve the meanings of individual words, compute the sense of each sentence, integrate the meanings of successive sentences, and incorporate background knowledge to construct a representation of the state of affairs described by the text. This representation, often called a mental model (Johnson-Laird, 1983) or situation model (Kintsch, 1998), encodes the causal relations between events, the goals of protagonists, and spatial and temporal information that is relevant to the story line (Zwaan & Radvansky, 1998).

Reading comprehension is a dynamic process that happens in real time. Thus, the efficiency with which these skills are executed is important. For example, slow and labored word reading will limit comprehension, because cognitive processing resources will be devoted to decoding the words on the page rather than understanding the meaning of the text (Perfetti, 1985). Reading comprehension is also an interactive process: The meaning of the text constructed so far will influence the meaning assigned to an individual word or sentence. For example, the meaning of the word *bank* in "She walked over to the bank" will differ according to the context (e.g., "Karen needed some cash" or "Karen wanted to feed the ducks"). Similarly, the meaning assigned to "Melissa was skating on thin ice" will differ depending on whether it is preceded by "The pond had begun to thaw" or "Melissa drove home, even though her headlights were broken." For these reasons, it is likely that the influences of specific language and cognitive skills on reading comprehension are not felt in isolation.

SKILLS RELATED TO SUCCESSFUL
READING COMPREHENSION

Children may fail to understand text for many reasons. The most common source of comprehension failure is a difficulty at the word level. For example, younger children and poor readers often experience reading comprehension difficulties because their word reading is slow or inefficient (Perfetti, 1985). However, a subset of children (approximately 10%

of those aged 8–11 years; Yuill & Oakhill, 1991) have below-age reading comprehension performance in the presence of age-appropriate word reading. Their listening comprehension is also impaired, which suggests that word-reading difficulties are not the source of their comprehension failure (Cain, Oakhill, & Bryant, 2000a). For these children, the reading comprehension deficit can be 18 months or greater (Cain & Oakhill, 2007). Although some children with reading comprehension difficulties may have semantic processing difficulties (Nation & Snowling, 1998), others show intact understanding of single written words (Cain et al., 2000a) and spoken words (Cain, Oakhill, & Lemmon, 2004).

In this section, we focus on investigations of comprehension-related skills in children aged 8 to 15 years selected for age-appropriate word-reading and vocabulary skills. Examples of such groups are shown in Table 7.1. Good word-reading and vocabulary skills are crucial for successful comprehension, and these skills are discussed elsewhere in this volume. Our investigations of poor comprehenders with good word-level skills have identified a wide range of skills, in addition to word reading and vocabulary knowledge, that are important for successful

TABLE 7.1. Characteristics of Good and Poor Comprehenders, Ages 9–10 Years

Variable	Poor comprehenders ($n = 14$)	Good comprehenders ($n = 14$)	$t(26)$
Variables commonly used to select and match groups			
Chronological age	9,08 (4.15)	9,08 (3.83)	< 1.0, ns
Gates–MacGinitie sight vocabulary	34.00 (2.04)	34.20 (2.75)	< 1.0, ns
Word reading accuracy in context	10, 07 (6.97)	10, 06 (7.05)	< 1.0, ns
Reading comprehension	7, 11 (5.33)	10, 07 (9.60)	= 10.71***
Number of stories	6.00 (0.00)	6.00 (0.00)	< 1.0, ns
Performance on other word-level tasks			
Graded Nonword Reading Test	18.64 (3.88)	19.07 (2.37)	< 1.0
BPVS	106.31 (6.30)	109.21 (3.45)	= 1.50, ns
CELF-R Word Association subtest	38.36 (7.56)	41.43 (7.15)	= 1.10, ns

Note. Where appropriate, ages are given as years, months (with standard deviations in months). Maximum score for Gates–MacGinitie sight vocabulary is 45. The word-reading accuracy and reading comprehension scores are the age-equivalent scores form the Neale Analysis of Reading Ability; the number of stories refers to the stories completed in this assessment. The scores of the Graded Nonword Reading Test (maximum = 24) and CELF-R Word Association Subtest are raw scores; those for the BPVS are standardized scores. BPVS, British Picture Vocabulary Scale; CELF-R, Clinical Evaluation of Language Fundamentals–Revised. Data from Cain, Oakhill, and Lemmon (2005).

reading comprehension and which should be considered as potential causal factors in successful comprehension development. We discuss these findings in three sections: comprehension of sentences; comprehension of text; memory and general knowledge.

Comprehension of Sentences

Comprehension at the sentence level provides a foundation for comprehension of larger units of prose. Readers need to understand the combined meaning of the words in a clause or sentence, and this often requires knowledge about specific syntactic structures and cohesive devices that cue how to integrate the information in individual sentences. Poor comprehenders' sentence-level comprehension has received little attention compared with the sentence-level skills of other populations, such as children with specific language impairment (Bishop, 1997). In this section, we consider two aspects of sentence-level comprehension: (1) understanding and knowledge of syntactic structures and (2) understanding and knowledge of specific types of cohesive cues, which guide the integration of clauses within a sentence and also between sentences.

Syntactic Knowledge

Many poor readers have difficulties with the comprehension of particular syntactic structures (Crain, 1989; Macaruso, Barshalom, Crain, & Shankweiler, 1989; Smith, Macaruso, Shankweiler, & Crain, 1989). Shankweiler and colleagues propose that sentence comprehension and reading ability are related because both rely on good phonological processing skills (Shankweiler, 1989). The argument is that poor readers find it hard to set up or maintain representations of verbal information in phonological short-term memory because of their phonological processing difficulties. Poor readers' difficulties are particularly pronounced for sentences with complex syntactic structures, such as relative clauses and passives, which have a high memory load. Shankweiler and colleagues have studied children with general reading difficulties: poor word reading and poor comprehension. So what about children who have poor comprehension but age-appropriate word-reading skills?

Early studies of children with specific reading comprehension difficulties indicated intact syntactic knowledge. For example, Yuill and Oakhill (1991) found no differences in performance on the Test for

Reception of Grammar (TROG; Bishop, 1982), a widely used assessment covering a range of syntactic constructions. Other work with poor comprehenders has revealed differences on the same measure (Nation, Clarke, Marshall, & Durand, 2004; but see Cain, Patson, & Andrews, 2005, for evidence of intact knowledge).

These discrepancies between studies are surprising because the TROG (and TROG-2; Bishop, 2003) is a widely used and reliable test instrument. One, not very interesting, reason for this discrepancy is that differences in the group selection criteria lead to the different outcomes. A more interesting possibility, which has important implications for identification and remediation of poor comprehension, is that the population of poor comprehension is heterogeneous: Not all children with poor comprehension have the same profile of skill strengths and weaknesses. Recent work indicates that some poor comprehenders have good syntactic comprehension, while others show weaknesses (Cain & Oakhill, 2006; Nation et al., 2004).

Another possibility is that poor comprehenders' syntactic development fails to thrive, perhaps because of limited reading experience. For example, Nation and colleagues have shown that poor comprehenders are less able than good comprehenders to derive the past tense of irregular verbs, structures that may be learned and practiced through reading (Nation, Snowling, & Clarke, 2005). If reading experience does play a role, deficits in syntactic skills might emerge later, rather than earlier, in children with comprehension difficulties. Indeed, our own work indicates that the relation between reading comprehension and syntactic knowledge may change over time: We found that syntactic knowledge (assessed with the TROG) did not predict concurrent reading comprehension skill in 7- to 8-year-olds (after controlling for IQ, vocabulary, and word-reading ability) but did explain significant variance in comprehension in the same children 1 year later (Oakhill, Cain, & Bryant, 2003).

Cohesive Cues

We now turn to the second aspect of sentence-level comprehension: understanding and knowledge of cohesive cues. Anaphors and interclausal connectives are cohesive devices that can aid the integration of successive clauses and sentences in a text. Both devices go beyond comprehension of individual sentences. For example, pronouns can refer back to protagonists and concepts introduced earlier in a text, for example, "Simon showed Hannah his new squash racquet. *She* thought *it* looked rather flash and wanted *one* too." Connectives can indicate relations between the events in different clauses and episodes, for example, "Charlie was late *because/so* he cycled to work."

Poor comprehenders have difficulties with anaphor production and comprehension. For example, they are more likely than good comprehenders to make errors on questions that can only be answered if the correct antecedent for a pronoun has been established (e.g., "Chris lent his coat to Kate because *she* was cold. Who was cold, Chris or Kate?"; Yuill & Oakhill, 1991; see also Oakhill & Yuill, 1986; Yuill & Oakhill, 1988b). Poor comprehenders are also less able to use the information provided by anaphors as they are reading to help them to integrate two sentences (e.g., "Justine had dinner with Joe in a restaurant. She chatted cheerfully with him"; Megherbi & Ehrlich, 2005).

Recent and ongoing work indicates difficulties with the use of interclausal connectives to link two clauses in a sentence. Poor comprehenders are less likely to supply the correct connective (e.g., *because, before, but*) in a cloze task (Cain, Patson, & Andrews, 2005). They are also less likely to use connectives such as *because* and *so* to indicate a causal relation between two events when producing a narrative (Cain, 2003).

Comprehension of Sentences: Summary

Poor comprehenders experience difficulties with comprehension of sentences. Some of these studies have assessed comprehension of spoken language, indicating that poor comprehenders' difficulties extend beyond written language processing. Poor comprehenders do not have short-term memory deficits, and we have found no evidence that children with specific reading comprehension difficulties have phonological processing deficits (Cain, Oakhill, & Bryant, 2000b) in contrast to the poor readers studied by Shankweiler and colleagues. Poor comprehenders do, however, have deficits on tasks that tap more complex memory skills requiring the simultaneous storage and processing of information (Yuill, Oakhill, & Parkin, 1989). It is not clear that such deficits can account for any difficulties with knowledge about specific syntactic structures or the purpose of interclausal connectives. However, on measures of anaphoric processing, poor comprehenders' difficulties are more pronounced when the anaphor and its antecedent are separated by several lines of text (Ehrlich, Remond, & Tardieu, 1999; Yuill & Oakhill, 1988b). Thus, when the processing demands of a task are high, as is the case in many natural reading situations where even a short story involves several paragraphs and episodes, a failure to use cohesive devices to guide integration may be more apparent.

Comprehension of Text

Successful reading (and listening) comprehension results in a representation of the meaning of a text that is integrated and coherent (Kintsch, 1998). This requires the reader to detect whether or not comprehension is adequate; if not, the reader may need to establish the link between two sentences or to generate inferences to make links between different parts of a text or to understand a character's motivations. In this section, we review the importance of three skills that aid the construction of a coherent and integrated representation of meaning: inference and integration, comprehension monitoring, and knowledge and use of story structure.

Inference and Integration

Authors do not make explicit every detail in a text. As a consequence, readers have to do some work in order to fully comprehend a text: They need to establish the links between successive sentences in order to integrate their meanings into a coherent whole, and they must generate inferences, often using general knowledge to fill in missing details. Inference and integration skills develop and improve over an extended period of time. Although young children between 6 and 8 years are capable of making inferences, differences in the time course and accuracy of inference making are apparent between the ages of 6 and 15 years and also between teenagers and adults (Barnes, Dennis, & Haefele-Kalvaitis, 1996; Casteel, 1993).

Cross-sectional studies comparing good and poor comprehenders matched for chronological age, word reading, and sight vocabulary demonstrate that poor comprehenders have difficulties with the integration of sentences and inference generation. Oakhill (1982) used a listening comprehension task to assess integration skills in good and poor comprehenders aged 7 to 8 years. The children heard sentences such as, "The boy was chasing the girl. The girl ran into the playground." The poor comprehenders were less likely to "falsely" recognize a test sentence, "The boy ran into the playground," presented after a delay than were good comprehenders, indicating that they were less likely to integrate the meanings of the two sentences in their memory-based model of the meaning of the text. In a different study, children read short stories followed by questions that could only be answered correctly if an inference was made. For example, in one story about a boy cycling to school, the sentence "John ran over some broken bottles and had to walk the rest of the way" supports the inference that John had to walk to school because the broken glass had caused a puncture in his bicycle tires. Poor comprehenders were less likely to make these inferences (Oakhill, 1984), even though the knowledge on which they are based is well within their grasp.

The poor comprehenders' difficulties cannot be attributed to poor memory for the text: Their recall of literal information is often good (Oakhill, 1982) and their inference-making difficulties are evident even when the written text is available to consult (Oakhill, 1984). Other work with good and poor comprehenders similarly finds that poor comprehenders' difficulties with inference and integration are not in line with their memory for explicit details in the text (Bowyer-Crane & Snowling, 2005).

Comprehension Monitoring

Inferences and integration are needed to make a text cohere, but readers can only actively generate an inference if they are monitoring their understanding of the text. If the current sentence cannot be integrated with the situation model that readers have constructed, they need to take remedial action, which can involve generating an inference to establish a link. Comprehension monitoring makes an important contribution to reading comprehension, and it develops during the years when reading fluency develops (Baker, 1984; Markman & Gorin, 1981).

Comprehension monitoring is commonly assessed by error detection tasks: Children read short texts containing different types of error. The errors may arise because of an internal inconsistency, where information is presented that contradicts an earlier statement in the text, or from an external inconsistency, where the information in the text conflicts with general knowledge. Another type of error used in such tasks is a nonsense word. Examples of the types of materials used in these tasks are provided in Figure 7.1. To do well on these tasks, readers must actively engage in the evaluation of their understanding; for example, an internal inconsistency will only be noticed if readers strive to integrate each successive sentence with the model of the text constructed so far.

Children with poor reading comprehension across a wide age range have difficulties with comprehension monitoring, as measured by error

Jill—used in our longitudinal study for 7- to 8-year-olds (time 1)
Last night Jill walked home through the woods.
She had just been to the cinema with her friends.
*There was no moonlight, so Jill could hardly see her way.
She walked along the path.
*The moon was so bright that it lit the way.
Jill lived at the other side of the woods.

Moles—used in our longitudinal study for 8- to 9-year-olds (time 1) and in cross-sectional work by Oakhill, Hartt, and Samols (2005)
Moles are small, brown animals and they live underground using networks of tunnels.
*Moles cannot see very well but their hearing and sense of smell are good.
They sleep in underground nests lined with grass, leaves, and twigs.
Moles use their front feet for digging and their short fur allows them to move along their tunnels either forward or backward.
They mainly eat worms but they also eat insects and snails.
*Moles can easily find food for their young because their eyesight is so good.

FIGURE 7.1. Examples of comprehension monitoring materials. Asterisks denote inconsistent lines.

detection tasks. For example, 10-year-old poor comprehenders are less likely to spot two contradictory sentences in a text (Oakhill, Hartt, & Samols, 2005) and 10- to 15-year-old French speakers are less likely to spot inconsistent anaphors (Ehrlich, 1996; Ehrlich et al., 1999). Ehrlich's work demonstrates the generality of poor comprehenders' difficulties since she has focused on expository, rather than narrative, text.

Knowledge and Use of Story Structure

Narrative is the most common genre in children's early literacy experience and is a form used in textual and picture books, children's television programs, films, and so on. Narratives comprise a series of interrelated episodes that include goal-directed actions and causally related events. Narrative comprehension in preschoolers and young children is considered a foundation for later reading comprehension skills because, to understand narratives, children have to monitor their understanding, generate inferences, identify the key points, and understand causal relations (Paris & Paris, 2003). These are the skills, among others, needed to construct an integrated and coherent situation model.

Narrative comprehension and understanding of story structure are often assessed with production tasks (Paris & Paris, 2003). On such measures, 7- to 8-year-olds with poor reading comprehension are less likely to produce causally related sequences of events than same-age peers, even when the story-telling task is supported by a series of pictures or a goal-directed title, such as "How the Pirates Lost Their Treasure" (Cain, 2003; Cain & Oakhill, 1996). Similar deficits have been found for written story production (Cragg & Nation, 2006). Poor comprehenders' difficulties extend beyond production tasks: They are poor at discriminating among the main point, the setting, and the main event of stories (Yuill & Oakhill, 1991), and their ability to correctly sequence short stories presented as individual sentences in an anagram task is poor (Cain & Oakhill, 2006). In contrast, their knowledge about the conventions used to begin and end stories is good (Cain & Oakhill, 1996).

Comprehension of Text: Summary

Compared with same-age peers, matched for word reading and sight vocabulary, poor comprehenders demonstrate deficits on tasks designed to measure inference and integration, comprehension monitoring, and knowledge and use of story structure. They make fewer constructive inferences that involve integrating information from different sentences in a text, and they are also less likely to generate simple inferences that involve the integration of information from the text with general knowledge. Their inference and integration skills may, in part, be limited by their poor comprehension monitoring: They are less likely to spot inconsistencies in a text and, therefore, less likely to detect when an inference is needed to make the text cohere. Finally, their ability to use knowledge about the causal structure of stories is impaired. All of these skills are important when constructing a representation of the meaning of the text that is internally consistent, integrated, and coherent in relation to the reader's world knowledge.

Memory and General Knowledge Memory

Memory

Memory is important for the skills discussed so far in the sections on sentence and text comprehension and for reading (and listening) comprehension in general. Skills such as the correct interpretation of an anaphor, the integration of sentences within a text, and the detection of an inconsistency between two sentences require the reader to store and coordinate the relevant information in memory. As stated earlier, reading comprehension is a dynamic and interactive process that occurs in real time. As readers process each new part of a text, they must be able to access several sources of information. These include the memory-based representation of its meaning constructed so far, readers' semantic knowledge about words, and general knowledge and relevant topic-specific knowledge. Readers also need to access the situation model stored in long-term memory in order to perform many assessments of comprehension such as question answering, recall, and summarization.

It is perhaps for these reasons that reading and listening comprehension are most strongly associated with performance on memory tasks that require the simultaneous processing and storage of information and are less strongly associated with simple measures of storage. Working memory capacity, measured by tasks such as sentence span, is associated with concurrent measures of children's and adults' reading and listening comprehension (Cain, Oakhill, & Bryant, 2004; Daneman & Merikle, 1996; Seigneuric, Ehrlich, Oakhill, & Yuill, 2000). In poor comprehenders, weaknesses in working memory are consistently found (Cain, 2006; De Beni, Palladino, Pazzaglia, & Cornoldi, 1998; Yuill et al., 1989), whereas deficits in short-term memory storage of words or digits are less common (Cain, 2006; Oakhill, Yuill, & Parkin, 1986; but see Nation, Adams, Bowyer-Crane, & Snowling, 1999). Working memory skills support essential comprehension-fostering skills such as inference and integration, comprehension monitoring, and structuring a coherent narrative, but they do not fully explain performance on such tasks (Cain, Oakhill, & Bryant, 2004; Oakhill et al., 2003).

General Knowledge

Different types of knowledge are essential for successful reading comprehension (Kintsch, 1998). Knowing the meanings of individual words enables sentence and text comprehension and is discussed in detail elsewhere in this volume. A reader must possess the requisite knowledge to generate particular inferences; inferences also rely on specific topic knowledge and general background knowledge. For these reasons, it seems likely that some of the comprehension failures associated with young readers and poor comprehenders may result from lack of relevant knowledge.

Barnes and colleagues (Barnes, Dennis, & Haefele-Kalvaites, 1996) have developed a paradigm in which the relevant knowledge base is first taught to children to make all things equal. They have shown that even when knowledge is held constant, younger children make fewer inferences than older children. Using the same paradigm with good and poor comprehenders, we have shown that poor comprehenders fail to generate inferences that are necessary to make sense of a text, even when they possess the requisite knowledge (Cain, Oakhill, Barnes, & Bryant, 2001). Similarly, we have found that poor comprehenders know that bicycles are pedaled, even though they may not infer that a bicycle was the most likely mode of transport when reading the sentence "He pedaled to school as fast as he could go" (Cain & Oakhill, 1999).

Memory and General Knowledge: Summary

Memory resources and key knowledge are essential for successful reading comprehension and may limit younger readers' and poor comprehenders' performance to a limited extent. However, carefully controlled studies have shown that neither measure can fully explain individual differences in reading comprehension performance.

METHODS TO STUDY CAUSALITY

Reading comprehension is a complex skill that requires the coordination and interaction of different language and cognitive skills and sources of knowledge. These different skills may be related to reading comprehension in one of four ways: A skill may be a prerequisite of reading comprehension, a facilitator, a consequence, or simply an incidental correlate (Ehri, 1979). Thus far, we have reviewed the evidence from correlational studies. Such studies cannot identify causal relations, even when there is a good theoretical reason to support a particular direction of causality. For example, inference generation is crucial to comprehension and is impaired in poor comprehenders. However, although good inferential skills seem a very plausible prerequisite or facilitator of comprehension, they may instead be the consequence of good comprehension skill: Perhaps the experience of reading and understanding text that comes from good word reading, vocabulary, and syntactic knowledge supports and develops inference making.

Three (complementary) ways have been used to explore the causes of poor reading comprehension: comparison of poor comprehenders with a younger comprehension–age match group, longitudinal studies, and training studies. Here we briefly describe the advantages and disadvantages of each design before reviewing the findings from research studies that have used these approaches.

The Comprehension–Age Match Design

The comprehension–age match design (CAM) is an adaptation of the reading–age match design, used widely in the study of word-reading difficulties (Bryant & Goswami, 1986). This design includes three groups of readers: good and poor comprehenders matched for chronological age, word reading, and sight vocabulary, as outlined in Table 7.1, and a group of children who are at the *same absolute level* of reading comprehension skill as the older poor comprehenders (Cain et al., 2000a; Stothard & Hulme, 1992). For the poor comprehenders in Table 7.1, an appropriate match would be children aged approximately 7 years 11 months, whose word reading and reading comprehension were age appropriate. As for the reading–age match design, the poor comprehenders (or readers) and the younger comprehension– (or reading–) age match group will have reached the same level of performance on the comprehension (or reading) test through slightly different routes. For example, studies using a reading–age match design find that groups of older and younger readers matched on single-word reading differ on phonological processing tasks (e.g., Bradley & Bryant, 1978).

The CAM design cannot be used to establish causality: It can rule out a causal link in one direction (e.g., from comprehension ability to the skill in question). To continue with our example of inferential processing, if we find that the younger CAM group generates more inferences from text than older poor comprehenders, we can rule out the possibility that superior inference skill arises from superior comprehension, because the CAM group and the poor comprehenders are matched on this measure. This is a strong test, because the CAM group is, necessarily, composed of younger children who have poorer word-reading skills than the poor comprehender group.

Longitudinal Studies

In a longitudinal study to identify causal influences on comprehension development, measures of reading comprehension and possible precursors or facilitators of comprehension are measured at different time points. The aim is to determine specific relations between one (or more) candidate causal skill and reading comprehension. With such studies, we can investigate which early component skills (or variables) are the best predictors of later reading comprehension level. We can also establish whether a particular skill (or variable) assessed at the outset of the study is a better predictor of later comprehension skill than comprehension at outset.

One limitation of the longitudinal design is that an early skill might be related to the later skill of interest through a mediating variable. For example, early phonological awareness may be found to be a strong predictor of later reading comprehension through the mediating influence of word reading; both reading comprehension and phonological awareness are strongly related to word reading. It is, therefore, important to take measures of likely mediating variables. However, resources are not unlimited and, when studying a complex behavior such as reading comprehension, the researcher must carefully choose which "control" variables to include. Another limitation is that it may not be possible to measure particular skills at the outset. For example, when studying which early language skills predict growth in reading comprehension, we cannot take a measure of reading comprehension at age 3 because children are not readers at this age. It is possible to take a measure of the underlying construct (e.g., listening comprehension) and to use this as a control of initial comprehension level (see Kendeou, Bohn-Gettler, White, & van den Broek, 2008, for an illustration of the efficacy of this approach).

Here, we provide a brief overview of the design of our own longitudinal study, which we also refer to in the appropriate sections that follow. This study provides data on the reading development of the same group of children over a 4-year period, from ages 7 to 8 (UK Year 3), 8 to 9 (Year 4), and 10 to 11 (Year 6). At each of these ages, we took measures of reading comprehension and word-reading accuracy, using the Neale Analysis of Reading Ability: Revised (Neale, 1997). We also took measures of general verbal ability (times 1 and 3 only), memory, and specific reading-related skills such as phonemic awareness (phoneme deletion), vocabulary (British Picture Vocabulary Scale; Dunn, Dunn, Whetton, & Pintillie, 1992), syntax (TROG, Bishop, 1982), and measures of three comprehension-related skills: inference making, comprehension monitoring (assessed by the ability to detect inconsistencies in text), and story structure understanding (assessed by the ability to reconstruct a story from a set of jumbled sentences). Thus, we included measures of IQ, memory, word- and sentence-level comprehension skills, and text/discourse-level comprehension skills. We believe that this study is unique in that it includes measures of these important subskills of comprehension rather than simply a global measure of narrative comprehension (or production). This study enables us to explore the relation between early skills and abilities and later reading ability (both word reading and comprehension). In this study, we were interested in particular in whether different subskills of comprehension independently account for variance in later comprehension skill.

We were able to retest a subset ($n = 56$) of these children again when they were aged 13 to 14. The Neale Analysis is not appropriate for this age range, so we used a different test: The Edinburgh Test (Educational Assessment Unit, University of Edinburgh, 1999), which is suitable for children up to age 16+. We used the sections of the test that measured skimming, vocabulary, and inferential comprehension. We were only able to give this age group a limited range of other assessments, but we do not detail those here because the data of primary interest are the relations between these children's earlier abilities and their subsequent comprehension at 13 to 14 years of age.

Training Studies

Training (or intervention) studies can test whether an impairment in a particular skill is a likely cause of poor comprehension. This design is regarded by some as the gold standard for establishing causality. A causal candidate of good comprehension is first identified on both theoretical and empirical grounds (e.g., inference making). If poor comprehenders trained to generate inferences improve not only on a subsequent test of inference making but also on a more general measure of reading comprehension skill, there is good reason to conclude that good inference making leads to good comprehension. The comparison group depends on the particular research question. For example, it could comprise poor comprehenders who received instruction in a different skill, if the effectiveness of different types of training is of interest.

Unfortunately, even training studies have their limitations: The benefits attributed to the training may actually have arisen because the training influenced a different skill that is also important for comprehension. For example, inference training might involve teaching children to identify clues in a text and to integrate this information with general knowledge. Such training might improve inference and integration skills, but it could benefit reading comprehension in general, because the training may have improved children's ability to identify the clues in the text, activate general knowledge, or monitor their comprehension and detect when an inference is needed. Thus, it is hard to identify the source of the benefit from a single training study, and training studies clearly need to be tightly controlled to enable sound theoretical conclusions.

Summary of Methods

Clearly, there is no single best design for identifying which skill deficits are causally implicated in comprehension difficulties. Research that includes the same variables in different designs and controls for the influence of different mediating variables is required to provide converging evidence for causal relations.

CAUSES OF COMPREHENSION FAILURE

In this section, we draw both on our own research and that of others that has investigated causal relations between inference making, comprehension monitoring, understanding text structure, and reading comprehension. We evaluate the evidence for causal relations from studies that have used the three designs that can address causality: the comprehension–age match comparison, training studies, and longitudinal studies.

Inference and Integration

We have investigated the possibility of a causal relation between inference-making skills and reading comprehension using all of the three designs outlined previously. In a CAM design, we compared good and poor comprehenders' ability to make two different types of inference, and to answer literal questions, with that of a younger comprehension–age match group (Cain & Oakhill, 1999). The two types of inferences tested were *text-connecting inferences*, which are required to integrate information from different parts of a text to establish coherence, and *gap-filling inferences*, which are needed to fill in missing details and to provide an integrated representation of the text as a whole. In the case of this latter type of inference, information from outside the text (general knowledge) needs to be incorporated with information provided by the text to "fill the gaps." An example of this type of story and questions to tap these inferences is provided in Figure 7.2.

In this study, as in all studies using the CAM design reported in this chapter, the good and poor comprehenders were 7 to 8 years old and the CAM group comprised 6 to 7 year olds who had normal word reading and comprehension ability for their age. The children read a set of short stories (individually, with the experimenter), each of which was followed by four inference questions (two of each of the types outlined previously) and two literal questions. The results showed that there

Jenny was late getting home from school on Friday and she was soaking wet when she walked through the door. She was angry because the bus had broken down.

Mom was just in the middle of a job when Jenny walked in. "Take off those wet clothes," Mom said. "I was just sorting out the blue items to do first. I can put your jumper in with them now. It will be ready to wear again by Monday." Jenny went upstairs to dry and change out of her wet clothes. But she left a puddle of water in the kitchen by the fridge where she had been standing. Mom looked for the cleaning equipment. She found the bucket in the cupboard under the stairs.

When Jenny came downstairs, Mom wasn't in the kitchen any longer. Perhaps she was sitting in the living room relaxing. Jenny knew that Mom was still working hard. There was a strange sound coming from the living room: click, click, click, over and over again. Jenny's Mom was making a Christmas present for her grandfather. The present would keep him warm in the winter months.

Questions to tap memory for literal information:

1. Who was the present for? Answer: Grandfather.
2. Where was the puddle of water? Answer: In the kitchen/by the fridge/where she had been standing.

Questions to tap the ability to generate inferences to integrate information between two sentences (text-connecting inferences):

1. Why was Jenny late home from school? Answer: The bus had broken down.
2. Where did her Mom look for the cleaning equipment? Answer: In the cupboard under the stairs.

Questions to tap the ability to generate inferences to fill in missing details (gap-filling inferences):

1. What job was Mom doing when Jenny got home? Answer: clothes washing.
2. What was Jenny's Mom making? Answer: a scarf/jumper/cardigan etc. (something knitted).

FIGURE 7.2. Examples of a story constructed to assess inference-making skill (adapted from Cain, Oakhill, & Bryant, 2004; Oakhill et al., 2003).

were no differences between any of the groups in ability to answer the literal questions. The skilled and less skilled groups, however, differed in their ability to answer both types of inference question, and the poor comprehenders performed worse than the CAM group in the case of the text-connecting inferences. Because these two groups were matched for comprehension ability, any difference in inference making cannot be attributed to reading comprehension skill. Thus, this pattern of results suggests, rather, that inference skills might be causally implicated in the development of reading comprehension.

This conclusion about likely direction of causality is supported by two training studies. In the first, Yuill and Joscelyne (1988) trained children (aged 7–8) to make inferences from "clue words" in texts that were written to be deliberately obscure. In one story, for instance, a boy is crying because "all his work had been broken by the wave" and his mother had "accidentally stepped on the only tower that was left," hints that the boy was upset because his sandcastle had been destroyed. Following the training, the children answered questions about further stories of a similar sort. The training benefit was significantly greater for the poor comprehenders than for the good comprehenders. In the second training study, Yuill and Oakhill (1988a) trained children of the same age to make lexical inferences of the same sort and also to generate questions to test their understanding. Thus, this training combined inference making and comprehension-monitoring skills. The poor comprehenders who had received such training (compared with a control group who received training in rapid decoding) made substantial gains on a subsequent standardized test of reading comprehension, whereas good comprehenders showed no such gains, presumably because they already possessed and used the skills being trained.

Our longitudinal study also enabled us to explore the relation between early inference skills and later comprehension ability. At the second and third time points, when the children were aged 8 to 9 and 10 to 11 years, respectively, we tested them on stories and questions that were very similar to those in the CAM study described previously. At the first time point, when the children were aged 7 to 8, we used a different task that assessed the children's ability to integrate separate sentences within a short text (see Oakhill, 1982). At each time point, we found that inference-making skill was strongly related to reading comprehension, even when concurrent word reading, vocabulary, and IQ had been controlled for. However, more important for the causal issue is the finding that inference-making skill at Time 2 was a significant predictor of reading comprehension skill 2 years later, over and above the contributions of word reading, vocabulary, and IQ and even when the autoregressive effect had been taken into account (see Oakhill & Cain, 2007, for a fuller account of these data). This pattern of results strongly implies that early inference skills are causally implicated in the development of reading comprehension.

A follow-up, when the children were aged 13 to 14, showed that inference making at the start of the study when children were aged 7 to 8 years was strongly related to overall comprehension score 6 years later. Further, we found that inference skill when the children were aged 10 to 11 years predicted significant independent variance in reading comprehension (a composite of the skimming and inference mea-

TABLE 7.2. Summary of Multiple Regression Analyses to Predict Reading at 13–14 Years from Variables Measured at 10–11 Years

Step	Variable	ΔR^2	p
Prediction of reading comprehension			
1	Verbal IQ	.470	< .001
2	Reading comprehension	.118	< .010
3	Working memory digit task	.098	< .001
4	Knowledge about story titles	.048	< .010
5	Comprehension monitoring	.024	< .050
6	Inference making	.024	< .050
Prediction of performance on pseudohomophone task			
1	Verbal IQ	.153	< .010
2	Word-reading accuracy	.094	< .050

Note. Steps 1 and 2 were fixed-order forced entry; the variables reported in steps 3–6 were the significant predictors, and a forward stepwise entry procedure was used. Total R^2 for reading comprehension = .89; total R^2 for pseudohomophone task = .25

sures) at 13 to 14 years even when verbal IQ and the autoregressor were controlled. These analyses are summarized in Table 7.2.

Comprehension Monitoring

There is very little work on the causal relations between comprehension monitoring and reading comprehension, and we know of no studies that have used the CAM design in this area. As mentioned previously, the study by Yuill and Oakhill (1988a) contained an element of comprehension monitoring, in that children had to consider their understanding of the text in order to generate sensible questions. However, attempts to teach comprehension monitoring skills alone, rather than in combination with inference training, have been less successful (Yuill & Oakhill, 1991). This lack of effect may be because the training was not sufficiently long, but it is more likely because comprehension monitoring is inextricably linked to comprehension and will not improve unless comprehension itself is improved by other means.

The National Reading Panel Reports of the Subgroups (National Institute of Child Health and Human Development, 2000) included a meta-analysis of studies that trained comprehension monitoring. Their conclusion was that, although such training can improve specific learning of the strategy trained, the evidence for it having an effect on its own is not compelling, and it is probably best used as one of a number of training strategies. In addition, only a few studies attempted to test transfer to standardized tests, and those that did so did not show reliable results.

Children's ability to monitor their comprehension was assessed in our longitudinal study using an inconsistency detection task. The children were presented with short texts, some of which contained a pair of contradictory sentences, and were required to identify the parts that did not make sense. Examples of the texts used for this type of assessment are given in Figure 7.1. The texts were similar in form at each time point but were made progressively longer as the children got older to ensure that they were sufficiently difficult.

At each of the first three time points in the study, performance on this monitoring task was related to concurrent comprehension skill, even after word-reading ability, vocabulary, and verbal IQ had been taken into account. We also found that early comprehension monitoring skill predicted later reading comprehension ability over and above the contribution of word reading, vocabulary, and verbal IQ and the autoregressive effect of earlier reading comprehension. Thus, the longitudinal data provide evidence that comprehension monitoring is causally implicated in the development of reading comprehension. In the later follow-up (at age 13–14), the measure of comprehension monitoring at age 7 to 8 was strongly correlated with later comprehension skill, and performance on the comprehension monitoring task at 10 to 11 years predicted significant independent variance in comprehension 3 years later even when verbal IQ and the autoregressor were controlled (see Table 7.2 for a summary).

Knowledge and Use of Text Structure/Narrative Skills

In our own work, we have focused on children's understanding of story structure in particular, because young children have more experience with this genre than expository texts. Two studies have explored the relation between reading comprehension and children's understanding of story structure. In both studies, we required children to orally produce stories (which were audio recorded and transcribed) as an indication of their ability. In the first study, the children's ability to produce well-constructed stories was compared in two different conditions: The children were given either a topic prompt such as "The Holiday" or a series of pictures and were asked to recount the story told by the pictures (Cain & Oakhill, 1996). The interest here is in the quality of the story structures produced by the three groups of children. The children's productions were scored based on a three-way classification that captured the level of interconnectedness and causal linkage in the productions. The categories used were nonstories, intermediate stories, and well-formed stories, and the children's productions were scored based on their classification. These scores were used as the dependent variable in the analyses of productions.

Overall, the poor comprehenders produced less well-structured stories than the good comprehenders, and in the topic prompt condition performed worse than the CAM group. This pattern of results did not arise simply because the poor comprehenders tended to produce rather short and incomplete stories. Indeed, in the topic prompt condition (the one that best discriminated between groups), the good comprehenders produced the shortest stories and the poor comprehenders the longest (with the CAM groups' stories intermediate in length). In a second study, which was designed to explore the support offered by the different types of prompts in more detail, we replicated the finding that the CAM group produced better structured stories than the poor comprehenders when provided with only a topic prompt (Cain, 2003).

The National Reading Panel Reports of the Subgroups (National Institute of Child Health and Human Development, 2000) also looked at story structure training as a specific instance of strategy training. About half of the 17 studies that met their criteria focused on poor readers, and it was the poor readers who benefited from this type of instruction. Instruction on the content and organization of stories was shown to improve the comprehension of stories as measured by the ability of readers to answer questions and recall what was read. Only two studies, however, demonstrated successful transfer to a standardized measure of reading comprehension.

The relation between narrative skills and later story comprehension has also been studied longitudinally; however, narrative skills are usually included as part of a language composite in such studies. For instance, Catts, Fey, Zhang, and Tomblin (1999) explored the contributions made by both phonological and oral language skills to reading and reading disability in a longitudinal study from kindergarten to second grade and used multiple regression analyses to assess the relative contributions of phonological and oral language abilities in predicting reading achievement. The oral language composite used by Catts et al. included measures of vocabulary and syntax, together with a narrative story task (which required the children to comprehend, organize, and retell a story read aloud to them) and was found to be a strong predictor of later reading comprehension. Phonological awareness and rapid naming also accounted for independent variance in reading comprehension in second grade, but over and above these, a composite of the oral language tasks (both receptive and expressive) accounted for a further 13.8% of variance. In addition, they found that the oral language composite (a mixture of vocabulary, grammar, and discourse skills) still accounted for significant unique variance in second-grade reading comprehension even after phonological skills and Full-Scale IQ had been taken into account. Unfortunately, however, it is impossible to determine from their analyses how much the different components of the composite contributed to the prediction.

Other studies have also explored the relation between oral language skills and later reading. Tabors, Snow, and Dickinson (2001), for instance, found consistent and strong correlations among oral narrative production, production of formal definitions, receptive vocabulary measured at age 5, and fourth- and seventh-grade reading comprehension. However, as with the study by Catts et al., it is not possible to disentangle the effect of the production task from that of the vocabulary tasks.

Van den Broek and colleagues (see, e.g., Kendeou et al., 2005; Kendeou, van den Broek, White, & Lynch, 2007; van den Broek et al., 2005) have conducted extensive investigations of narrative skills and comprehension development. They have directly tested the idea that comprehension skills generalize across different media and related assessments of comprehension in different media to language skills, exploring their contribution to later reading comprehension. In their longitudinal study, two cohorts of children (aged 4 and 6 at the outset) were tested on their recall and factual and inferential comprehension of both aurally presented and televised stories. These assessments were repeated every 2 years, and when the children reached 8 and 10 years, their recall and comprehension of written stories were also assessed.

Within each age group, the comprehension of aural and televised stories was highly correlated, and in the older children all three types of comprehension were interrelated. In all age groups, comprehension skills were not related to basic language skills such as phonological awareness, letter and word awareness, and word recognition, but they were related to vocabulary skills. Thus, the narrative skills and the skills related to word recognition develop relatively independently from an early age. The authors also explored the extent to which early narrative skills predict later comprehension. They found that narrative comprehension in preschool (age 4) accounted for significant variance in narrative comprehension of both audio and television stories at age 6. Similarly, narrative comprehension at 6 was predictive of comprehension of audio and televised stories at age 8 and also reading comprehension (comprehension and recall of a narrative). Furthermore, early comprehension predicted later comprehension over and above basic language skills and vocabulary. However, it should be noted that expressive language skills were not controlled for, and both early comprehension skills and later reading comprehension were measured in part by children's spoken (i.e., expressive) summaries.

These results demonstrate that narrative language skills develop even before reading begins and that there are commonalities in comprehension processes and abilities across different media. This conclusion is inconsistent with the widely held view that reading comprehension develops once decoding is in place, suggesting, rather, that reading comprehension has its roots in early language comprehension skills. Indeed, the authors showed that comprehension (across different media) and word identification at age 6 made independent contributions to reading comprehension at age 8.

In our own longitudinal study, it was not possible to include a story production task (as in the CAM study) because of the time it would have taken to record, transcribe, and score the individual productions. We, therefore, adapted a task used originally by Stein and Glenn (1982) to assess children's ability to structure stories (a story anagram task). In our version of the task, the children were presented with three short stories, which had been cut up into their constituent sentences. The sentences were presented on individual strips of paper, the order of which had been randomized, and the child's task was to rearrange the sentences into the correct story order. The length of the stories was increased as the children got older, to increase the difficulty of the task. To assess how well each child performed on each story, we calculated concordance ratings, which reflect the degree to which the child's ordering of the sentences matches the correct ordering (where a score of 1 would indicate a perfect correlation between the correct order and the child's order). We also obtained measures of children's understanding of story structure conventions at each time point, such as the sorts of information conveyed by story titles and what might be expected at the beginnings and ends of stories. We refer to this measure as the titles task for brevity.

The children's performance on the story anagram task correlated significantly with reading comprehension at each time point but only explained unique variance in reading comprehension (over and above the control variable of word reading, vocabulary, and IQ) at the third time point (when the children were 10–11 years old). The measures of knowledge about the information provided by titles, beginnings, and endings were more strongly related to concurrent measures of reading comprehension skill. Longitudinally, knowledge about the information in story titles at 7 to 8 years predicted reading comprehension skill 1 year later over and above the control variables and the autoregressor. Similarly, performance on the story anagram task when children were aged 7 to 8 years predicted reading comprehension 1 and also 3 years later over and above the control variables. Thus, these measures of story structure understanding seem to be tapping into a skill that is causally implicated in the development of effective reading comprehension.

When we assessed reading skills at 13 to 14 years, earlier measures of story structure knowledge predicted later comprehension. Scores on both the story anagram task and the knowledge about title task measured when children were 7 to 8 years were strongly correlated with comprehension ability. In regression analyses, the knowledge of titles task emerged as an independent predictor and accounted for significant variance in later comprehension skill, after controlling for verbal IQ and the autoregressor. In addition, performance on the extended version of the titles task taken at 10 to 11 years of age predicted significant independent variance in later comprehension after these controls (see Table 7.2 for a summary).

AN INTEGRATED MODEL
OF COMPREHENSION DEVELOPMENT

Thus far, we have presented the findings from our longitudinal study that relate to the three specific subskills outlined earlier: inference and integration, comprehension monitoring, and knowledge of text structure. The results of multiple regression were applied to a causal path diagram to show the pattern and strength of relations among the various skills across time. A preliminary account of the results of these analyses can be found in Oakhill and Cain (2007) and Perfetti, Landi, and Oakhill (2005). The final path diagram (with only significant paths included) is shown in Figure 7.3.

The results can be summarized briefly as follows. Initial reading comprehension skill was a strong predictor of later comprehension, and verbal ability (vocabulary and verbal IQ) also made significant unique contributions to the prediction of comprehension ability across

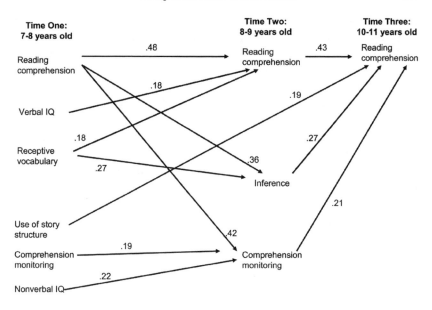

FIGURE 7.3. Path diagram to show the significant relations between skills and knowledge at time 1 to time 3. Standardized beta weights are shown.

time. Nevertheless, three distinct predictors of reading comprehension emerged, either through direct or indirect links: answering inferential questions, monitoring comprehension, and understanding story structure. These factors predicted comprehension at a later time even after the autoregressive effect of comprehension (the prediction of comprehension at later times from comprehension at earlier times) was controlled. In competition with the other variables, the assessment of working memory did not emerge as an independent predictor of comprehension across time.

In the follow-up 6 years later, early assessments of all three skills were related to later comprehension. It was not possible to extend the path analyses to include the later time point because the measures were not the same in the older children. However, because the path analyses provide us with a picture of which variables account for comprehension skill up to age 11, we included the measures from the third time point (age 10–11) as predictors of comprehension (and decoding) skill at age 13–14. A multiple regression analysis, with the combined skimming and inferential comprehension measures on the Edinburgh Test as the dependent variable, showed that, after controlling for verbal IQ and comprehension at 10 to 11 years, the titles measure of story structure understanding, comprehension monitoring, inference skills, and digit working memory each accounted for significant independent variance in the outcome measure. This model accounted for 89% of the variance in time 4 comprehension skill (see Table 7.2).

With word-reading accuracy as the dependent variable, the pattern was quite different. The significant predictors were previous measures of reading accuracy and a phoneme deletion measure taken at the outset when children were 7 to 8 years. The path analyses are presented in Figure 7.4. Initial phoneme deletion was also a strong and significant predictor of performance on a decoding task (pseudohomophone recognition) at the final test point (age 13–14), and word-reading accuracy at 10 to 11 years was a significant predictor of performance on the pseudohomophone task when children were aged 13 to 14, over and above the effect of verbal IQ.

From these analyses, a picture of skill development emerges in which certain components of comprehension are predictive of general comprehension skill. Early abilities in inference skill, comprehension monitoring, and story structure understanding predict performance on a later global assessment of comprehension skill independently of the contribution of earlier comprehension skill. There is also a clear dissociation between the skills that predict reading comprehension and those that predict word-reading accuracy.

The inclusion of the relevant autoregressor (i.e., the measure of the skill being predicted, in this case comprehension, at an earlier time point) in the prior analyses is particularly important for causal hypotheses. De Jong and van der Leij (2002) have argued that any additional

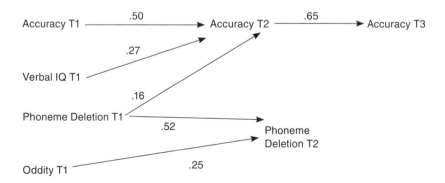

FIGURE 7.4. Path diagram to show the relations between skills from time 1 (7–8 years) to time 3 (10–11 years) word-reading accuracy. Standardized beta weights are shown.

effects of variables after the inclusion of the autoregressive effect can be taken as support for a causal relation between those variables and the outcome measure. To make this more concrete, in the analyses described previously, we found that inference skill accounted for variance in reading comprehension at a later time point over and above the autoregressive effect of reading comprehension. This result rules out the possibility that the relation between earlier inference skills and reading comprehension at 10 to 11 years was due simply to their association with earlier reading comprehension.

This longitudinal study confirms the importance of a set of higher level comprehension components, which, on theoretical grounds, one would expect to be important in the growth of reading comprehension skill. In addition, it is clear that early comprehension skill and early comprehension-related skills have far-reaching implications and are strong predictors of comprehension skill even after 6 years.

IMPLICATIONS FOR TRAINING AND REMEDIATION

The skills that we have identified as likely causal factors in comprehension development, and that might, therefore, be targeted for training, are inference making, comprehension monitoring, and understanding story structure. Indeed, our own and others' training studies have shown that training in these component skills can have substantial effects on improving comprehension.

However, although these factors predicted statistically independent portions of variance in later comprehension skill, there are obvious reasons why they might be interlinked. For instance, if comprehenders have a good understanding of how a story is typically structured and good monitoring skills, they will use those skills to assess how the story is developing, whether there are deviations from the expected structure, and whether inferences are required to make links between ideas in the text. There is also evidence for the separability of these skills. Kendeou et al. (2008) assessed inference and narrative comprehension using aural and televised stories in two cohorts of children aged 4 and 6 years. These skills were assessed once more 2 years later. Narrative comprehension was assessed through recall of story events, recall of causally related events, and correct answers to open-ended questions. Inference skills were assessed by calculating the total number of inferences included in free recall and answers to questions. At each time point, inference generation predicted unique variance in narrative comprehension over and above basic language skills such as phonological awareness, word identification, and vocabulary.

The relation among inference making, comprehension monitoring, story production, and comprehension could be partly mediated by the readers' standard for coherence (van den Broek, Risden, & Husebye-Hartman, 1995). For comprehension to develop satisfactorily, readers must adopt a high standard of coherence. In other words, they must care whether or not the text makes sense and must strive to derive a clear, complete, and coherent *situation model* of the text. When coherence is a goal, inferences will be made to keep the text coherent, inconsistencies between text elements or between text elements and readers' knowledge will be resolved rather than ignored or unnoticed, and the point and structure of the text as a whole will be appreciated by the readers and will, in turn, guide and reinforce their comprehension. Given these considerations, the question of how training might best be implemented becomes more complex. Should the skills and abilities that we have identified be trained separately, or should these be part of a broader package of skills, which take as their starting point that the goal of comprehension is a structured and coherent text? Our view is that teaching children to improve their standard for coherence is about as intangible as teaching them to improve their comprehension and that the best way forward is probably to teach comprehension skills separately, all the while encouraging the children to work toward an integrated and complete model of the text as a whole.

Our longitudinal study, in particular, provides a clear indication that separable components of comprehension skill can be identified and that these make independent contributions to the development of comprehension skill over and above the effect of initial comprehension ability. Our conclusions from these studies about which component skills might usefully be trained are very much in line with the conclusions of the National Reading Panel study (National Institute of Child Health and Human Development, 2000). The National Reading Panel identified more than 200 studies of comprehension instruction that met their methodological criteria. Of the 16 different categories of text comprehension instruction they identified, seven were deemed to have solid scientific evidence for their effectiveness in training comprehension in non-impaired readers. Interestingly, these include *use of graphic and semantic organizers* and *use of story structure*, both of which might be expected to develop understanding of text structure; *summarization*, where children are taught to integrate ideas, and *question answering* (both of which might be expected to improve children's awareness of the need for integration and inferences); *comprehension monitoring;* and *question generation,* which might be expected to improve both inference and monitoring skills. The seventh type of instruction, *cooperative learning,* might incorporate any, or all, of these elements. The panel noted that these types of instruction are effective when used alone, but that many are more effective when used together as part of a multiple-strategy method. It seems to us that an important question for future research in this area is whether comprehension strategies are trained individually or as part of a package of skills.

REFERENCES

Baker, L. (1984). Children's effective use of multiple standards for evaluating their comprehension. *Journal of Educational Psychology, 76,* 588–597.

Barnes, M. A., Dennis, M., & Haefele-Kalvaitis, J. (1996). The effects of knowledge availability and knowledge accessibility on coherence and elaborative inferencing in children from six to fifteen years of age. *Journal of Experimental Child Psychology, 61*(3), 216–241.

Bishop, D. (1982). *Test for Reception of Grammar.* Manchester, UK: Chapel Press.

Bishop, D. V. M. (1997). *Uncommon understanding: Development and disorders of language comprehension in children.* Hove, UK: Psychology Press/Erlbaum.

Bishop, D. V. M. (2003). *Test for Reception of Grammar–2.* New York: Harcourt Assessment.

Bowyer-Crane, C., & Snowling, M. (2005). Assessing children's inference generation: What do tests of reading comprehension measure? *British Journal of Educational Psychology, 75,* 189–201.

Bradley, L., & Bryant, P. E. (1978). Difficulties in auditory organisation as a possible cause of reading backwardness. *Nature, 271,* 746–747.

Bryant, P., & Goswami, U. (1986). Strengths and weaknesses of the reading level design: A comment on Backman, Mamen & Ferguson. *Psychological Bulletin, 100,* 101–103.

Cain, K. (2003). Text comprehension and its relation to coherence and cohesion in children's fictional narratives. *British Journal of Developmental Psychology, 21,* 335–351.

Cain, K. (2006). Individual differences in children's memory and reading comprehension: An investigation of semantic and inhibitory deficits *Memory, 14,* 553–569.

Cain, K., & Oakhill, J. (1996). The nature of the relationship between comprehension skill and the ability to tell a story. *British Journal of Developmental Psychology, 14,* 187–201.

Cain, K., & Oakhill, J. V. (1999). Inference making and its relation to comprehension failure. *Reading and Writing, 11,* 489–503.

Cain, K., & Oakhill, J. (2006). Profiles of children with specific reading comprehension difficulties. *British Journal of Educational Psychology, 76,* 683–696.

Cain, K., & Oakhill, J. (2007). Reading comprehension difficulties: Correlates, causes, and consequences. In K. Cain & J. Oakhill (Eds.), *Children's comprehension problems in oral and written language: A cognitive perspective.* New York: Guilford Press.

Cain, K., Oakhill, J. V., Barnes, M. A., & Bryant, P. E. (2001). Comprehension skill, inference making ability and their relation to knowledge. *Memory & Cognition, 29,* 850–859.

Cain, K., Oakhill, J. V., & Bryant, P. E. (2000a). Investigating the causes of reading comprehension failure: The comprehension-age match design. *Reading and Writing, 12,* 31–40.

Cain, K., Oakhill, J. V., & Bryant, P. E. (2000b). Phonological skills and comprehension failure: A test of the phonological processing deficit hypothesis. *Reading and Writing, 13,* 31–56.

Cain, K., Oakhill, J., & Bryant, P. E. (2004). Children's reading comprehension ability: Concurrent prediction by working memory, verbal ability, and component skill. *Journal of Educational Psychology, 96,* 671–681.

Cain, K., Oakhill, J., & Lemmon, K. (2004). Individual differences in the inference of word meanings from context: The influence of reading comprehension, vocabulary knowledge, and memory capacity. *Journal of Educational Psychology, 96,* 671–681.

Cain, K., Oakhill, J., & Lemmon, K. (2005). The relation between children's reading comprehension level and their comprehension of idioms. *Journal of Educational Psychology, 90,* 65–87.

Cain, K., Patson, N., & Andrews, L. (2005). Age- and ability-related differences in young readers' use of conjunctions. *Journal of Child Language, 32*(4), 877–892.

Casteel, M. A. (1993). Effects of inference necessity and reading goal on children's inference generation. *Developmental Psychology, 29,* 346–357.

Catts, H., Fey, M. E., Zhang, X., & Tomblin, J. B. (1999). Language basis of reading and reading disabilities: Evidence from a longitudinal investigation. *Scientific Studies of Reading, 3,* 331–361.

Cragg, L., & Nation, K. (2006). Exploring written narrative in children with poor reading comprehension. *Educational Psychology, 26,* 55–72.

Crain, S. (1989). Why poor readers misunderstand spoken sentences. In D. Shankweiler & I. Y. Liberman (Eds.), *Phonology and reading disability: Solving the reading puzzle.* Ann Arbor: University of Michigan Press.

Daneman, M., & Merikle, P. M. (1996). Working memory and language comprehension: A meta-analysis. *Psychonomic Bulletin and Review, 3,* 422–433.

De Beni, R., Palladino, P., Pazzaglia, F., & Cornoldi, C. (1998). Increases in intrusion errors and working memory deficit of poor comprehenders. *Quarterly Journal of Experimental Psychology: Human Experimental Psychology, 51A,* 305–320.

de Jong, P. F., & van der Leij, A. (2002). Effects of phonological abilities and linguistic comprehension on the development of reading. *Scientific Studies of Reading, 6,* 51–77.

Dunn, L. M., Dunn, L. M., Whetton, C., & Pintillie, D. (1992). *British Picture Vocabulary Scale.* Windsor: NFER-Nelson.

Educational Assessment Unit, University of Edinburgh. (1999). *Edinburgh Reading Test* (2nd ed.). London: Hodder Education.

Ehri, L. C. (1979). Linguistic insight: Threshold of reading acquisition. In T. G. Waller & G. E. MacKinnon (Eds.), *Reading research: Advances in theory and practice* (Vol. 1). New York: Academic Press.

Ehrlich, M. F. (1996). Metacognitive monitoring in the processing of anaphoric devices in skilled and less-skilled comprehenders. In C. Cornoldi & J. Oakhill (Eds.), *Reading comprehension difficulties: Processes and intervention.* Mahwah, NJ: Erlbaum.

Ehrlich, M. F., Remond, M., & Tardieu, H. (1999). Processing of anaphoric devices in young skilled and less skilled comprehenders: Differences in metacognitive monitoring. *Reading and Writing, 11*, 29–63.

Johnson-Laird, P. N. (1983). *Mental models: Towards a cognitive science of language, inference, and consciousness.* Cambridge, UK: Cambridge University Press.

Kendeou, P., Bohn-Gettler, C., White, M., & van den Broek, P. (2008). Children's inference generation across different media. *Journal of Research in Reading, 31*, 259–272.

Kendeou, P., Lynch, J. S., van den Broek, P., Espin, C., White, M., & Kremer, K. E. (2005). Developing successful readers: Building early narrative comprehension skills through television viewing and listening. *Early Childhood Education Journal, 33*, 91–98.

Kendeou, P., van den Broek, P., White, M. J., & Lynch, J. S. (2007). Comprehension in preschool and early elementary children: Skill development and strategy interventions. In D. S. McNamara (Ed.), *Reading comprehension strategies: Theories, interventions, and technologies.* Mahwah, NJ: Erlbaum.

Kintsch, W. (1998). *Comprehension: A paradigm for cognition.* New York: Cambridge University Press.

Macaruso, P., Barshalom, E., Crain, S., & Shankweiler, D. (1989). Comprehension of temporal terms by good and poor readers. *Language and Speech, 32*, 45–67.

Markman, E. M., & Gorin, L. (1981). Children's ability to adjust their standards for evaluating comprehension. *Journal of Educational Psychology, 73*, 320–325.

Megherbi, H., & Ehrlich, M. F. (2005). Language impairment in less skilled comprehenders: The on-line processing of anaphoric pronouns in a listening situation. *Reading and Writing, 18*, 715–753.

Nation, K., Adams, J. W., Bowyer-Crane, C. A., & Snowling, M. J. (1999). Working memory deficits in poor comprehenders reflect underlying language impairments. *Journal of Experimental Child Psychology, 73*, 139–158.

Nation, K., Clarke, P., Marshall, C. M., & Durand, M. (2004). Hidden language impairments in children: Parallels between poor reading comprehension and specific language impairment? *Journal of Speech, Language, and Hearing Research, 47*(1), 199–211.

Nation, K., & Snowling, M. J. (1998). Semantic processing and the development of word-recognition skills: Evidence from children with reading comprehension difficulties. *Journal of Memory and Language, 39*, 85–101.

Nation, K., Snowling, M. J., & Clarke, P. (2005). Production of the English past tense by children with language comprehension impairments. *Journal of Child Language, 32*(1), 117–137.

National Institute of Child Health and Human Development. (2000). *Report of the National Reading Panel. Teaching children to read: An evidence-based assessment of the scientific research literature on reading and its implications for reading instruction.* Washington, DC: US Government Printing Office.

Neale, M. D. (1997). *The Neale Analysis of Reading Ability–Revised (NARA-II).* Windsor, UK: NFER-Nelson.

Oakhill, J. V. (1982). Constructive processes in skilled and less-skilled comprehenders' memory for sentences. *British Journal of Psychology, 73,* 13–20.

Oakhill, J. V. (1984). Inferential and memory skills in children's comprehension of stories. *British Journal of Educational Psychology, 54,* 31–39.

Oakhill, J. V., & Cain, K. (2007). Issues of causality in children's reading comprehension. In D. S. McNamara (Ed.), *Reading comprehension strategies: Theory, interventions and technologies.* Mahwah, NJ: Erlbaum.

Oakhill, J. V., Cain, K., & Bryant, P. E. (2003). The dissociation of word reading and text comprehension: Evidence from component skills. *Language and Cognitive Processes, 18,* 443–468.

Oakhill, J., Hartt, J., & Samols, D. (2005). Levels of comprehension monitoring and working memory in good and poor comprehenders. *Reading and Writing, 18,* 657–713.

Oakhill, J. V., & Yuill, N. M. (1986). Pronoun resolution in skilled and less skilled comprehenders: Effects of memory load and inferential complexity. *Language and Speech, 29,* 25–37.

Oakhill, J. V., Yuill, N. M., & Parkin, A. (1986). On the nature of the difference between skilled and less-skilled comprehenders. *Journal of Research in Reading, 9,* 80–91.

Paris, A. H., & Paris, S. G. (2003). Assessing narrative comprehension in young children. *Reading Research Quarterly, 38,* 36–76.

Perfetti, C. A. (1985). *Reading ability.* New York: Oxford University Press.

Seigneuric, A., Ehrlich, M.-F., Oakhill, J. V., & Yuill, N. M. (2000). Working memory resources and children's reading comprehension. *Reading and Writing, 13,* 81–103.

Shankweiler, D. (1989). How problems of comprehension are related to difficulties in decoding. In D. Shankweiler & I. Y. Liberman (Eds.), *Phonology and reading disability: Solving the reading puzzle.* Ann Arbor: University of Michigan Press.

Smith, S. T., Macaruso, P., Shankweiler, D., & Crain, S. (1989). Syntactic comprehension in young poor readers. *Applied Psycholinguistics, 10,* 420–454.

Stein, N. L., & Glenn, C. G. (1982). Children's concept of time: The development of story schema. In W. Friedman (Ed.), *The development of psychology of time* (pp. 255–282). New York: Academic Press.

Stothard, S. E., & Hulme, C. (1992). Reading comprehension difficulties in children: The role of language comprehension and working memory skills. *Reading and Writing, 4,* 245–256.

Tabors, P. O., Snow, C. E., & Dickinson, D. K. (2001). Homes and schools together: Supporting language literacy with language. In D. K. Dickinson & P. O. Tabors (Eds.), *Beginning literacy with language*. Baltimore, NJ: Brookes Publishing.

Van den Broek, P., Kendeou, P., Kremer, K., Lynch, J. S., Butler, J., White, M. J., et al. (2005). Assessment of comprehension abilities in young children. In S. Stahl & S. Paris (Eds.), *Children's reading comprehension and assessment*. Mahwah, NJ: Erlbaum.

Van den Broek, P. W., Risden, K., & Husebye-Hartman, E. (1995). The role of readers' standards for coherence in the generation of inferences during reading. In R. F. Lorch & E. J. O'Brien (Eds.), *Sources of coherence in reading*. Mahwah, NJ: Erlbaum.

Yuill, N., & Joscelyne, T. (1988). Effect of organizational cues and strategies on good and poor comprehenders' story understanding. *Journal of Educational Psychology, 80*, 152–158.

Yuill, N. M., & Oakhill, J. V. (1988a). Effects of inference awareness training on poor reading comprehension. *Applied Cognitive Psychology, 2*, 33–45.

Yuill, N., & Oakhill, J. (1988b). Understanding of anaphoric relations in skilled and less skilled comprehenders. *British Journal of Psychology, 79*, 173–186.

Yuill, N., & Oakhill, J. (1991). *Children's problems in text comprehension: An experimental investigation*. Cambridge, UK: Cambridge University Press.

Yuill, N. M., Oakhill, J. V., & Parkin, A. J. (1989). Working memory, comprehension skill and the resolution of text anomaly. *British Journal of Psychology, 80*, 351–361.

Zwaan, R. A., & Radvansky, G. A. (1998). Situation models in language comprehension and memory. *Psychological Bulletin, 123*, 162–185.

8

Reading Comprehension and Vocabulary

What's the Connection?

Kate Nation

> Twas brillig, and the slithy toves
> Did gyre and gimble in the wabe:
> All mimsy were the borogoves,
> And the mome raths outgrabe.
> "Beware the Jabberwock, my son!
> The jaws that bite, the claws that catch!
> Beware the Jubjub bird, and shun
> The frumious Bandersnatch!"
> —Extract from *Jabberwocky* (*Through the Looking-Glass,*
> *and What Alice Found There* by Lewis Carroll, 1872)

It has been known for a long time that vocabulary knowledge and reading comprehension are strongly correlated (e.g., Davis, 1944; Thorndike, 1973). Reading *Jabberwocky* tells us quite a lot about this relationship, as does Alice's response to reading the poem:

> "It seems very pretty," she said when she had finished it, "but it's rather hard to understand!" (You see she didn't like to confess even to herself, that she couldn't make it out at all.) "Somehow it seems to fill my head with ideas—only I don't exactly know what they are! However, somebody killed something: that's clear, at any rate...."

176

A moment of introspection about *Jabberwocky* indicates that the relationship between reading comprehension and vocabulary is likely to be rich, interactive, and complex. On the one hand, it is clear that vocabulary is needed for comprehension. Without doubt, our lack of knowledge concerning the meaning of individual words impedes our understanding. At the same time, however, it is equally clear that we can construct some meaning from the text, despite the fact that many of the words are nonsense. In turn, this constructed meaning provides an emerging context that helps us construe possible meanings to some of the individual words.

These introspections are consistent with a very large number of studies that have observed a close relationship between reading comprehension and vocabulary knowledge. Across the age span, individuals with better vocabulary knowledge tend to show advanced reading comprehension relative to peers with less well-developed vocabulary knowledge. Reviewing this evidence, Tannenbaum, Torgesen, and Wagner (2006) reported that the correlation between reading comprehension and vocabulary varied between approximately .3 to .8. The correlation strengthens as children get older (Torgesen, Wagner, Rashotte, Burgess, & Hecht, 1997), and factors such as test format and the dimension of word knowledge being assessed also impact the magnitude of the correlation. Limitations in vocabulary knowledge have been suggested to be a putative cause of reading comprehension failure (e.g., Cromley & Azevedo, 2007), and many interventions for poor reading comprehension involve strategies designed to increase vocabulary knowledge (e.g., Beck, Perfetti, & McKeown, 1982). This aim of this chapter is to explore the links between vocabulary knowledge and reading comprehension, with particular reference to children identified as having specific deficits in reading comprehension. Before discussing this group of children in some detail, it is useful to review two general (and interrelated) issues. First, why might reading comprehension and vocabulary be associated? Second, which aspects of the reading comprehension process might be most closely related to vocabulary knowledge?

WHY ARE READING COMPREHENSION AND VOCABULARY KNOWLEDGE ASSOCIATED?

It is very clear that reading comprehension and vocabulary knowledge are closely associated. What is less clear is how this association is best interpreted. One interpretation sees individual differences in reading ability being responsible for individual differences in vocabulary knowledge. According to this view, children learn the meaning of new words via reading, among other strategies. Consequently, better readers will develop larger vocabularies over time, whereas poor readers, who read less, lack print exposure, and this serves to hamper vocabulary development (e.g., Cunningham & Stanovich, 1991, 1997; Nagy & Anderson, 1984; Nagy & Scott, 2000). An alternative view sees individual differences in vocabulary knowledge being responsible for individual differences in reading comprehension. On this view, if children have limited vocabulary knowledge or if they are unable to access word meanings rapidly and efficiently, this will be detrimental to their reading comprehension (e.g., Beck et al., 1982; Daneman & Green, 1986). Longitudinal studies provide evidence to support both of these explanations, with vocabulary knowledge predicting growth in reading comprehension and reading comprehension itself predicting growth in vocabulary knowledge (e.g., de Jong & van der Leij, 2002; Muter, Hulme, Snowling, & Stevenson, 2004; Seigneuric & Ehrlich, 2005).

An additional possibility is that vocabulary and reading are related because they share common processes. Vocabulary growth requires the development of mappings between the semantic meaning of a word and its phonological form (McGregor, 2004), and, in a similar vein, reading depends on the development of mappings among semantic, phonological, and orthographic units of representation (Plaut, McClelland, Seidenberg, & Patterson, 1996; Perfetti, 2007). Within this view, specific underlying processes may be impaired in poor readers, and it is these weaknesses that lead to *both* poor reading and poor vocabulary. For example, Sternberg and Powell (1983) suggested that the relationship among reading comprehension, vocabulary, and general intelligence may be mediated by the ability to acquire new information from context. Domain-general cognitive skills such as working memory may also serve to mediate the relationship between vocabulary and reading comprehension.

COMPONENT READING SKILLS

Reading comprehension is a complex skill (Kintsch & Rawson, 2005; Perfetti, Landi, & Oakhill, 2005). Readers need to recognize or decipher individual words, access their meanings, and interpret grammatical structure. Rarely is a text completely literal: Readers need to draw on general knowledge and an appreciation of pragmatic factors to understand the intended message. Successful reading demands that readers construct a coherent and integrated mental representation of the text, rich in referential relations (e.g., Gernsbacher, 1990; Kintsch, 1998; van den Broek, 1994).

Given that vocabulary correlates with reading comprehension, an important question is whether there are particular aspects of the reading comprehension process that are more closely correlated with vocabulary. To illustrate, consider a child who has great difficulty reading words. They are slow, inaccurate, and effortful. Not surprisingly, they also have difficulty understanding text. They also show low-for-age vocabulary knowledge. Here we observe an association between poor reading comprehension and poor vocabulary, but it is impossible to know whether this is a consequence of vocabulary being associated with the child's word-reading problems or with comprehension-level problems, or both.

It is helpful to think about reading comprehension as comprising two sets of component parts: One set concerned with recognizing printed words and the other concerned with understanding the message that the print conveys (e.g., Hoover & Gough, 1990). From this perspective, it is possible to ask whether vocabulary shares its association with reading comprehension via word-level reading, comprehension-level processes, or both. Ricketts, Nation, and Bishop (2007) investigated this question by assessing vocabulary knowledge and component-reading skills in a group of 8- to 9-year-old children. They found that vocabulary was important for both aspects of reading. In terms of word-level reading, vocabulary knowledge was most associated with reading words rather than nonwords, particularly words with irregular or unusual print–sound correspondences. Vocabulary also showed a moderate to strong correlation with reading comprehension, and regression analyses revealed that vocabulary knowledge accounted for a large portion of unique variance (17.8%) in reading comprehension, even after variance associated with chronological age, nonverbal IQ, and word-level reading was controlled.

Further discussion of the association between vocabulary and word-level reading can be found elsewhere (e.g., Nation, 2008), but for present purposes, Ricketts et al.'s findings are important because they show that the association between vocabulary and reading comprehension is not just a consequence of factors associated with word-level reading. Instead, something more specific about the comprehension process appears to be related to children's vocabulary knowledge.

CHILDREN WITH POOR
READING COMPREHENSION

Who Are Poor Comprehenders?

Many children who have difficulties understanding written text will also have difficulty reading the words in the text (e.g., Perfetti, 1985, 2007). However, given that the correlation between word reading and reading comprehension is far from perfect (e.g., Juel, Griffith, & Gough, 1986, report correlations of .74 and .69 for first- and second-grade children), it is not that rare to find children who perform adequately in one component but not the other. The focus of the remainder of this chapter is on children who appear to show selective impairments of reading comprehension. That is, their word-reading accuracy is within the normal range for their age, but their comprehension of what is read is substantially below average. Studies of such children allow us to explore the relationship between comprehension processes and vocabulary in a relatively clean way, independent of the processes that might be related to individual differences in word-reading ability.

Oakhill and colleagues (Oakhill, 1994; Yuill & Oakhill, 1991) were the first to describe children who obtained normal-for-age-text reading accuracy but showed impaired reading comprehension. At a simple level of description level, these children (who are referred to in this chapter as "poor comprehenders") read accurately but have specific difficulty understanding what they read. Typically, poor comprehenders are rare in clinically referred samples of children with reading difficulties (e.g., Leach, Scarborough, & Rescorla, 2003; Shankweiler et al., 1999). However, this is probably a reflection of referral bias. Also, the nature of finding children with specific comprehension difficulties will be tightly constrained by the nature of the reading comprehension test used to select and define groups (e.g., Keenan, 2006). Repeatedly, we find that when populations of 7- to 10-year-old children have been screened in the United Kingdom, approximately 10% can be classified as poor comprehenders (Nation & Snowling, 1997; Stothard & Hulme, 1992; Yuill & Oakhill, 1991). A similar profile of poor reading is also seen in adulthood (Perfetti, Wlotko, & Hart, 2005; Landi & Perfetti, 2007) and has been reported in children learning to read languages other than English (e.g., Cornoldi, de Beni, & Pazzaglia, 1996; De Beni, Palladino, Pazzaglia, & Cornoldi, 1998; Megherbi & Erlich, 2004).

There is a growing literature documenting poor comprehenders' abilities and disabilities; comprehensive reviews are provided by

Cain and Oakhill (2007) and Nation (2005). Although many questions remain, a number of consistent findings have been reported. One consistent finding is that, unlike children with poor word reading, poor comprehenders do not show impairments in phonological awareness or phonological processing (Cain, Oakhill, & Bryant, 2000; Nation, Clarke, Marshall, & Durand, 2004; Nation & Snowling, 1998). They do, however, show impairments in listening comprehension (Nation & Snowling, 1997; Yuill & Oakhill, 1991) and in oral language more generally (Nation et al., 2004). Poor comprehenders show a variety of text-level impairments such as problems with making inferences, using cohesive devices, and monitoring comprehension (Bowyer-Crane & Snowling, 2005; Cain & Oakhill, 1999; Cain, Oakhill, Barnes, & Bryant, 2001). Narrative comprehension and production are compromised (Cain, 1999; Cragg & Nation, 2006), and there is also evidence of impairments in working memory, particularly verbal working memory (Cain, 2006; Nation, Adams, Bowyer-Crane, & Snowling, 1999; Yuill, Oakhill, & Parkin, 1989).

Poor Comprehenders and Vocabulary: Correlate, Cause, or Consequence?

Given that reading comprehension is closely associated with vocabulary knowledge, one might expect poor comprehenders to show impairments in vocabulary. There is some evidence suggesting that they do. For example, Nation and Snowling (1998) investigated poor comprehenders' semantic skills: their knowledge of and sensitivity to word meanings. Poor comprehenders were slower and less accurate at judging whether pairs of words were synonymous, and they generated fewer exemplars than their peers in a category fluency task. Poor comprehenders are also slower and less accurate at providing the name for objects pictured on a computer screen, especially if the items are low in frequency (Nation, Marshall, & Snowling, 2001). Mild to moderate deficits in expressive and receptive vocabulary as measured by standardized tests have also been observed (Catts, Adlof, & Weismer, 2006; Nation et al., 2004; Ricketts et al., 2007).

These data appeal to the view that poor reading comprehension may be a consequence of lack of vocabulary knowledge. However, there are a number of reasons why this conclusion is likely to be only partially correct. First, not all poor comprehenders show poor vocabulary on standardized tests (Cain, Lemmon, & Oakhill, 2004), consistent

with the more general observation that poor comprehenders are a heterogeneous group, and that there are likely to be multiple routes to
comprehension failure (Cain & Oakhill, 2007; Nation, 2005). Second, it
is clear that poor comprehenders' difficulties with text-level processes
remain, even when care is taken to make sure that they are familiar
with all of the relevant vocabulary and background knowledge (Cain
et al., 2001). Third, and most importantly, vocabulary weaknesses in
poor comprehenders may be as much a consequence of the reading
comprehension impairment as a cause. Without longitudinal data, it
is impossible to assess issues of causality. However, given the highly
reciprocal relationship between reading comprehension and vocabulary described earlier, it seems likely that reciprocal links will be seen
when longitudinal data charting the early development of comprehension and vocabulary are examined in children with a poor comprehender reading profile.

A rather different approach to investigating the relationship
between vocabulary and reading comprehension is provided by studies examining new vocabulary learning in poor comprehenders. These
studies are interesting because they address learning—how vocabulary
is acquired and how children may differ in this—rather than the product
of learning—how many words a child knows according to a standardized instrument. Broadly, these studies can be separated into two types:
those investigating whether meaning can be inferred from context and
those investigating lexical learning. Because these studies stem from
different theoretical backgrounds, it is more straightforward to consider
them in detail separately before considering synergies between them.

Inferring Meaning from Context

Context provides a powerful cue to discovering the meaning of new
words. Indeed, given the number of words that children acquire and the
speed with which they learn them, something other than direct learning must be taking place. There is good evidence that young children
draw on a variety of contextual cues to support vocabulary learning
(Bloom, 2000; Tomasello, 2003). Once children begin to learn to read,
text provides many opportunities for vocabulary development, and it
is known that reading provides a more effective context for learning
new words than oral conversation (Nagy & Anderson, 1984). A single
encounter with a new word in text can be enough to allow its meaning
to be inferred and learned (Nagy, Herman, & Anderson, 1985), although
multiple encounters in different contexts are likely to be needed too, if

readers are to develop a full appreciation of the range of nuances in meaning a word may have (Nagy & Scott, 2000).

Given that poor comprehenders have difficulty making inferences and constructing a well-integrated and coherent representation of the meaning of text, it is reasonable to expect that they may have difficulty inferring the meaning of new words from context. This prediction was assessed by Cain et al. (2004a). Children read short stories containing a single exposure to novel word. The meaning of the novel word could be inferred from information contained immediately after the novel word (near condition) or following a few filler sentences (far condition). After reading the story, poor comprehenders were less able to explain the meaning of the novel word than control children, especially in the far condition. These findings suggest that poor comprehenders are less skilled at inferring the meaning of new words from context, especially when the processing demands of the task are high, that is, when information across sentences needs to be remembered and integrated, if word meaning is to be inferred.

Cain et al. (2004a) also investigated poor comprehenders' ability to learn the meaning of new words via direct instruction. In this condition, children were read a definition that explained the meaning of the new word explicitly, for example, "a small bouncy ball is called a *wut*." Those poor comprehenders who showed relative weaknesses in existing vocabulary knowledge (as assessed by the British Picture Vocabulary Scales, a UK version of the Peabody Picture Vocabulary Test) were poor at learning new words via direct instruction; those poor comprehenders with good-for-age vocabulary as assessed by the standardized test were able to learn the meaning of new words via direct instruction as well as control children.

In summary, Cain et al.'s study provides evidence that poor comprehenders are less able to infer the meaning of new words from text. This is an important finding, and a worrying one with respect to the longer term outcome for poor comprehenders. It suggests that their vocabulary will decline with age, relative to controls, because they fail to acquire the meanings of new words from their encounters with text. Although impairments in inferring the meaning of new words were pervasive across all children with poor reading comprehension (Cain et al., 2004a), only some poor comprehenders showed difficulty learning new vocabulary via direct instruction. This finding suggests that some children with poor reading comprehension may have additional difficulty establishing new lexical representations, an issue we now address.

Lexical Learning in Poor Comprehenders

Perfetti, Wlotko, and Hart (2005) investigated individual differences in learning the meanings of new words in college students who differed in reading comprehension skill. Skilled and less skilled comprehenders were provided with definitions for very rare and previously unfamiliar words such as *gloaming* and *flexion*. Learning was assessed via a meaning judgment task. Less skilled comprehenders made significantly more errors, suggesting that they learned the new words less well than skilled comprehenders. In addition, Perfetti et al. examined event-related potential (ERP) responses to the newly acquired words. Skilled comprehenders showed a greater familiarity response (indexed as a P600 marker of episodic memory) to new words and a different N400 response showing that they were more sensitive to the meaning of the newly acquired words than less skilled comprehenders.

Nation, Snowling, and Clarke (2007) also investigated individual differences in lexical learning. Building on an earlier study by Aguiar and Brady (1991), we examined phonological learning (mappings between a new phonological label and its referent) and semantic learning (mappings between meaning and form). Given the profile of language strengths and weaknesses revealed by previous studies of poor comprehenders, we made specific predictions concerning poor comprehenders' lexical learning. Given that poor comprehenders have normal phonological skills (e.g., Cain et al., 2000; Stothard & Hulme, 1995), we predicted that they would show normal phonological learning. They did. They took a similar number of trials to learn to associate a new label such as *corbelyeon* with a picture of a novel referent. In contrast to normal phonological learning, we predicted that poor comprehenders would show impaired semantic learning, following our earlier observations of semantic weaknesses (in synonym judgment, for example; Nation & Snowling, 1998). Consistent with this prediction, poor comprehenders learned less about the meaning of the new referents and were less able to recall the correct name for an object, given its definition. The poor comprehenders also appeared to have difficulty consolidating the meanings of newly acquired items, and their recall of these was poorer than that of skilled comprehenders 1 week after training.

Ricketts, Bishop, and Nation (2008) extended these findings by examining poor comprehenders' learning of new orthographic forms (i.e., written words). They contrasted orthographic learning and semantic learning across the same items by the same children. Orthographic learning was defined as the ease of learning the new spelling–sound

relations associated with each of the new words. Here, poor comprehenders learned the new orthographic forms as readily as control children. Semantic learning was defined as the ability to associate meaning
with the new orthographic forms. Poor comprehenders were less able
to correctly pair the newly acquired words with their correct referents
1 week after training, demonstrating weaknesses in this aspect of word
learning.

Taken together, these three studies (Perfetti, Wlotko, & Hart, 2005;
Nation et al., 2007; Ricketts et al., 2007) show that children and adults
with poor reading comprehension are less adept at learning new words.
More specifically, the aspect of learning that appears to be most frag-
ile concerns meaning. In all three studies, less skilled comprehenders
made some links between new words and their semantic properties.
Importantly, however, there was evidence of some difficulties with
developing rich and durable semantic representations. Such differences
in lexical learning might be responsible for the vocabulary deficits that
characterize some poor comprehenders, including those with lower
levels of existing vocabulary knowledge who failed to benefit from
direct instruction strategies in Cain et al.'s (2004a) study.

What do these studies of vocabulary learning in people with reading comprehension impairments tell us? Most generally, they again
highlight the complex and highly reciprocal relationship between reading comprehension and vocabulary. To some extent, they also show the
limitations of trying to address issues of causality or developmental
primacy in terms of what came first, comprehension deficit or vocabulary deficit. Clearly, reading comprehension will fail if a child does
not understand the meaning of enough of the words in a text, just as
our own comprehension of "Jabberwocky" is compromised. One could
argue that because many poor comprehenders have low vocabulary
knowledge, this is sufficient to explain their reading comprehension
deficit. However, the question then arises as to why poor comprehenders have weak vocabulary knowledge. Cain et al.'s study lends
support to the idea that an individual's ability to learn new words or
acquire new information from context mediates the high correlations
observed among verbal ability, reading comprehension, and vocabulary knowledge (e.g., Sternberg & Powell, 1983). In turn, this demonstrates how higher level processes such as the ability to make inferences
and integrate information within a text can influence the acquisition of
basic lower level knowledge, such as the meaning of a new word. Not-
withstanding this, it also seems clear that children with strong vocabulary knowledge will be well placed to engage in higher level processes

as they read (Perfetti, 2007). Thus, it is perhaps not surprising to find that children who are poor at making inferences tend to have weaker vocabulary skills relative to children who are skilled at making inferences and vice versa.

Flexibility, Efficiency, and Online Processing

So far, this chapter has considered vocabulary as a variable that indexes the number of words a child knows. Very clearly, however, this is far too simplistic. To support comprehension, vocabulary knowledge also needs to be flexible and efficient. Let us take each of these issues in turn.

Flexibility is important because children need to know more about a word than its pronunciation and its standard dictionary definition (Miller, 1999). They need to learn that words can have more than one meaning or can be associated with different senses. To capture fully the subtleties of word meaning, children need to be sensitive to both the range of information a word can denote and to the context in which it occurs, so that the precise meaning of a particular word in a particular context can be comprehended and other irrelevant meanings be inhibited (e.g., Gernsbacher & Faust, 1991). We know that some poor comprehenders show lower levels of vocabulary knowledge than control children (e.g., Cain et al., 2004a; Nation & Snowling, 1998; Ricketts et al., 2007); there is also evidence that they have some difficulty with flexibility too. Multiple Meanings is a subtest of The Test of Word Knowledge (TOWK; Wiig & Secord, 1992), in which children are presented a set of words with multiple meanings (e.g., *bat*) and are required to provide two distinct definitions for each word (e.g., the thing you hit a ball with and an animal that flies). Poor comprehenders perform less well on this test than controls, scoring in the below- to low-average range according to standardized norms (Nation & Snowling, 1998; Ricketts et al., 2007). Similarly, poor comprehenders have difficulty with comprehending figurative language (Nation et al., 2004) and processing idioms (Cain, Oakhill, & Lemmon, 2005). A goal for future work is to understand why poor comprehenders find these tasks difficult.

Related to flexibility is efficiency. Even if children know the meaning of a word, if they are slow to access or process its meaning, this may well have consequences for ongoing comprehension. Using a variety of behavioral and ERP measures, Landi and Perfetti (2007) found that less skilled college-age comprehenders showed differences in efficiency when making meaning decisions about pairs of words. Similarly, children identified as poor comprehenders show differences in patterns of semantic priming compared with their peers (Nation & Snowling, 1999). An important feature of both of these studies is that they used simple vocabulary, well within the range of participants (e.g., *dog, cat, brother, sister*). Despite this, reader group differences were seen in priming between pairs of words and the time taken to make meaning judgments (and in underlying ERP signatures). This suggests that possession of vocabulary knowledge for a word is not an all-or-nothing factor. Instead, as Perfetti (2007, p. 359) notes, what is important is "the ability to retrieve word identities that provide the meanings the reader needs in a given context."

This conclusion leads to a rather different perspective on the relationship between reading comprehension and vocabulary knowledge. Rather than think about whether vocabulary weaknesses can cause comprehension impairments or whether lack of comprehension can lead to vocabulary deficits, a more profitable approach may be to try to understand more about how children process language as they read. To date, most research has assessed reading comprehension and vocabulary knowledge offline. Typically, children are asked to read stories and answer questions about them or are asked to provide definitions of words or to match words to pictures. Although these methods reveal whether or not a child has a comprehension or vocabulary problem, they cannot tell us *why*. Take, as an example, a child who finds it difficult to comprehend sentences containing ambiguous words. This could be a reflection of lack of knowledge, because perhaps the child only knows one meaning. Alternatively, it could be a difficulty with using context to activate the appropriate meaning or a difficulty with using context to inhibit or suppress contextually irrelevant interpretations. Offline measures that ask children to answer questions or provide definitions can only ever measure the endpoint of comprehension, not the actual process itself.

In contrast to offline tasks, online tasks allow inferences to be made about the processing of language itself, not just its endpoint. Our understanding of the temporal dynamics of sentence processing in skilled adults has long been informed by online measures such as reading time (Rayner, 1998). To borrow an example from Altmann (1997), when participants read a sentence such as "Sam told the writer that he couldn't understand to get some help from a decent editor," eye movements during the reading of "to get" are disturbed, relative to when they read the same words in the almost identical sentence: "Sam asked the writer that he couldn't understand to get some help from a decent editor." This is because in the first sentence the verb *told* sets up an expectation that the word *that* will introduce a message rather than an embedded clause. Disruptions to eye movements are indicative of the processing difficulty participants experience as they read something that is not expected.

Very few studies have used eye movement methods to track reading processes in typically developing children (see Joseph et al., 2008, for a recent findings). At the time of this writing, there have been no published reports of such studies with poor comprehenders. Yet the utility of eye movement methodology to the study of children with poor reading comprehension is obvious. Potentially, these reports provide opportunities to understand more about the interactions between word knowledge and comprehension as children read. More generally, they can tell us precisely when comprehension breaks down and perhaps point to the reasons why (Nation, 2008b; Rapp, Van den Broek, McMaster, Kendeou, & Espin, 2007).

An example of the utility of online methods is provided by a study that used eye movement methodology to explore individual differences in comprehension processes when children listened to spoken language. Nation, Marshall, and Altmann (2003) used the visual word paradigm to assess poor comprehenders' sensitivity to verb argument structure. This paradigm (e.g., Tanenhaus, Spivey-Knowlton, Eberhard, & Sedivy, 1995) involves recording participants' eye movements as they view a visual scene, which might comprise an array of real objects or objects presented on a computer screen. At the same time, they are listening to spoken stimuli that describe aspects of the visual scene. Because participants tend to look at objects that serve as potential referents for the linguistic expressions they hear, eye movements can reveal how long participants take to establish reference. Experimental manipulations (of the language or of the scene) then allow the experimenter to compare processing in different conditions, moment by moment, as the language unfolds in real time, allowing competing hypotheses to be evaluated.

As noted earlier, to fully capture of the subtleties of word meaning, children need to be sensitive to the range of information a word can denote so that the precise meaning of a particular word in a particular context can be comprehended. Our experiment used the visual world paradigm to investigate one aspect of this: sensitivity to verb argument structure. When listening to a sentence such as "Jane watched her mother eat the cake," 10-year-old children fixated the picture of the cake (the only edible object in the array) well before the acoustic onset of the word *cake*. In more neutral sentences such as "Jane watched her mother choose the cake," the probability of looking at the cake (relative to other objects in the visual array that also could have been chosen) only increased once the acoustic token of the word *cake* began to unfold. This demonstrates that skilled comprehenders are highly sensitive to information contained in verbs and that this information is used to guide subsequent processing.

How about poor comprehenders? Interestingly, poor comprehenders also showed this effect, suggesting that they too were very rapidly able to integrate information contained in the verb with contextual information provided by the visual scene. However, although less skilled comprehenders showed equal sensitivity to the contextual constraints offered by verbs, they also made more eye movements overall. We suggested that this may reflect difficulties in memory (with more looks being needed to refresh traces of either the language or the objects in the scene) or possibly differences in allocation of attentional resources in children. This suggestion raises the possibility that less skilled comprehenders construct their initial sentence representations adequately but that differences arise later in processing. For example, they may fail to integrate, elaborate, and link new information into their developing representations of the text. Eye movement methodology offers excellent potential for exploring these possibilities further (see also Rapp et al., 2007).

SUMMARY

There are close and intimate links between reading comprehension and vocabulary. This is nicely illustrated when we consider children with poor reading comprehension, many of whom have concomitant weaknesses in vocabulary. It is possible that lack of vocabulary may be at least in part causally implicated in their reading comprehension deficit. Equally, however, it is important to remember that lack of vocabulary knowledge may be a consequence of reading comprehension impairments. There are few longitudinal studies of poor comprehenders, but it seems likely that when more longitudinal data are available, reciprocal links between reading comprehension and vocabulary will be evident. Experiments have revealed that many poor comprehenders find it difficult to infer the meaning of new words from context, and some show impairments in lexical learning. These findings hint at potential causes of vocabulary weaknesses and potential starting points for effective intervention. They also highlight reciprocal interactions between high-level skills such as inference and low-level skills such as vocabulary. Very few studies have examined reading processes in children using online methods such as eye tracking. These methods offer great promise for revealing the underlying processes and strategies that guide children's comprehension as they read text and for revealing how these differ in children who fail to comprehend.

ACKNOWLEDGMENT

Preparation of this chapter was supported by a grant from the Economic and Social Research Council.

REFERENCES

Aguiar, L., & Brady, S. (1991). Vocabulary acquisition and reading ability. *Reading and Writing, 3*(3–4), 413–425.

Altmann, G. T. M. (1997). *The ascent of Babel.* Oxford, UK: Oxford University Press.

Beck, I. L., Perfetti, C. A., & McKeown, M. G. (1982). Effects of long-term vocabulary instruction on lexical access and reading comprehension. *Journal of Educational Psychology, 74*(4), 506–521.

Bloom, P. (2000). *How children learn the meanings of words.* Cambridge, MA: MIT Press.

Bowyer-Crane, C., & Snowling, M. J. (2005). Assessing children's inference generation: What do tests of reading comprehension measure? *British Journal of Educational Psychology, 75*, 189–201.

Cain, K. (1999). Ways of reading: How knowledge and use of strategies are related to reading comprehension. *British Journal of Developmental Psychology, 17*, 293–309.

Cain, K. (2006). Individual differences in children's memory and reading comprehension: An investigation of semantic and inhibitory deficits. *Memory, 14*(5), 553–569.

Cain, K., Lemmon, K., & Oakhill, J. (2004a). Individual differences in the inference of word meanings from context: The influence of reading comprehension, vocabulary knowledge, and memory capacity. *Journal of Educational Psychology, 96*, 671–681.

Cain, K., & Oakhill, J. V. (1999). Inference making ability and its relation to comprehension failure in young children.

Cain, K., & Oakhill, J. (2007). *Children's comprehension problems in oral and written language: A cognitive perspective.* New York: Guildford Press.

Reading and Writing, 11(5–6), 489–503.

Cain, K., Oakhill, J. V., Barnes, M. A., & Bryant, P. E. (2001). Comprehension skill, inference-making ability, and their relation to knowledge. *Memory & Cognition, 29*(6), 850–859.

Cain, K., Oakhill, J., & Bryant, P. (2000). Phonological skills and comprehension failure: A test of the phonological processing deficit hypothesis. *Reading and Writing, 13*(1–2), 31–56.

Cain, K., Oakhill, J. V., & Elbro, C. (2003). The ability to learn new word meanings from context by school-age children with and without language comprehension difficulties. *Journal of Child Language, 30*(3), 681–694.

Cain, K., Oakhill, J., & Lemmon, K. (2005). The relation between children's reading comprehension level and their comprehension of idioms. *Journal of Experimental Child Psychology, 90*(1), 65–87.

Carretti, B., Cornoldi, C., De Beni, R., & Romano, M. (2005). Updating in working memory: A comparison of good and poor comprehenders. *Journal of Experimental Child Psychology, 91*(1), 45–66.

Catts, H. W., Adlof, S. M., & Weismer, S. E. (2006). Language deficits in poor comprehenders: A case for the simple view of reading. *Journal of Speech Language and Hearing Research, 49*(2), 278–293.

Cornoldi, C., De Beni, R., & Pazzaglia, F. (1996). Profiles of reading comprehension difficulties. In C. Cornoldi & J. Oakhill (Eds.), *Reading comprehension dificulties: Processes and inteventions* (pp. 113–136). Mahwah, NJ: Erlbaum.

Cragg, L., & Nation, K. (2006). Exploring written narrative in children with poor reading comprehension. *Educational Psychology, 21*(1), 55–72.

Cromley, J. G., & Azevedo, R. (2007). Testing and refining the direct and inferential mediation model of reading comprehension. *Journal of Educational Psychology, 99*(2), 311–325.

Cunningham, A. E., & Stanovich, K. E. (1991). Tracking the unique effects of print exposure in children—Associations with vocabulary, general knowledge, and spelling. *Journal of Educational Psychology, 83*, 264–274.

Cunningham, A. E., & Stanovich, K. E. (1997). Early reading acquisition and its relation to reading experience and ability 10 years later. *Developmental Psychology, 33*(6), 934–945.

Daneman, M., & Green, I. (1986). Individual differences in comprehending and producing words in context. *Journal of Memory and Language, 25*(1), 1–18.

Davis, F. B. (1944). Fundamental factors in reading comprehension. *Psychometrika, 9*, 185–197.

De Beni, R., Palladino, P., Pazzaglia, F., & Cornoldi, C. (1998). Increases in intrusion errors and working memory deficit of poor comprehenders. *Quarterly Journal of Experimental Psychology. A, Human Experimental Psychology, 51*(2), 305–320.

De Jong, P. F., & van der Leij, A. (2002). Effects of phonological abilities and linguistic comprehension on the development of reading. *Scientific Studies of Reading, 6*(1), 51–77.

Gernsbacher, M. A. (1990). *Language comprehension as structure building*. Hillsdale, NJ: Erlbaum.

Gernsbacher, M. A., & Faust, M. E. (1991). The mechanism of suppression—A component of general comprehension skill. *Journal of Experimental Psychology: Learning, Memory, and Cognition, 17*(2), 245–262.

Hoover, W. A., & Gough, P. B. (1990). The simple view of reading. *Reading and Writing, 2*, 127–160.

Joseph, H. S. S. L., Liversedge, S. P., Blythe, H. I., White, S. J., Gathercole, S. E., & Rayner, K. (2008). Children's and adults' processing of anomaly and implausibility during reading: Evidence from eye movements. *Quarterly Journal of Experimental Psychology, 61*, 708–723.

Juel, C., Griffith, P. L., & Gough, P. B. (1986). Acquisition of literacy—A longitudinal study of children in first and second grade. *Journal of Educational Psychology, 78*(4), 243–255.

Keenan, J. (2006). *How comparable are reading comprehension tests?* Paper presented at the meeting of the Society for the Scientific Study of Reading, Vancouver.

Kintsch, W. A. (1998). *Comprehension: A paradigm for cognition.* Cambridge, UK: Cambridge University Press.

Kintsch, W., & Rawson, K.A. (2005). Comprehension. In M. J. Snowling & C. Hulme (Eds.), *The science of reading* (pp. 209–226). Oxford, UK: Blackwell.

Landi, N., & Perfetti, C. A. (2007). An electrophysiological investigation of semantic and phonological processing in skilled and less-skilled comprehenders. *Brain and Language, 102*(1), 30–45.

Leach, J. M., Scarborough, H. S., & Rescorla, L. (2003). Late-emerging reading disabilities. *Journal of Educational Psychology, 95*, 211–224.

McGregor, K. K. (2004). Developmental dependencies between lexical semantics and reading. In C. A. Stone, E. R. Silliman, B. J. Ehren, & K. Apel (Eds.), *Handbook of language and literacy: Development and disorders* (pp. 302–317). New York: Guilford Press.

Megherbi, H., & Ehrlich, M. F. (2004). Listening comprehension in first-grade skilled and less-skilled comprehenders for written texts. *Annee Psychologique, 104*(3), 433–489.

Miller, G. A. (1999). On knowing a word. *Annual Review of Psychology, 50*, 1–19.

Muter, V., Hulme, C., Snowling, M. J., & Stevenson, J. (2004). Phonemes, rimes, vocabulary, and grammatical skills as foundations of early reading development: Evidence from a longitudinal study. *Developmental Psychology, 40*, 665–681.

Nagy, W. E., & Anderson, R. C. (1984). How many words are there in printed school English. *Reading Research Quarterly, 19*(3), 304–330.

Nagy, W. E., Herman, P. A., & Anderson, R. C. (1985). Learning words from context. *Reading Research Quarterly, 20*(2), 233–253.

Nagy, W. E., & Scott, J. A. (2000). Vocabulary processes. In M. L. Kamil, P. Mosenthal, P. D. Pearson, & R. Barr (Eds.), *Handbook of reading research* (Vol. 3, pp. 269–284). Mahwah, NJ: Erlbaum.

Nation, K. (2005). Children's reading comprehension difficulties. In M. J. Snowling & C. Hulme (Eds.), *The science of reading* (pp. 248–265). Oxford, UK: Blackwell.

Nation, K. (2008a). Learning to read words. *Quarterly Journal of Experimental Psychology, 61*(8), 1121–1133.

Nation, K. (2008b). Using eye-movements to investigate developmental language disorders. In C. F. Norbury, J. B. Tomblin & D. V. M. Bishop (Eds.), *Understanding developmental language disorders* (pp. 39–52). Hove, UK: Psychology Press.

Nation, K., Adams, J. W., Bowyer-Crane, C. A., & Snowling, M. J. (1999). Working memory deficits in poor comprehenders reflect underlying language impairments. *Journal of Experimental Child Psychology, 73*(2), 139–158.

Nation, K., Clarke, P., Marshall, C. M., & Durand, M. (2004). Hidden language impairments in children: Parallels between poor reading comprehension and specific language impairment. *Journal of Speech, Language and Hearing Research, 47*, 199–211.

Nation, K., Marshall, C. M., & Altmann, G. T. M. (2003). Investigating individual differences in children's real-time sentence comprehension using language-mediated eye movements. *Journal of Experimental Child Psychology, 86*, 314–329.

Nation, K., Marshall, C. M., & Snowling, M. J. (2001). Phonological and semantic contributions to children's picture naming skill: Evidence from children with developmental reading disorders. *Language and Cognitive Processes, 16*(2–3), 241–259.

Nation, K., & Snowling, M. (1997). Assessing reading difficulties: The validity and utility of current measures of reading skill. *British Journal of Educational Psychology, 67*(3), 359–370.

Nation, K., & Snowling, M. J. (1998). Semantic processing and the development of word-recognition skills: Evidence from children with reading comprehension difficulties. *Journal of Memory and Language, 39*(1), 85–101.

Nation, K., & Snowling, M. J. (1999). Developmental differences in sensitivity to semantic relations among good and poor comprehenders: Evidence from semantic priming. *Cognition, 70*(1), B1–13.

Nation, K., Snowling, M. J., & Clarke, P. (2007). Dissecting the relationship between language skills and learning to read: Semantic and phonological contributions to new vocabulary learning in children with poor reading comprehension. *Advances in Speech Language Pathology, 9*(2), 131–139.

Oakhill, J. V. (1994). Individual differences in children's text comprehension. In M. A. Gernsbacher (Ed.), *Handbook of psycholinguistics* (pp. 821–848). San Diego, CA: Academic Press.

Perfetti, C. A. (1985). *Reading ability*. New York: Oxford University Press.

Perfetti, C. (2007). Reading ability: Lexical quality to comprehension. *Scientific Studies of Reading, 11*(4), 357–383.

Perfetti, C. A., Landi, N., & Oakhill, J. (2005). The acquisition of reading comprehension skill. In M. J. Snowling & C. Hulme (Eds.), *The science of reading* (pp. 227–247). Oxford, UK: Blackwell.

Perfetti, C. A., Wlotko, E. W., & Hart, L. A. (2005). Word learning and individual differences in word learning reflected in event-related potentials. *Journal of Experimental Psychology: Learning, Memory, and Cognition, 31*, 1281–1292.

Plaut, D. C., McClelland, J. L., Seidenberg, M. S., & Patterson, K. (1996). Understanding normal and impaired word reading: Computational principles in quasi-regular domains. *Psychological Review, 103*, 56–115.

Rapp, D. N., van den Broek, P., McMaster, K. L., Kendeou, P., & Espin, C. A. (2007). Higher-order comprehension processes in struggling readers: A perspective for research and intervention. *Scientific Studies of Reading, 11*(4), 289–312.

Rayner, K. (1998). Eye movements in reading and information processing: 20 years of research. *Psychological Bulletin, 124*, 372–422.

Ricketts, J., Bishop, D. V. M., & Nation, K. (2008). Investigating orthographic and semantic aspects of word learning in poor comprehenders. *Journal of Research in Reading, 31*, 117–135.

Ricketts, J., Nation, K., & Bishop, D. V. M. (2007). Vocabulary is important for some, but not all reading skills. *Scientific Studies of Reading, 11*(3), 235–257.

Seigneuric, A., & Ehrlich, M. F. (2005). Contribution of working memory capacity to children's reading comprehension. *Reading and Writing, 18*, 617–656.

Shankweiler, D., Lundquist, E., Katz, L., Stuebing, K. K., Fletcher, J. M., Brady, S., et al. (1999). Comprehension and decoding: Patterns of association in children with reading difficulties. *Scientific Studies of Reading, 3*, 69–94.

Sternberg, R. J., & Powell, J. S. (1983). Comprehending verbal comprehension. *American Psychologist, 38*, 878–893.

Stothard, S. E., & Hulme, C. (1992). Reading comprehension difficulties in children—The role of language comprehension and working memory skills. *Reading and Writing, 4*(3), 245–256.

Stothard, S. E., & Hulme, C. (1995). A comparison of phonological skills in children with reading comprehension difficulties and children with decoding difficulties. *Journal of Child Psychology and Psychiatry and Allied Disciplines, 36*(3), 399–408.

Tanenhaus, M. K., Spivey-Knowlton, M. J., Eberhard, K. M., & Sedivy, J. C. (1995). Integration of visual and linguistic information in spoken language comprehension. *Science, 268*(5217), 1632–1634.

Tannenbaum, K. R., Torgesen, J. K., & Wagner, R. K. (2006). Relationships between word knowledge and reading comprehension in third-grade children. *Scientific Studies of Reading, 10*(4), 381–398.

Thorndike, R. L. (1973). *Reading comprehension education in fifteen countries.* New York: Wiley.

Tomasello, M. (2003). *Constructing a language: A usage-based theory of language acquisition.* Cambridge, UK: Cambridge University Press.

Torgesen, J. K., Wagner, R. K., Rashotte, C. A., Burgess, S. R., & Hecht, S. A. (1997). Contributions of phonological awareness and rapid automatic naming ability to the growth of word-reading skills in second- to fifth-grade children. *Scientific Studies of Reading, 1*, 161–185.

Van den Broek, P. (1994). Comprehension and memory of narrative texts: Inferences and coherence. In M. A. Gernsbacher (Ed.), *Handbook of psycholinguistics* (pp. 539–588). San Diego, CA: Academic Press.

Wiig, E. H., & Secord, W. (1992). *Test of Word Knowledge.* Austin, TX: Psychological Corporation.

Yuill, N., & Oakhill, J. V. (1991). *Children's problems in text comprehension.* Cambridge, UK: Cambridge University Press.

Yuill, N., Oakhill, J., & Parkin, A. (1989). Working memory, comprehension ability and the resolution of text anomaly. *British Journal of Psychology, 80*, 351–361.

9

Examining the Decision Reliability and Validity of Three Reading Fluency Measures for Predicting Outcomes on Statewide Reading Accountability Tests

Jose M. Castillo, Joseph K. Torgesen,
Kelly A. Powell-Smith, *and* Stephanie Al-Otaiba

In our increasingly educated and technologically advanced society, good reading skills have become essential. However, according to the 2001 American Management Association Survey on Workplace Testing, 34.1% of applicants tested by respondent firms lacked the basic reading skills necessary for the jobs they sought. Of the firms that responded to this survey, 84.6% did not hire skill-deficient applicants (American Management Association, 2001). Yet far too many students lack basic reading skills. Of the nations' fourth graders, 36% performed below the basic level on the National Assessment of Educational Progress. For minority students, the statistics are even worse: 59% of African American students and 58% of Hispanic students performed below basic (Grigg, Donahue, & Dion, 2007). These data provide clear evidence that immediate and intensive intervention is needed to prevent the emergence of reading difficulties and their associated detrimental consequences. Compounding the problem of large numbers of children experiencing reading failure is the fact that research has shown that

children who get off to a poor start in reading almost always continue
to be poor readers (Francis, Shaywitz, Stuebing, Shaywitz, & Fletcher,
1994; Good, Simmons, & Smith, 1998; Juel, 1988; Torgesen & Burgess,
1998).

In light of this research, recent legislation was passed to address
the reading crisis facing our nation. For example, a goal of the No Child
Left Behind Act (NCLB; 2002) is for all children to read at grade level
by the end of third grade starting in 2013. To document improvements
in reading outcomes, statewide tests are required each year from third
to eighth grades. State-mandated reading measures used for accountability purposes have primarily assessed reading comprehension skills.
These outcome assessments are used in some states to grade schools
and retain students who score below a specified performance criterion.
The first "high-stakes" outcome measures are usually administered in
third grade.

Demonstrating reading proficiency requires students to begin
acquiring and integrating myriad skills and strategies (National Institute of Child Health and Human Development, 2000) years before the
administration of statewide assessments. Differences in the language
development, exposure to text, background knowledge, development
of phonemic awareness, and decoding skills, among others, necessitate
that educators use techniques that identify students at risk for reading
difficulties as early as possible so that instruction can be matched to
their needs. It is this need that led us to design and conduct the study
that is described in this chapter. First, the rationale for the development
and use of efficient early identification measures is described in more
detail. Next, the measures examined and how their utility was investigated are discussed. Finally, we present the results of the study and
some potential implications for research and practice.

RATIONALE FOR EFFICIENT
EARLY IDENTIFICATION MEASURES

The development of reliable, efficient, and valid measures for early
identification and prevention of reading difficulties is critical because
of the timing of administration and importance placed on statewide accountability tests (Buly & Valencia, 2002; Good, Simmons, &
Kame'enui, 2001). Early identification measures must be reliable and
valid indicators of early reading growth. Such measures must be efficient, easy to use, dynamic (i.e., sensitive to small changes in perfor-

mance), as well as predictive of reading comprehension skills to be of greatest use in assisting educators in preventing future reading difficulties. One method for early identification that has been examined by researchers is reading fluency.

Types of Reading Fluency Measures

A widely accepted way to measure reading fluency is words read correctly per minute in connected text (i.e., oral reading fluency; ORF). Typically, ORF measures are administered beginning in first grade. Importantly, ORF measures are efficient, easy to use, dynamic, reliable, and valid. Researchers have demonstrated that oral reading rate and accuracy are reliable indicators of overall reading ability (Deno, Marston, Shinn, & Tindal, 1983; Deno, Mirkin, & Chiang, 1982). Measures of ORF, like Reading Curriculum-Based Measurement (R-CBM) (Deno, 1985; Marston, 1989; Shinn, 1989, 2002), have been well established as technically adequate and useful for ongoing progress monitoring for more than 30 years (Hasbrouk & Tindal, 1992; Shinn, 1989; Shinn, Good, Knutson, Tilly, & Collins, 1992).

A large body of research has documented the technical adequacy of R-CBM (see Marston, 1989, for details). In fact, ORF measures like R-CBM are highly correlated with reading comprehension, with most correlations ranging from .73 to .91 in elementary school (e.g., Fuchs, Fuchs, & Maxwell, 1988; Shinn et al., 1992; Hintze, Shapiro, Conte, & Basile, 1997; Fuchs, Fuchs, Hosp, & Jenkins, 2001). The well-documented relationship between ORF and reading comprehension provides strong evidence supporting the use of ORF as an indicator of overall reading development. Notably, the technical qualities of ORF hold true whether the probes are pulled directly from a specific curriculum or not (i.e., are generic; Fuchs & Deno, 1994; Henson & Powell-Smith, 2007; Powell-Smith & Bradley-Klug, 2001). One example of a set of widely used generic ORF probes is the Dynamic Indicators of Basic Early Literacy Skills (DIBELS; Good & Kaminski, 2001; Kaminski, Cummings, Powell-Smith, & Good, 2008).

A second way in which oral reading fluency is measured is through word lists. Word lists are used to measure context-free fluency, or the fluency with which students read a list of printed words. Some researchers have argued that list fluency measures may not be as strongly related to reading comprehension outcomes as oral reading fluency measures (Perfetti, 1995). Fuchs et al. (2001) and Jenkins, Fuchs, van der Broek, Espin, and Deno (2003) reported a correlation of .83 between text fluency (i.e., R-CBM) and reading comprehension, whereas the correlation between list fluency and reading comprehension was .53.

However, one potential limitation to the findings reported by Fuchs et al. (2001) and Jenkins et al. (2003) is that the words on the list fluency measure were at the same level of difficulty, which may have artificially limited the range of individual differences on the test. In fact, Torgesen, Wagner, and Rashotte (1999) have reported higher correlations with reading comprehension measures using the Test of Word Reading Efficiency (TOWRE). These correlations ranged from .50 to .87, with most correlations above .75. The TOWRE measures the fluency with which children read words in lists that increase gradually in difficulty. Such a measure is potentially useful for screening, pre–post testing, and progress monitoring.

Despite the attractive qualities of measuring reading fluency using ORF probes and word lists, one drawback does exist: the potential for inefficiency. These measures require individual administration. When time for instructions and transition are taken into account, administration of these measures may take 3 to 5 minutes per student. Teachers must find ways to manage their classrooms while they complete the assessment. Thus, the seemingly simple administration of a 45-second to 1-minute assessment can become an arduous task when teachers attempt to screen large numbers of their students.

To improve efficiency when screening a large number of students, group-administered measures of reading fluency have been developed. In this study, we used an experimental version of the Test of Critical Early Reading Skills (TOCERS; Torgesen & DeGraff, 2002), which is a group-administered fluency measure. The TOCERS is one subtest within a battery of group-administered tests designed to monitor early reading development. When administering the TOCERS, each student receives a form with five lists composed of real and nonreal words. The student's task is to go through each list and mark as many real words as possible in 90 seconds.

Notably, the link between a brief group-administered measure of fluency, like the TOCERS, and reading comprehension has not been validated. In addition to uncertain criterion validity, group measures of reading fluency have other drawbacks. Student performance on these measures may be less reliable than student performance on individual administrations, particularly at lower grade levels. For example, a student may lose concentration, causing the obtained score to be an inaccurate estimate of the child's true skill. In addition, the utility of these measures for intervention planning may be limited. For instance, if a child performs poorly on a group-administered test, the teacher will have little, if any, qualitative information about why performance was low. Another potential problem is related to face validity. It is possible that a concern may be raised regarding the task demands (e.g., crossing off real words on a page) being somewhat removed from the more authentic demands of reading connected text.

Evaluating Reading Fluency Measures

Although examining the relationship between measures of reading fluency and tests of reading comprehension is important when considering decision validity, correlations should not be used as the sole criterion for validating fluency measures. Decision validity refers to the appropriateness of using assessment data for a specific decision purpose. According to Barnett, Macmann, and Carey (1992), both conceptual and empirical evidence should be examined when the decision validity of an assessment procedure is the concern. Therefore, researchers interested in the utility of reading fluency measures also should examine the diagnostic efficiency of the measures for correctly classifying outcomes on tests of reading comprehension.

McGlinchey and Hixson (2004) examined the decision validity of DIBELS ORF probes for predicting outcomes on the Michigan Assessment of Educational Performance (MEAP), Michigan's statewide reading assessment relative to NCLB. The MEAP is administered to students in the spring of fourth grade in Michigan schools. Over an 8-year period, DIBELS ORF probes were administered to fourth-grade students at three points during the school year: once each in the fall, winter, and spring. While examining the decision validity of the probes, the authors found moderate to moderately strong correlations between DIBELS ORF and the MEAP. The authors also found that the proportions of students identified by the DIBELS ORF probes as likely to pass or fail the MEAP were above the passing and failure base rates, respectively, in the sample. Overall, DIBELS ORF correctly classified student outcomes at a rate significantly above chance. Thus, the moderate to moderately strong correlations and diagnostic efficiency of DIBELS ORF probes provided evidence for the decision validity of the measure.

Although previous research has examined the decision validity of ORF for predicting outcomes on statewide assessments (McGlinchey & Hixson, 2004), little research on the decision validity of alternate measures of reading fluency (i.e., list and group fluency measures) has been conducted. Thus, we do not know whether the relationship between the alternate fluency measures and reading comprehension tests and the diagnostic efficiency of the alternate measures for classifying outcomes on statewide reading assessments are strong enough to warrant consideration. Another question to be examined is whether the administration of various fluency measures leads to different screening decisions. Barnett and MacMann (1992) referred to this comparison of screening decisions as decision reliability. Decision reliability is defined as the "consistency of classifications or other socially important outcomes across such factors as alternative assessment instruments, methods, raters, and occasions of measurement" (Barnett & MacMann, 1992, p. 432). What is of primary interest here is whether the same students would be identified as at risk by the various fluency measures.

Because of conflicting findings in the literature regarding list fluency's relationship with reading comprehension, the need for efficiency in schools, and the emergence of group fluency measures, research examining the decision reliability and validity of various types of reading fluency measures is needed. To begin addressing this need, we asked the following questions:

1. How are ORF, list fluency, and group fluency measures differentially related to reading comprehension?
2. How efficient are the measures at classifying student outcomes on statewide reading assessments?
3. To what extent are the screening decisions for the three types of reading fluency measures different?

What follows is a description of the methods we used to address the three questions, including the participants sampled, reading fluency measures and statewide assessments used, and the administration and data analysis procedures utilized.

METHODS

Participants

The study was conducted in two elementary schools in a small city in the Southeast United States. We selected the two schools because they varied in ethnic and socioeconomic diversity and recruited first, second, and third graders to participate. Students from school 1 were recruited through a larger research project occurring at the school, while letters requesting permission were sent home to the parents of the students from school 2. At school 1 (n = 38 first graders, 42 second graders, and 42 third graders), approximately 5% of the students were Caucasian, while the remaining 95% were predominantly African American. Eighty-three percent of the students at this school were eligible for free or reduced lunch. Conversely, at school 2 (n = 53, 48, and 59 first, second, and third graders, respectively), approximately 79% of the students were Caucasian, while the remaining 21% were of Asian American, Hispanic, or African American descent, and only 9% were eligible to receive free or reduced lunch. The participants were selected from all students attending the schools because we wanted to obtain a sample with a full range of reading ability. Thus, data from the two schools were aggregated to achieve a sample that was heterogeneous in terms of socioeconomic status and ethnicity. A total of 91 first graders, 90 second graders, and 101 third graders participated.

Measures

©DIBELS ORF—Fifth Edition

The DIBELS ORF (fifth edition; Good & Kaminski, 2001). This measure, which is similar to R-CBM (Deno, 1985; Shinn, 1989), consists of grade-level generic reading passages. Students typically are administered three passages and the median score is used. Each student is assessed individually according to standardized procedures. The measures are scored by counting the number of words read correctly in 1 min. Words considered to be read correctly are those read correctly within the context of the sentence. Hesitations of 3-second omissions, and mispronunciations are scored as incorrect. Passages in this study were administered to all participants using standardized DIBELS ORF procedures.

    The DIBELS ORF measure has demonstrated reliability and validity for its intended purposes. Alternate-form reliability coefficients range from .89 to .96, with a median of .94 (Good, Kaminski, Smith, & Bratten, 2008). Concurrent validity data with the Test of Oral Reading Fluency yielded coefficients ranging from .92 to .96, with a median of .95 (Good et al., 2008). Notably, research consistently has shown that ORF is an accurate predictor of outcomes on statewide reading assessments (e.g., Barger, 2003; Buck & Torgesen, 2003; Good, Simmons, & Kame'enui, 2001; Shapiro, Keller, Lutz, Santoro, & Hintze, 2006; Shaw & Shaw, 2002; Van der Meer, Lentz, & Stollar, 2005).

TOWRE—Sight Word Efficiency

This TOWRE Sight Word Efficiency subtest consists of a list of real printed words administered to each student individually. Each student is provided with a practice list that contains several real words. After reading from this list, each student has 45 seconds to read as many words as possible aloud from the test list. A valid response includes any word read correctly. Any word pronounced incorrectly is marked with a slash. In addition, a hesitation of 3 seconds counts as an incorrect response. Examiners score this measure by counting the total number of words read correctly in 45 seconds. Research has demonstrated high levels of reliability for the measure. For the 6- to 9-year age group, a test–retest reliability coefficient of .97 and alternate-form reliability coefficients ranging from .93 to .97 have been reported (Torgesen et al., 1999). Standardized administration and scoring procedures were followed during this study (Torgesen, et al., 1999).

TOCERS Real and Nonreal Word Lists

The TOCERS Real and Nonreal Word Lists subtest is an experimental group-administered measure that consists of a form with five lists of both real and nonreal words. Each student receives a practice form and is asked to complete it. The class receives 30 seconds to mark as many real words as possible on this short list and is then shown the correct responses. Following this demonstration, the students are told to begin the test. The students have 90 seconds to mark as many real words as possible on the form. A correct response includes any real words marked with a slash. The score for the TOCERS is calculated by examining each column separately. The score in each column is the total number of real words marked correctly minus nonwords marked incorrectly times the ratio of real to nonreal words in that column. The scores for each column are then added together to obtain the total score. Relatively high reliability coefficients have been found for this measure. Alternate-form reliability coefficients of .85 in first grade, .91 in second grade, and .93 in third grade have been demonstrated (Torgesen & DeGraff, 2002). Standardized administration and scoring procedures were followed during this study (Torgesen & DeGraff, 2002).

Stanford Achievement Test—Ninth Edition (SAT-9)

First- and second-grade students in the study received the SAT-9. This is a published norm-referenced test that primarily assesses reading comprehension. Many school districts in the state of Florida used the measure to track the progress of its first- and second-grade students before the release of the 10th edition of the Stanford Achievement Test series. The series has a demonstrated history of high technical quality (Wisconsin Center for Education Research, n.d.). Scores were reported as scale scores and percentiles.

Florida Comprehensive Assessment Test—Sunshine State Standards (FCAT SSS)

The FCAT SSS was administered to the third-grade students in the study. The subtest is one of two that is administered from the FCAT to assess reading outcomes in third grade. The FCAT SSS is a criterion-referenced measure of reading comprehension that is used to help determine the extent to which students are meeting the reading objectives set forth by the Florida Department of Education. It is Florida's statewide assessment relative to NCLB. Standard scores and achievement levels were reported. Reliability indices for the FCAT exceed .90. Concurrent validity estimates range from .70 to .81 (Florida Department of Education, 2004).

Examiner Training and Reading Fluency Measure Administration Procedures

Four upper-division undergraduate psychology majors and one upper-division undergraduate education major administered and scored the measures. Two sessions were held to train the five examiners to administer and score the individual measures. The first training session occurred 2 weeks before testing and took approximately 2 hours to complete. During this session, the examiners were trained on testing procedures and administration and scoring rules. The examiners also practiced administering and scoring the measures until all examiners met a 100% criterion of scoring accuracy. The fluency with which each of three modeled passages was read was varied. The examiners scored each modeled passage and discussed differences from the trainer's template. Finally, several passages were read to the examiners, who scored them until each of them reached a 100% accuracy criterion. A second training session, 1 hour in length, occurred 1 week before testing began. Testing procedures and administration and scoring rules were reviewed. Also, the examiners received additional practice.

Joseph K. Torgesen, one of the authors of the TOCERS, trained one of the examiners to administer and score the measure. A 30-minute training session provided instruction on the standardized administration and scoring procedures for the measure. The examiner was told to read the directions printed on the examiner copy of the test booklet and to use the template provided to score the protocols. At the conclusion of the session, the examiner received the test booklets, including the standardized directions and scoring templates, for the TOCERS.

The examiners administered the three reading fluency measures to all participants. Both forms A and B of the TOWRE and TOCERS were used. The DIBELS ORF benchmark passages for end-of-year monitoring in each grade level were administered. The participants were tested with all of the reading fluency measures in May, approximately 1 month after administration of the SAT-9 and FCAT SSS. The examiners gave the group-administered and individual tests to each participant in two sessions. During the group testing, each class was administered forms A and B of the TOCERS. During individual testing, the examiners administered TOWRE forms A and B and the three DIBELS ORF probes to the students.

Group testing occurred within the participants' classrooms at both schools. Individual testing occurred within the media center at school 1. At school 2, individual testing occurred within two empty classrooms. One examiner scored along with another examiner for approximately 10% of the participants to calculate interscorer reliability for the individually administered measures. For each DIBELS ORF passage and TOWRE form, the number of words read correctly was used to calculate interscorer correlations. Interscorer reliability for the DIBELS and the TOWRE was high, with reliability coefficients exceeding .99.

Data–Analytic Procedures

In all the analyses we conducted, the score used for the DIBELS passages was the median of the three passages. Similarly, the mean of forms A and B for each participant formed the score for the alternate measures of reading fluency (i.e., the TOWRE and TOCERS).

We began examining the decision validity of the different types of reading fluency measures by conducting correlational analyses across grade levels. Correlations between each of the reading fluency measures and the tests of reading comprehension described previously were derived. Next, we compared the correlations in a pairwise fashion using a test for dependent r's to determine whether the differences were statistically significant (Steiger, 1980). We used a Bonferoni adjustment to control for Type I error. We divided the alpha level of .05 by the number of analyses conducted to reduce the chance that statistically significant results would be found by chance. Because nine pairwise comparisons were made across the three grade levels, we used an alpha level of .006 to determine whether a significant difference existed. Finally, we examined the pairwise comparisons to determine which fluency measure(s) had the strongest relationship with the tests of reading comprehension.

To address the diagnostic efficiency of the reading fluency measures (the second component of our decision validity analysis), we conducted two analyses per grade level. First, the diagnostic efficiency of the measures for identifying students significantly at risk for failing the statewide assessments was examined. Any student who scored at or below the 20th percentile in the sample for each of the fluency measures was identified as significantly at risk. Second, we examined the diagnostic efficiency of the fluency measures for identifying students at risk for performing below grade level. Any student who scored below the 40th percentile in the sample for each of the measures was identified as at risk for scoring below grade level on the statewide assessment. We chose at or below the 20th percentile and below the 40th percentile because they typically are used to identify significant risk and grade-level performance, respectively (J. K. Torgesen, personal communication, 2005).

In first and second grades, we compared screening decisions to outcomes on the SAT-9. We used the SAT-9 percentiles obtained from the schools as the marker for student outcomes on the statewide reading assessment. The same approach and rationale just described were used to establish cutoffs for the statewide assessment. Scores at or below the 20th percentile were considered failing, and scores below the 40th percentile were considered below grade-level performance. For third grade, we compared the screening decisions with outcomes on the FCAT SSS. We used the achievement levels derived from the FCAT SSS in the analyses. A score within the level 1 range corresponded with below basic performance and was considered failing by the state of Florida. An achievement level of 2 corresponded with basic performance and was the lowest passing score. Achievement levels 3, 4, and 5 corresponded with grade-level performance (Florida Department of Education, 2002).

Six statistical indices were used to determine the diagnostic efficiency of each of the measures:

1. Sensitivity: Of individuals *who truly have poor reading skills* (TP; students who perform below the score cut point on the state-

wide assessment), what proportion are identified as having reading difficulties (or at risk for reading difficulties) by the screening test? Sensitivity is represented by the following formula (TP = true positive; FN = false negative):

$$\frac{TP}{TP + FN}$$

2. Specificity: Of individuals *who truly do not have poor reading skills* (*TN*; students who perform above the score cut point for the statewide assessment), what proportion are identified as not having reading difficulties (or are screened as not at risk) on the screening test? Specificity is represented by the following formula (TN = true negative; FP = false positive):

$$\frac{TN}{FP + TN}$$

3. Positive predictive power (PPP) is the ratio of true positives (i.e., those who truly have poor reading skills) compared with all positives (e.g., TP/TP + FP).
4. Negative predictive power (NPP) is the ratio of true negatives (i.e., those who truly do not have poor reading skills) compared with all negatives (e.g., TN/TN + FN).
5. Overall correct classification (OCC) is the proportion of agreement between the screening decisions and outcomes on the statewide assessment.
6. Cohen's (1960) kappa is the degree to which the reading fluency measures correctly classified statewide reading assessment outcomes significantly above chance.

To address the decision reliability of the measures, we compared the screening decisions made by each of the measures across individual students. Across grade levels and performance criteria on the statewide assessments, the percentage of identical screening decisions was calculated and compared in a pairwise fashion. Thus, we compared the number of identical screening decisions across individual students for the DIBELS and TOWRE, the DIBELS and TOCERS, and the TOWRE and TOCERS. This analysis provides practical information on the degree to which the fluency measures would typically identify similar students as at risk.

RESULTS

Data obtained from each participating school were combined when conducting the analyses examining the decision validity and reliability of the fluency measures. Scores on the measures indicated that, as a group, the students in the sample performed slightly above average. For example, on average, participants in the study scored above the DIBELS benchmarks and the mean standard score for the TOWRE in all three grade levels examined. Table 9.1 includes the descriptive statistics for each of the fluency and comprehension measures.

TABLE 9.1. Descriptive and Inferential Statistics across Grades

Statistic	Grade 1[a]	Grade 2[b]	Grade 3[c]
Descriptives[d]			
SAT-9 and FCAT SSS	580.10 (55.09)	621.60 (51.29)	321.50 (72.92)
DIBELS	76.91 (33.49)	114.06 (42.62)	139.78 (40.99)
TOWRE	46.35 (12.97)	58.91 (12.44)	64.57 (9.89)
TOCERS	41.54 (14.35)	44.20 (14.42)	48.18 (11.20)
Correlation (r)[e]			
DIBELS * SAT-9/FCAT SSS	.78**	.78**	.64**
TOWRE * SAT-9/FCAT SSS	.78**	.62**	.45**
TOCERS * SAT-9/FCAT SSS	.49**	.53**	.24*
z scores for tests of differences between r's[f]			
DIBELS versus TOWRE	0.45	3.59***	3.91***
DIBELS versus TOCERS	4.26***	3.99***	4.15***
TOWRE versus TOCERS	4.68***	1.26	2.19*

Note. SAT-9, Stanford Achievement Test—Form 9 (Wisconsin Center for Educational Research, n.d.); FCAT SSS, Florida Comprehensive Assessment Test—Sunshine State Standards (Florida Department of Education, 2004); DIBELS, Dynamic Indicators of Basic Early Literacy Skills (Good & Kaminski, 2001); TOWRE, Test of Word Reading Efficiency (Torgesen et al., 1999); TOCERS, Test of Critical Early Literacy Skills (Torgesen & DeGraff, 2002).

[a]The SAT-9 was administered as the statewide assessment; $n = 91$.

[b]The SAT-9 was administered as the statewide assessment; $n = 90$.

[c]The FCAT SSS was administered as the statewide assessment; $n = 101$.

[d]Values represent means, with standard deviation in parentheses.

[e]Correlation is between the fluency measure and the statewide assessment administered.

[f]z scores were calculated by comparing the correlation between one fluency measure and the statewide assessment and another fluency measure and the statewide assessment.

*$p < .05$; **$p < .01$; ***$p < .001$.

Decision Validity

Relationship between Reading Fluency and Reading Comprehension Tests

Correlations among the reading fluency and reading comprehension tests, as well as the z values from the test of dependent r's are reported by grade level in Table 9.1. Correlations for all the fluency measures with the tests of reading comprehension were significant across grade levels. Across grades, the DIBELS ORF produced moderately strong correlations, the TOWRE moderate to moderately strong correlations, and the TOCERS low to moderate correlations with the tests of reading comprehension. The correlation coefficients for each of the measures appeared to be lower in third grade than in first and second grades.

Next, we conducted tests for dependent r's to determine whether the measures were differentially related to the statewide tests of reading comprehension. For the first-grade sample, the TOCERS was significantly less correlated with the SAT-9 than were the other measures. When the correlation between the TOCERS and the SAT-9 was compared with those between the SAT-9 and the other measures, z values of 4.26 and 4.68 (p's < .001) were obtained. The comparison of correlation coefficients between the individually administered measures produced no significant differences.

For the sample of second- and third-grade students, DIBELS ORF produced the highest correlations with the tests of reading comprehension. When the correlation between DIBELS ORF and the SAT-9 was compared with those between the SAT-9 and the alternate measures in second grade, z values of 3.59 and 3.99 (p's < .001) were obtained. When the correlation between DIBELS ORF and the FCAT SSS was compared with those between the FCAT SSS and the alternate measures in third grade, z values of 3.91 and 4.15 (p's < .001) were obtained. The comparison of correlation coefficients between the alternate measures produced no significant differences in either grade.

Therefore, in regard to the relationships between the three types of reading fluency measures and the statewide reading assessments, DIBELS ORF produced higher correlation coefficients with the SAT-9 and FCAT SSS than the alternate measures for the second- and third-grade samples. No significant differences were found between the correlations for the alternate reading fluency measures in second and third grades. For the first-grade sample, the TOWRE was as highly correlated with the SAT-9 as DIBELS ORF. The TOCERS produced the lowest correlation with the SAT-9.

Diagnostic Efficiency

To further examine the decision validity of the reading fluency measures, we investigated diagnostic efficiency. The number of true positives, false positives, true negatives, and false negatives were used to calculate the diagnostic efficiency statistics for each measure. These raw data (i.e., the true positives, false positives, true negatives, and false negatives) for first grade used to identify significantly at-risk readers (i.e., a score at or below the 20th percentile) are presented in Table 9.2 as an example. The remaining raw data are available from Jose M. Castillo. The following diagnostic efficiency statistics were examined: sensitivity, specificity, PPP, NPP, and OCC. Cohen's (1960) kappa was calculated as well to determine whether the measures correctly classi-

TABLE 9.2. Number of True Positives, True Negatives, False Positives, and False Negatives When Screening for Students Significantly at Risk for Failure on the SAT-9

| Fluency measure | SAT-9 (20th percentile) | | |
	≤ 20th percentile	> 20th percentile	Total
DIBELS			
≤ 20th percentile	n = 4 a	n = 14 b	n = 18
> 20th percentile	n = 1 c	n = 72 d	n = 73
Total	n = 5	n = 86	N = 91
TOWRE			
≤ 20th percentile	n = 4 a	n = 14 b	n = 18
> 20th percentile	n = 1 c	n = 72 d	n = 73
Total	n = 5	n = 86	N = 91
TOCERS			
≤ 20th percentile	n = 3 a	n = 16 b	n = 19
> 20th percentile	n = 2 c	n = 70 d	n = 72
Total	n = 5	n = 86	N = 91

Note. Sensitivity = $a/(a + c)$; specificity = $d/(d + b)$; positive predictive power = $a/(a + b)$; failure base rate = $(a + c)/N$; negative predictive power = $d/(c + d)$; passing base rate = $(b + d)/N$; overall correct classifications = $(a + d)/N$. SAT-9, Stanford Achievement Test—Form 9 (Wisconsin Center for Educational Research, n.d.); DIBELS, Dynamic Indicators of Basic Early Literacy Skills (Good & Kaminski, 2001); TOWRE, Test of Word Reading Efficiency (Torgesen et al., 1999); TOCERS, Test of Critical Early Literacy Skills (Torgesen & DeGraff, 2002).

fied student outcomes at a rate significantly above chance. A summary of the diagnostic efficiency statistics for each measure in first, second, and third grades can be found in Tables 9.3, 9.4, and 9.5, respectively.

For DIBELS ORF, sensitivity estimates ranged from .64 to .94 across grade levels and performance criteria, with the majority of estimates exceeding .75. The measure's PPP ranged from .22 to .54, with the majority of the values exceeding .40. All PPP values exceeded the base rate of students who did not achieve the specified performance criterion in the sample. Specificity estimates ranged from .71 to .87, with the majority exceeding .75. NPP estimates ranged from .92 to .99. All NPP estimates exceeded the base rate of students who achieved or exceeded the performance criterion in the sample. OCC rates ranged from .73 to .86. Finally, Cohen's (1960) kappa estimates ranged from .29 to .49 (p's < .001), indicating that DIBELS ORF correctly classified students at rates ranging from 29 to 49% above chance.

For the TOWRE, sensitivity estimates ranged from .57 to .88 across grade levels and performance criteria. All sensitivity estimates in first and second grades exceeded .75, whereas the estimates in third grade were below .75. PPP estimates ranged from .22 to .49, with all values exceeding the base rate of students who failed to meet the specified performance criterion in the sample. Specificity estimates ranged from .68 to .87, with the majority exceeding .75. The measure's NPP ranged from .88 to .99. All NPP values exceeded the base rate of students who

TABLE 9.3. Diagnostic Efficiency Statistics for Three Reading Fluency Measures in First Grade

Measure	Sensitivity	Specificity	PPP	NPP	FBR	PBR	OCC	Kappa
		SAT-9 (20th percentile)						
DIBELS	.80	.84	.22	.99	.05	.95	.84	.29***
TOWRE	.80	.84	.22	.99	.05	.95	.84	.29***
TOCERS	.60	.81	.16	.97	.05	.95	.80	.18*
		SAT-9 (40th percentile)						
DIBELS	.78	.71	.40	.93	.20	.80	.73	.36***
TOWRE	.83	.71	.42	.95	.20	.80	.74	.40***
TOCERS	.61	.68	.32	.88	.20	.80	.67	.22*

Note. SAT-9, Stanford Achievement Test—Form 9 (Wisconsin Center for Educational Research, n.d.); DIBELS, Dynamic Indicators of Basic Early Literacy Skills (Good & Kaminski, 2001); TOWRE, Test of Word Reading Efficiency (Torgesen et al., 1999); TOCERS, Test of Critical Early Reading Skills (Torgesen & DeGraff, 2002); PPP, positive predictive power; NPP, negative predictive power; FBR, failure base rate; PBR, passing base rate; OCC, overall correct classifications.

*p < .05; ***p < .001.

TABLE 9.4. Diagnostic Efficiency Statistics for Three Reading Fluency Measures in Second Grade

Measure	Sensitivity	Specificity	PPP	NPP	FBR	PBR	OCC	Kappa
		SAT-9 (20th percentile)						
DIBELS	.88	.85	.37	.99	.09	.91	.86	.45***
TOWRE	.88	.87	.39	.99	.09	.91	.87	.47***
TOCERS	.75	.85	.33	.97	.09	.91	.84	.39***
		SAT-9 (40th percentile)						
DIBELS	.94	.73	.44	.98	.19	.81	.77	.47***
TOWRE	.76	.68	.36	.93	.19	.81	.70	.31***
TOCERS	.76	.68	.36	.93	.19	.81	.70	.31***

Note. SAT-9, Stanford Achievement Test—Form 9 (Wisconsin Center for Educational Research, n.d.); DIBELS, Dynamic Indicators of Basic Early Literacy Skills (Good & Kaminski, 2001); TOWRE, Test of Word Reading Efficiency (Torgesen et al., 1999); TOCERS, Test of Critical Early Reading Skills (Torgesen & DeGraff, 2002); PPP, positive predictive power; NPP, negative predictive power; FBR, failure base rate; PBR, passing base rate; OCC, overall correct classifications.

***p < .001.

met the specified performance criterion. OCC rates ranged from .70 to .87. Finally, Cohen's (1960) kappa estimates ranged from .29 to .47 (*p*'s < .001), indicating that the TOWRE correctly classified students at rates ranging from 29 to 47% above chance across grade levels.

For the TOCERS, sensitivity estimates ranged from .36 to .76, with the majority of the values exceeding .50. PPP estimates ranged from .16 to .36, with all values exceeding the base rate of students who did not achieve the specified performance criterion in the sample. The measure's specificity ranged from .64 to .85, with the majority exceeding .75. The NPP estimates ranged from .79 to .97. All NPP values exceeded the base rate of students who achieved or exceeded the specified performance criterion in the sample. OCC rates ranged from .60 to .84. Finally, Cohen's (1960) kappa estimates ranged from .18 to .39 (*p*'s < .05) in first and second grades. The kappa coefficients of .12 (*p* = .21) and .16 (*p* = .11) obtained in third grade were not statistically significant. Therefore, in first and second grades, the TOCERS correctly classified students at rates ranging from 21 to 39% above chance, while the measure's correct classification was not statistically significantly above chance in third grade.

Decision Reliability

To examine the decision reliability of the three fluency measures, we compared the screening decisions for each of the measures with the

TABLE 9.5. Diagnostic Efficiency Statistics for Three Reading Fluency Measures in Third Grade

Measure	Sensitivity	Specificity	PPP	NPP	FBR	PBR	OCC	Kappa
		FCAT SSS						
DIBELS	.64	.87	.45	.94	.14	.86	.84	.44***
TOWRE	.57	.85	.38	.92	.14	.86	.81	.34***
TOCERS	.36	.83	.25	.89	.14	.86	.76	.16
		FCAT SSS						
DIBELS	.81	.76	.54	.92	.26	.74	.77	.49***
TOWRE	.69	.75	.49	.88	.26	.74	.73	.39***
TOCERS	.50	.64	.33	.79	.26	.74	.60	.12

Note. FCAT SSS, Florida Comprehensive Assessment Test—Sunshine State Standards (Florida Department of Education, 2004); DIBELS, Dynamic Indicators of Basic Early Literacy Skills (Good & Kaminski, 2001); TOWRE, Test of Word Reading Efficiency (Torgesen et al., 1999); TOCERS, Test of Critical Early Reading Skills (Torgesen & DeGraff, 2002); PPP, positive predictive power; NPP, negative predictive power; FBR, failure base rate; PBR, passing base rate; OCC, overall correct classification.
***$p < .001$.

individual student as the unit of analysis. Table 9.6 contains the data for the percentage of agreements among the measures across grade levels and performance criteria. The percentage of agreements appeared to vary by comparison with the highest agreement between DIBELS ORF and the TOWRE. The measures agreed on a screening decision for approximately 84 to 96% of students across grade levels and performance criteria, with slightly higher agreement in first grade. The percentages of agreement among DIBELS ORF and TOCERS and the TOWRE and TOCERS were lower. Both comparisons yielded agreements ranging from approximately 63 to 81% of the time, with slightly lower agreement in third grade. Across all comparisons, the percentage of agreements was lower when screening for grade-level performance (i.e., the 40th percentile).

DISCUSSION

Our primary focus was related to the decision validity of the three reading fluency measures in terms of predicting outcomes on two school-administered tests of reading comprehension: the SAT-9 and FCAT SSS. Results of a correlational analysis revealed that the DIBELS ORF, TOWRE, and TOCERS produced moderately strong correlations, moderate to moderately strong correlations, and low to moderate cor-

TABLE 9.6. Percentage of Identical Screening Decisions among Reading Fluency Measures by Performance Criteria and Grade Level

Grade	20th percentile	40th percentile
Grade 1		
DIBELS TOWRE	95.60	92.31
DIBELS TOCERS	81.32	76.92
TOWRE TOCERS	81.32	80.22
Grade 2		
DIBELS TOWRE	87.78	84.44
DIBELS TOCERS	81.11	75.56
TOWRE TOCERS	82.22	73.33
Grade 3		
DIBELS TOWRE	91.09	84.16
DIBELS TOCERS	76.24	63.37
TOWRE TOCERS	79.21	63.37

Note. DIBELS, Dynamic Indicators of Basic Early Literacy Skills (Good & Kaminski, 2001); TOWRE, Test of Word Reading Efficiency (Torgesen et al., 1999); TOCERS, Test of Critical Early Reading Skills (Torgesen & DeGraff, 2002).

relations, respectively, across grade levels. DIBELS ORF produced the highest correlation coefficients in second and third grades, while both DIBELS ORF and the TOWRE produced the highest correlations in first grade. For each of the measures, the correlations with the tests of reading comprehension appeared lower in third grade than in first and second grades.

We also examined the diagnostic efficiency of the measures. DIBELS ORF produced the highest sensitivity and specificity estimates (most exceeded .75), followed by the TOWRE (many of the sensitivity and specificity estimates exceeded .75, but fewer estimates reached that level than the DIBELS), and then the TOCERS (some exceeded .75). PPP and NPP estimates for each of the measures exceeded the base rate of students who failed to achieve and achieved the specified performance criterion (e.g., significantly at risk, grade level), respectively. Kappa estimates indicated that the DIBELS ORF and TOWRE correctly classified students at rates statistically significantly above chance across all three grade levels. For the TOCERS, kappa estimates indicated that the measure correctly classified students at rates statistically significantly above chance in first and second grades but not in third grade.

Another analysis we conducted focused on the decision reliability of the three fluency measures. It appeared that the DIBELS ORF and TOWRE produced the highest percentages of agreement across grade levels and performance criteria. Little difference was observed between the other two comparisons (i.e., a comparison of the percentages of agreement between the DIBELS ORF and TOCERS and the TOWRE and TOCERS). Both individually administered measures agreed less often with the TOCERS, with slightly lower agreements found in third grade. Across all comparisons, the percentage of agreements was slightly lower when screening for grade-level performance.

The correlational and diagnostic efficiency findings for DIBELS ORF were consistent with prior findings. Correlations in first and second grades were consistent with the myriad studies demonstrating a strong relationship between R-CBM and reading comprehension (e.g., Deno et al., 1982; Fuchs et al., 1988, Shinn et al., 1992). Although the correlations between DIBELS ORF and the FCAT SSS in third grade were slightly lower than the .73 to .91 reported in the aforementioned seminal studies, they were consistent with those reported for other statewide assessments (Schatsneider, Torgeson, Buck, & Powell-Smith, 2004; Shapiro, Edwards, Lutz, & Keller, 2004).

The diagnostic efficiency statistics were largely consistent with those reported by previous research as well (McGlinchey & Hixson, 2004), with the exception of the PPP estimates. PPP estimates ranged from .22 to .54 across grade levels, which were below that reported for DIBELS ORF by McGlinchey and Hixson (2004). However, these lower estimates appear to be a result of the lower base rate of students who performed below the performance criteria in the sample. According to Streiner (2003), as the prevalence of a problem drops within the population, the PPP of the screening instrument decreases, whereas the proportion of false-positive results increases. In the McGlinchey and Hixson study, the base rate of not achieving a satisfactory score was 54%, while the base rates in the current study ranged from 5 to 26%. Therefore, the lower PPP estimates in the current study may be attributed to the lower base rate of students who did not achieve a satisfactory score. Despite the lower estimates, all PPP estimates exceeded the base rate of students who scored below the performance criteria. In addition, the DIBELS ORF accurate classifications of approximately 75 to 86% of student outcomes across grade levels and performance criteria were significantly above chance. Kappa estimates were similar to those reported by McGlinchey and Hixson. Therefore, our findings corroborate the finding that oral reading fluency probes are valid indicators of reading fluency *and* reading comprehension.

With respect to the correlations between list fluency and reading comprehension, the findings in this study differed slightly from those reported by Fuchs et al. (2001) and Jenkins et al. (2003). Correlations in this study appeared higher at first and second grades. In fact, correlations between DIBELS ORF and the SAT-9 and the TOWRE and the SAT-9 were not statistically significantly different in first grade. However, the correlation obtained between the TOWRE and the FCAT SSS in third grade was similar to the list fluency correlation reported by previous research.

One potential hypothesis for this finding involves other subcomponents besides word recognition that Perfetti (1995) suggested can become automatized (e.g., integrating propositions within text and within background knowledge, inferencing). Because first-grade students typically do not start reading connected text until the winter of first grade (Good et al., 1998), it is plausible that these students have not had the practice opportunities for the additional subcomponents to become automatized by the end of the year. The differences among the correlations between DIBELS ORF and the reading comprehension measures and the TOWRE and the reading comprehension measures in second and third grades provide potential support for this hypothesis. Thus, the correlational data from second and third grades are more consistent with the findings from Fuchs et al. (2001), Jenkins et al. (2003), and Perfetti (1995).

Despite the lower correlations in second and third grades, the diagnostic efficiency statistics for the TOWRE indicated an improvement in the accuracy of student outcomes classification over what would be expected by chance. The majority of sensitivity and specificity estimates exceeded .75, while all PPP and NPP estimates exceeded the base rate of students who failed to achieve or achieved the performance criteria, respectively. Once again, the high proportion of false-positive results was likely impacted by the low base rates of students not achieving a satisfactory score in the sample (Streiner, 2003). In addition, the list fluency measure's accurate classifications of approximately 70 to 87% of student outcomes across grade levels and performance criteria were significantly above chance, with kappa coefficients similar to those reported for DIBELS ORF. Across grade levels, the TOWRE produced high percentages of identical screening decisions with the DIBELS ORF as well. Thus, the moderate to moderately strong correlations and improvements in student outcomes classifications indicate that the TOWRE may be a valid indicator of performance on statewide reading assessments. The strongest case for the TOWRE may be in first grade; however, because the correlations and diagnostic efficiency statistics were the most similar to the DIBELS ORF probes. These results are also consistent with the work of Perfetti (1995).

The findings for the TOCERS were mixed regarding its relationship with reading comprehension and diagnostic efficiency. In first and second grades, the TOCERS produced correlations within the moderate range with the SAT-9. However, the measure produced low correlations with the FCAT SSS in third grade. Across grade levels, the TOCERS was less correlated with the tests of reading comprehension than the DIBELS ORF probes.

Regarding the diagnostic efficiency of the TOCERS, many of the sensitivity and specificity estimates were below .75. However, all PPP and NPP estimates exceeded the base rate of students who failed to achieve and achieved satisfactory scores, respectively. The PPP estimates for the TOCERS were also lower than might be expected given the low base rate of students scoring unsatisfactorily. The measure's rate of correct classifications seemed to be consistent with the correlational analysis. In first and second grades, the TOCERS correctly classified students at rates significantly above chance. In third grade, the group fluency measure's rates of correct classification were not significantly above chance. In addition, the proportion of identical screening decisions among the TOCERS and the individually administered measures appeared to be lower than the proportion of identical screening decisions between the DIBELS ORF and the TOWRE. These results suggest that the TOCERS may not be as valid an indicator of reading comprehension performance as the other fluency measures examined in this study. However, the moderate correlations and improvements in student outcomes classifications found in first and second grades provide a rationale for further examining the utility of group fluency measures as an indicator of reading comprehension. Additional research, perhaps using different types of fluency tasks, is needed before more definitive statements can be made.

Interestingly, all three fluency measures produced lower correlations with the tests of reading comprehension in third grade. One reason for the significant drop in the magnitude of the correlations could be measurement differences between the SAT-9 and FCAT SSS. The FCAT SSS contains performance items not included on the SAT-9. The difference in response demands may be due to increasing expectations for vocabulary knowledge and verbal reasoning skills. Studies have found that the amount of variance in reading comprehension accounted for by reading fluency is greatest in early elementary school and decreases in higher grades (e.g., Schatschneider, Buck, et al., 2004). In other words, although reading fluency remains a significant predictor, variables such as vocabulary and verbal reasoning skills account for increasingly more variance in higher grades. Clearly, more research is needed to investigate the reason for the decline in correlations across grade levels.

Implications for Research and Practice

A 1-min timed measure of oral reading fluency (e.g., R-CBM, DIBELS ORF) is one of the most common ways to measure reading fluency. Findings from this study are consistent with two decades of research on ORF (e.g., Fuchs et al., 1988; Shinn et al., 1992; Hintze et al., 1997; Fuchs et al., 2001; McGlinchey & Hixson, 2004), suggesting that ORF is a reliable correlate of reading comprehension and an efficient predictor of student outcomes, supporting its use as a dynamic indicator of students' overall reading skill, including comprehension. Because these tasks take approximately 1 min to administer, with careful planning and classroom management they can be administered to an entire class of students with minimal disruption to classroom routine.

Another potential way in which reading fluency can be measured is using word lists such as those found in the TOWRE. Results of the decision validity and reliability analyses suggest that word lists such as the TOWRE may lead to accurate screening decisions. Jenkins et al. (2003) suggested some utility for using list fluency measures to examine the function of reading fluency deficits. In their study, Jenkins et al. found that context-free (i.e., list) fluency made a larger contribution to context fluency for less fluent readers than for more fluent readers. For more fluent readers, comprehension processes made a larger contribution. Therefore, it may be possible to use list fluency measures to determine whether a student's fluency with sight words is contributing to context fluency difficulties. These findings and the two alternate forms provided in the TOWRE suggest that screening, infrequent progress monitoring (i.e., pre–post testing), and perhaps diagnostic assessment are possibilities.

Because individually administered measures, such as ORF probes and word lists, take approximately 1 min to administer to each student and must be given individually, some educators may view them as impractical for classroom use. Alternative methods of screening students that take less time to administer to a group do exist. One such experimental measure is the TOCERS. The decision validity and reliability analyses conducted on the TOCERS suggested some potential for use as a screener. Correlations between the TOCERS and the SAT-9 in first and second grades were moderate. Diagnostic efficiency statistics suggested that use of the TOCERS correctly classified student outcomes on the statewide assessment above chance. However, the correlations were lower at third grade and the measure did not correctly classify student outcomes significantly above chance. In addition, correlations across all grade levels were significantly lower overall than the individually administered measures, particularly the DIBELS ORF. Diagnostic efficiency statistics, particularly sensitivity and kappa estimates, for the TOCERS generally appeared lower than those produced by the individually administered measures as well. These preliminary correlational and diagnostic efficiency findings may be a reason for caution when administration of the TOCERS is considered. However, because the TOCERS takes approximately 1.5 min to administer to an entire class compared with 3 to 5 min per student for the individually administered measures, the moderate correlations and improvement in student outcomes classifications in first and second grades suggest that future research should be conducted on group measures.

Another published group measure that could be examined is the Test of Silent Word Reading Fluency (TOSWRF; Mather, Hammill, Allen, & Roberts, 2004). For this test, students are given 3 min to separate as many real words as possible on a form that has lines of real words on it but no spaces between the words. Students are to place a slash between each word. The score is the number of words separated correctly. Reliability for this measure is relatively high and correlations between the TOSWRF and reading comprehension tests (e.g., SAT-9) range from moderate to high (Mather et al., 2004). Future research could examine the validity of the TOSWRF to determine its utility as a measure of reading fluency and an indicator of overall reading proficiency.

Given the focus on statewide assessments in NCLB and the reauthorization of the Individuals with Disabilities Education Improvement Act of 2004 that support the use of a Response-to-Intervention model, the findings in this study are very timely and relevant to school personnel responsible for implementing or evaluating interventions. With the increased focus on using evidence-based interventions that has arisen from this legislation, educators will be called on to assist teachers with testing, developing interventions, monitoring student progress, and interpreting progress data. The validity of ORF for the aforementioned uses has been repeatedly documented in the literature. For example, scores on ORF can be compared with empirically derived benchmarks (i.e., DIBELS ORF) or local norms (i.e., R-CBM) to determine whether a student needs further testing or intervention. Importantly, these ORF measures can be used to determine intervention effectiveness through their use for more frequent progress monitoring (e.g., weekly if needed). Benchmarks can be used to develop goals, and data from progress monitoring can be used to determine whether students' rates of progress are on track to meet those goals.

List fluency measures such as the TOWRE may have utility in the process of developing evidence-based interventions as well. Given the apparent importance of developing sight word fluency to reading fluency (Jenkins et al., 2003) and the importance of reading fluency to overall reading proficiency, as well as the comparable diagnostic efficiency statistics reported in this study, both screening and monitoring student performance in this domain may prove useful.

Although certainly more efficient in terms of administration, the group measure examined in this study produced lower correlations with reading comprehension and was less efficient in terms of classifying student outcomes. In addition, no theoretical link between group fluency measures and reading proficiency has been posited. However, more research is needed on the relationship between group measures and tests of reading comprehension and the diagnostic efficiency of group fluency measures before more definitive statements can be made. Such data, along with the information presented on the other methods of measuring reading fluency, may be useful to school personnel.

Limitations and Directions for Future Research

One limitation to this study is that the measures were administered at the end of the year. Thus, it provides information on the concurrent validity rather than the predictive validity of these reading fluency measures. Future research should address the measures' validity for predicting statewide reading assessment outcomes. In particular, longitudinal work is needed to examine how reading fluency measures administered in first or second grades predict performance on statewide reading assessments. Another limitation is that the measures were administered approximately 1 month after the statewide assessments. Because reading fluency grows rapidly in the primary grades (Deno, Fuchs, Marston, & Shinn, 2001; Shapiro, 2004), the reading fluency of the students may have grown as much as 10 words per minute between the administrations of the statewide assessments and fluency measures. However, because the intent of this study was to examine the criterion and decisional validity of the reading fluency measures and all of the measures were subject to this limitation, the results of the study should not have been impacted greatly.

Despite these limitations, the study described in this chapter suggests that each of the three types of reading fluency measures examined may have utility in schools. Although more research is needed to determine the relationships of the different fluency measures with reading comprehension and their utility in terms of predicting outcomes on statewide assessments, the extant research suggests that measures of reading fluency exhibit much potential in terms of predicting whether students are likely to become proficient readers. Given the increased demands for higher performance that educators and students must respond to, it is vital that tools that efficiently allow educators to identify students at risk for reading difficulties are identified and used.

REFERENCES

American Management Association. (2001). *American Management Association Survey on Workplace Testing: Basic skills, job skills, psychological measurement–Summary of findings.* New York: Author.

Barger, J. (2003). *Comparing the DIBELS Oral Reading Fluency indicator and the North Carolina End of Grade Reading Assessment* (technical report). Asheville: North Carolina Teacher Academy.

Barnett, D. W., & Macmann, G. M. (1992). Decision reliability and validity: Contributions and limitations of alternative assessment strategies. *The Journal of Special Education, 25,* 431–452.

Barnett, D. W., Macmann, G. M., & Carey, K. T. (1992). Early intervention and the assessment of developmental skills: Challenges and directions. *Topics in Early Childhood Special Education, 12*(1), 21–43.

Buck, J., & Torgesen, J. (2003). *The relationship between performance on a measure of oral reading fluency and performance on the Florida Comprehensive Assessment Test* (Tech. Rep. No. 1). Tallahassee: Florida Center for Reading Research.

Buly, M. R., & Valencia, S. W. (2002). Below the bar: Profiles of students who fail state reading assessments. *Educational Evaluation and Policy Analysis, 24*(3), 219–239.

Cohen, J. (1960). A coefficient of agreement for nominal scales. *Educational and Psychological Measurement, 20,* 37–46.

Deno, S. L. (1985). Curriculum-based measurement: The emerging alternative. *Exceptional Children, 52,* 219–232.

Deno, S. L., Fuchs, L. S., Marston, D., & Shinn, M. (2001). Using curriculum-based measurement to establish growth standards for students with learning disabilities. *School Psychology Review, 30*(4), 507–524.

Deno, S. L., Marston, D., Shinn, M., & Tindal G. (1983). Oral reading fluency: A simple datum for scaling reading disability. *Topics in Learning and Learning Disabilities, 2*(4), 53–59.

Deno, S. L., Mirkin, P., & Chiang, B. (1982). Identifying valid measures of reading. *Exceptional Children, 49*, 36–45.

Florida Department of Education. (2002, May). *Understanding FCAT reports 2002*. Retrieved April 2, 2004, from *www.firn.edu/doe/sas/fcat/pdf/fcrpdes.pdf*.

Florida Department of Education. (2004, April). *Assessment & accountability briefing book*. Retrieved August 28, 2005, from *fcat.fldoe.org/pdf/fcataabb.pdf*.

Francis, D. J., Shaywitz, S. E., Stuebing, K. K., Shaywitz, B. A., & Fletcher, J. M. (1994). Measurement of change: Assessing behavior over time and within a developmental context. In G. R. Lyon (Ed.), *Frames of reference for the assessment of learning disabilities: New views on measurement issues* (pp. 29–58). Baltimore, MD: Brookes.

Fuchs, L. S., & Deno, S. L. (1994). Must instructionally useful performance assessment be based in the curriculum? *Exceptional Children, 61*, 15–24.

Fuchs, L. S., Fuchs, D., Hosp, M. K., & Jenkins, J. R. (2001). Oral reading fluency as an indicator of reading competence: A theoretical, empirical, and historical analysis. *Scientific Studies of Reading, 5*(3), 239–256.

Fuchs, L. S., Fuchs, D., & Maxwell, L. (1988). The validity of informal reading comprehension measures. *Remedial and Special Education, 9*, 20–28.

Good, R. H., & Kaminski, R. A. (2001). *Dynamic indicators of basic early literacy skills* (5th ed.). Eugene, OR: Institute for the Development of Educational Achievement.

Good, R. H., Kaminski, R. A., Smith, S., & Bratten, J. (2008). *Technical adequacy of second grade DIBELS oral reading fluency passages* (Tech. Rep. No. 8). Eugene: University of Oregon.

Good, R. H., Simmons, D. C., & Kame'enui, E. J. (2001). The importance and decision-making utility of a continuum of fluency-based indicators of foundational reading skills for third-grade high-stakes outcomes. *Scientific Studies of Reading, 5*(3), 257–288.

Good, R. H., Simmons, D. C., & Smith, S. B. (1998). Effective academic interventions in the United States: Evaluating and enhancing the acquisition of early reading skills. *School Psychology Review, 27*(1), 45–56.

Grigg, W., Donahue, P., & Dion, G. (2007). *The nation's report card: 12th-grade reading and mathematics 2005* (NCES Rep. No. 2007-468). Washington, DC: U.S. Government Printing Office.

Hasbrouk, J. E., & Tindal, G. (1992). Curriculum based oral reading fluency for students in grades 2 through 5. *Teaching Exceptional Children, 24*, 41–44.

Henson, K., & Powell-Smith, K. A. (2007). *Assessing student reading progress: A comparison of generic and curriculum-based reading probes*. Manuscript under review.

Hintze, J. M., Shapiro, E. S., Conte, K. L., & Basile, I. M. (1997). Oral reading fluency and authentic reading material: Criterion validity of the technical features of CBM survey-level assessment. *School Psychology Review, 26*(4), 535–553.

Individuals with Disabilities Education Improvement Act, U.S.C. H. R. 1350 (2004).

Jenkins, J. R., Fuchs, L. S., van der Broek, P., Espin, C., & Deno, S. L. (2003).

Sources of individual differences in reading comprehension and reading fluency. *Journal of Educational Psychology, 95*(4), 719–729.

Juel, C. (1988). Learning to read and write: A longitudinal study of 54 children from first through fourth grades. *Journal of Educational Psychology, 80*, 437–447.

Kaminski, R. A., Cummings, K. D., Powell-Smith, K. A., & Good, R. H. III. (2008). Best practices in using Dynamic Indicators of Basic Early Literacy Skills (DIBELS®) for formative assessment and evaluation. In A. Thomas & J. Grimes (Eds.), *Best practices in school psychology-V* (pp. 1181–1204). Bethesda, MD: National Association of School Psychologists.

Marston, D. B. (1989). Curriculum-based measurement: What is it and why do it? In M. R. Shinn (Ed.), *Curriculum-based measurement: Assessing special children* (pp. 18–78). New York: Guilford Press.

Mather, N., Hammill, D. D., Allen, E. A., & Roberts, R. (2004). *Test of Silent Word Reading Fluency.* Austin, TX: PRO-ED.

McGlinchey, M. T., & Hixson, M. D. (2004). Using curriculum-based measurement to predict performance on state assessments in reading. *School Psychology Review, 33*(2), 193–203.

National Institute of Child Health and Human Development. (2000). *Report of the National Reading Panel. Teaching children to read: An evidence-based assessment of the scientific research literature on reading and its implications for reading instruction* (NIH Publication No. 00-4769). Washington, DC: U.S. Government Printing Office.

No Child Left Behind Act, U.S.C. 115 STAT. 1426 (2002).

Perfetti, C. A. (1995). Cognitive research can inform reading education. *Journal of Research in Reading, 18*(2), 106–115.

Powell-Smith, K. A., & Bradley-Klug, K. L. (2001). Another look at the "C" in CBM: Does it really matter if curriculum-based measurement reading probes are curriculum-based? *Psychology in the Schools, 38*(4), 299–312.

Schatsneider, C., Buck, J., Torgesen, J., Wagner, R., Hassler, L., Hecht, S., et al. (2004). *A multivariate study of individual differences in performance on the reading portion of the Florida Comprehensive Assessment Test: A brief report* (Tech. Rep. No. 5). Tallahassee: Florida Center for Reading Research.

Schatsneider, C., Torgeson, J., Buck, J., & Powell-Smith, K. A. (2004, February). *Individual differences in FCAT performance.* Paper presented at the 12th annual Pacific Coast Research Conference, Coronado, CA.

Shapiro, E. S. (2004). *Academic skill problems: Direct assessment and intervention* (3rd ed.). New York: Guilford Press.

Shapiro, E. S., Edwards, L., Lutz, J. G., & Keller, M. (2004, March). *Curriculum-based measurement predicted outcomes on high stakes testing—Reading and math outcomes in Pennsylvania.* Paper presented at the meeting of the National Association of School Psychologists, Dallas, TX.

Shapiro, E. S., Keller, M. A., Lutz, J. G., Santoro, L. E., & Hintze, J. M. (2006). Curriculum-based measures and performance on state assessment and standardized tests. *Journal of Psychoeducational Assessment, 24*(1), 19–35.

Shaw, R., & Shaw, D. (2002). *DIBELS oral reading fluency-based indicators of third grade reading skills for Colorado State Assessment Program (CSAP)* (technical report). Eugene: University of Oregon.

Shinn, M. R. (Ed.). (1989). *Curriculum-based measurement: Assessing special children.* New York: Guilford Press.

Shinn, M. R. (2002). Best practices in using curriculum-based measurement in a problem-solving model. In a. Thomas & J. Grimes (Eds.), *Best practices in school psychology IV* (pp. 671–697). Bethesda, MD: National Association of School Psychologists.

Shinn, M. R., Good, R. H., Knutson, N., Tilly, W. D., & Collins, V. L. (1992). Curriculum-based measurement of oral reading fluency: A confirmatory analysis of its relation to reading. *School Psychology Review, 21,* 459–479.

Steiger, J. H. (1980). Tests for comparing elements of a correlation matrix. *Psychological Bulletin, 87,* 245–251.

Streiner, D. L. (2003). Diagnosing tests: Using and misusing diagnostic and screening tests. *Journal of Personality Assessment, 81*(3), 209–219.

Torgesen, J. K., & Burgess, S. R. (1998). Consistency of reading-related phonological processes throughout early childhood: Evidence from longitudinal-correlational and instructional studies. In J. L. Metsala & L. C. Ehri (Eds.), *Word recognition in beginning literacy* (pp. 161–188). Mahwah, NJ: Erlbaum.

Torgesen, J. K., & DeGraff, A. (2002). *Test of Critical Early Reading Skills.* Unpublished manuscript, Florida State University.

Torgesen, J. K., Wagner, R. K., & Rashotte, C.A. (1999). *Test of Word Reading Efficiency.* Austin, TX: PRO-ED.

Van der Meer, C. D., Lentz, F. E., & Stollar, S. (2005). *The relationship between oral reading fluency and Ohio proficiency testing in reading* (technical report). Eugene: University of Oregon.

Wisconsin Center for Education Research. (n.d.). *Common measures of general achievement.* Retrieved August 28, 2005, from *www.wcer.wisc.edu/cce/documents/common_measures_of_gen_ach.pdf.*

PART IV

BIOLOGICAL-BASED APPROACHES

10

Assessment and Etiology of Individual Differences in Reading Comprehension

Janice M. Keenan, Richard K. Olson,
and Rebecca S. Betjemann

W oody Allen once commented on his reading comprehension after taking a speed reading course, "I've read *War and Peace*; it's about Russia!" Intended as a criticism of speed reading, this comment also raises the issue of what it means to adequately comprehend what one has read. We laugh because we know that comprehension of this weighty tome involves more than knowing that it is about Russia. But because comprehension is such a complex process, it is not easy to say exactly what would constitute evidence of comprehending it. That is the difficulty that confronts researchers and clinicians concerned with comprehension assessment.

One of the consequences of this ambiguity about how best to evaluate comprehension is the variety of tests that have emerged for assessing it. Although there has been a tendency in the field to regard differences between these tests as basically format differences that have consequences mainly for ease of administration or scoring, what we show in this chapter is that the consequences are much more significant than that. Different tests can lead to very different outcomes both for clinical diagnosis and for research questions. We illustrate how serious the implications of these test differences are by showing their impact on how we understand the biological underpinnings of reading skill in terms of genetic influences. The bottom line is both a cautionary one—comprehension tests cannot be considered interchangeable—and a positive one—test differences highlight the different components of comprehension, which brings us closer to understanding how best to evaluate comprehension and understand its etiology.

OVERVIEW OF ASSESSMENT
AND ETIOLOGY ISSUES

As any teacher knows, as well as any parent who has had more than one child, there are large differences between children in skills such as how quickly they learn to read, how readily they comprehend what they read, and how easy it is for them to attend to information. The basic question driving our research is to understand these individual differences. What causes these differences to develop? How are the cognitive processes different? What are ways to help those who have deficits? We are part of a team of researchers, called the Colorado Learning Disabilities Research Center (CLDRC), which is one of four research centers funded by the National Institutes of Health to study individual differences and deficits in skills related to learning (cf. DeFries et al., 1997; Olson, 2006).

At the CLDRC we are trying to determine the extent to which individual differences and deficits in reading and related skills are driven by genetic and environmental factors. Our approach is to study twins because twins allow us to separate how genes and environments each contribute to behavior. We compare the similarities of identical twins with those of fraternal twins to estimate the relative influences of genes, shared family environment, and nonshared environment.

Reading comprehension is a major focus of our work (cf. Keenan, Betjemann, Wadsworth, DeFries, & Olson, 2006). Among the goals of this research are to (1) determine the influence of genes and environment on individual differences in comprehension, and (2) study the component skills of comprehension to determine the extent to which these skills share a common genetic basis or whether there are independent sets of genes associated with each.

Because reading comprehension is such a central focus of our work, we assess our twins on five different measures of reading comprehension. We use so many tests because we want to have a broad and representative assessment of comprehension skill. By testing a child on many different tests and using a composite across those tests, we can feel more confident about the validity of our assessment and thus the validity of the genetic analyses.

Our use of multiple assessments turned out to be very serendipitous. It allowed us to discover that comprehension tests are not all that comparable (Keenan, Betjemann, & Olson, 2008). We found that the intercorrelations among our reading comprehension tests were rather modest. Our investigations into why that was so revealed that there are large differences between the tests in the component skills of comprehension that they assess; thus, even though all purport to measure comprehension, they are not all measures of the same process.

Our finding that reading comprehension tests are not very comparable was rather surprising to us because there is such a tendency in both clinical practice and in research to assume that tests of comprehension available on the market are interchangeable. One goal of this chapter is to illustrate the differences between the tests in the skills they assess and thus show why these tests are not interchangeable. We do that by summarizing the major findings from Keenan et al. (2008), including how there can be developmental differences in what some tests measure. Another equally important goal is to show the impact of these test differences for research. We do this by demonstrating how, in our research on genetic and environmental influences on reading comprehension, we obtain a very different answer to one of the central questions—do word reading skill and comprehension skill depend on the same genes?—depending on which tests are used to assess comprehension.

OUR READING COMPREHENSION TESTS

When we selected the reading comprehension tests we use in our behavioral genetic study of reading comprehension, there was no information available about the types of comprehension skills assessed by each test. We suspect this was because of a tendency to think of comprehension as a unified skill back when these tests were developed, and thus it was assumed that any test that measured comprehension measured the same thing as any other test of it. Without benefit of research about the comprehension skills assessed by any of the tests to guide our selection, we selected tests for our battery by attempting to cover a range of test formats. Our reasoning was that different formats might involve different task demands and different task demands might tap a broader range of skills.

The reading comprehension tests in our battery are the Gray Oral Reading Test–3 (GORT-3; Wiederholt & Bryant, 1992), the Qualitative Reading Inventory–3 (QRI-3; Leslie & Caldwell, 2001), the Woodcock–Johnson Passage Comprehension subtest (WJPC) from the Woodcock–Johnson Tests of Achievement–III (Woodcock, McGrew, & Mather, 2001), and the Reading Comprehension subtest from the Peabody Individual Achievement Test (PIAT; Dunn & Markwardt, 1970), which is identical in format to the PIAT-R and PIAT-R/NU (Markwardt, 1989, 1997).[1]

These tests cover a range of test format options. We have two tests that are silent reading (WJPC and PIAT) and two that are oral reading (GORT and QRI). The passage length varies from a single sentence (PIAT and many WJPC texts) to long passages up to 785 words (QRI). The types of tasks used to assess comprehension include (1) picture selection in the PIAT, where the child must select from among four pictures the one that best represents the meaning of the sentence just read; (2) the cloze technique in the WJPC, wherein the child is presented with a text in which one word is omitted and the child demonstrates understanding by providing the missing word; (3) multiple-choice comprehension questions in the GORT; (4) open-ended, short-answer questions in the QRI, some of which are literal and some inferential; and finally, because the QRI involves two assessments of comprehension, (5) retelling the passage in the QRI.

INTERCORRELATIONS AMONG READING COMPREHENSION TESTS

Table 10.1 presents the correlations among our reading comprehension tests. They range from a low of .31 for the correlation of the GORT with the QRI Retellings to a high of .70 for the correlation between the PIAT and the WJPC. In general, except for the correlation between the PIAT and the WJPC, the correlations among the tests are rather modest given that they all purport to be measures of the same construct. Even the correlation between the two assessments of the QRI, which both assess comprehension of the same passage, is only .41. These modest correlations suggest that our reading comprehension assessments may be measuring different component skills of comprehension. To investigate what those components might be, we performed an exploratory factor analysis on our tests.

TABLE 10.1. Intercorrelations among Reading Comprehension Tests

	GORT	QRI-R	QRI-Qs	PIAT	WJPC
GORT	1.0				
QRI-Retell	.31	1.0			
QRI-Qs	.38	.41	1.0		
PIAT	.51	.45	.44	1.0	
WJPC	.54	.48	.45	.70	1.0

Note. GORT, Gray Oral Reading Test–3; QRI, Qualitative Reading Inventory–3; R, Retelling Subtest; Q, Comprehension Questions Subtest; PIAT, Peabody Individual Achievement Test; WJPC, Woodcock–Johnson Passage Comprehension Subtest. Adapted from Keenan, Betjemann, and Olson (2008). Copyright 2008 by Taylor & Francis. Adapted by permission.

FACTOR ANALYSIS OF READING COMPREHENSION TESTS

The factor analysis included not only our five reading comprehension assessments, but also three other measures. One was a composite of listening comprehension tests, many of which were simply the oral equivalent of the reading comprehension tests in our battery. The other two measures were a composite of the child's word-reading skill and a measure of their nonword decoding skill.

Two factors emerged from this factor analysis. One we refer to as a comprehension factor because all of the reading comprehension tests, as well as the listening comprehension composite, loaded on it. The other factor we refer to as decoding because the tests loading most heavily on it were the word- and nonword-reading measures.

What was most interesting was that, although all of the reading comprehension tests loaded on the comprehension factor, the factor loadings for the PIAT and the WJPC were much lower than for the other tests. These two tests, but none of the other reading comprehension measures, also loaded highly on the decoding factor. In fact, the PIAT and the WJPC loaded considerably higher on decoding than on comprehension, suggesting that they are measuring decoding more than comprehension skills.

REGRESSION ANALYSES OF COMPONENT SKILLS

Because our factor analysis suggested that decoding skills might be more important to the PIAT and the WJPC than to our other tests of reading comprehension, we used hierarchical regression to examine how much of the variance in performance on each test was accounted for by word decoding and by listening comprehension. The results are shown in Figure 10.1, which displays the amount of variance in each of the five reading comprehension measures that is unique to word decoding, unique to listening comprehension, and shared between the two.

Two findings are most salient from Figure 10.1. One is that more total variance is accounted for in the PIAT and the WJPC than the other three measures. The other is that this is because most of the variance in these two tests is accounted for by word decoding and its shared variance with listening comprehension. Only 5% of the variance on the PIAT and 7% on the WJPC are accounted for independently by listening comprehension skills. Thus, the answer to our question of whether reading comprehension tests differ in the degree to which they assess component skills appears to be "yes," because the PIAT and WJPC are more sensitive to individual differences in decoding skill than are the GORT and the QRI measures.

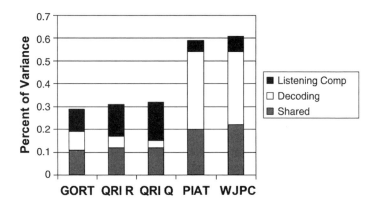

FIGURE 10.1. The proportion of total variance in each of the reading comprehension tests that was accounted for independently by word-decoding skill, by listening comprehension skill, or shared. GORT, Gray Oral Reading Test–3; QRI, Qualitative Reading Inventory–3; R, Retelling Subtest; Q, Comprehension Questions Subtest; PIAT, Peabody Individual Achievement Test; W-J, Woodcock–Johnson Passage Comprehension Subtest. Adapted from Keenan, Betjemann, and Olson (2008). Copyright 2008 by Taylor & Francis. Adapted by permission.

DEVELOPMENTAL DIFFERENCES

Another question that we examined is the extent to which there are developmental differences in what a test measures. Because the children in our sample range in age from 8 to 18 years, we could determine whether differences between the tests in what predicted reading comprehension differed with developmental level. Developmental differences were assessed both as a function of chronological age and of reading ability, defined by raw scores on the PIAT Word Recognition test.

The top half of Figure 10.2 displays the amount of variance accounted for in each test by decoding and listening separately for the two halves of our sample. Using a median split on age, the mean age for the *younger* group was 9.1 years and for the *older* group, 13.1 years. It is well known that decoding skill accounts for more variance in reading comprehension when children are younger than when they are older (Hoover & Tunmer, 1993), and the results from each of our tests show that same pattern. What is new in our results is that there are such large discrepancies across tests in these developmental differences. As this figure shows, there are dramatic differences across tests as a function of age in the amount of variance accounted for by word decoding. These developmental differences are large on the PIAT and WJPC but small on the GORT and QRI measures.

Whereas the top half of Figure 10.2 shows developmental trends across chronological age, the bottom half shows them across reading age (i.e., as a function of word reading ability), using raw scores on the PIAT word recognition test. The pattern for reading age is similar to what we found for chronological age. The difference between the two ability groups is most evident in the larger amount of variance independently accounted for by decoding skill in the children with lower word reading ability. This is most apparent on the PIAT and WJPC, where the amount of variance accounted for independently by decoding declines from .48 for low ability to .12 for high ability on the PIAT and from .36 to .16, respectively, on the WJPC. Thus, we are seeing evidence once again that the PIAT and WJPC differ from the other tests not just in terms of how much of their variance is accounted for by decoding skill, but also because what they measure depends on developmental level. If children are young or have low word reading ability, these tests are largely assessments of decoding skill, whereas for more advanced readers they also assess listening comprehension skills.

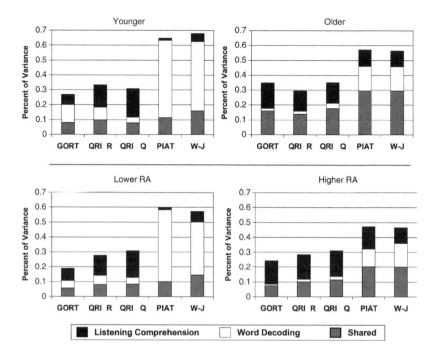

FIGURE 10.2. The proportion of total variance in each of the reading comprehension tests that was accounted for independently by word decoding skill, by listening comprehension skill, or shared for groups defined by chronological age (top figures), and reading age on PIAT word reading (bottom figures). RA, reading age; GORT, Gray Oral Reading Test–3; QRI, Qualitative Reading Inventory–3; R, Retelling Subtest; Q, Comprehension Questions Subtest; PIAT, Peabody Individual Achievement Test; W-J, Woodcock–Johnson Passage Comprehension Subtest. Adapted from Keenan, Betjemann, and Olson (2008). Copyright 2008 by Taylor & Francis. Adapted by permission.

CAN TEST FORMAT DIFFERENCES
EXPLAIN TEST OUTCOME DIFFERENCES?

We concluded in Keenan et al. (2008) that, although format differences underlie the differences between the tests in their sensitivity to word decoding skills, they are not the format differences that researchers have previously focused on. Previous research had suggested that cloze tests differ from other comprehension tests in that most of the variance in cloze tests is accounted for by decoding skill (Nation & Snowling,

1997; Francis, Fletcher, Catts, & Tomblin, 2005). What we found, however, is that it was not just the test using a cloze format, the WJPC, that was so heavily influenced by decoding skill. The PIAT, which uses multiple-choice selection of pictures representing the meaning of the sentence, showed the same pattern as the WJPC's cloze test format. Thus, some other factor besides the format of the test item appears to be responsible for a comprehension test being heavily influenced by decoding skill. Keenan et al. suggested that this factor might be the passage length.

Keenan et al. (2008) noted that the texts in the PIAT and the WJPC are all quite short. The PIAT uses only single sentences; and most of the WJPC items involve just two-sentence passages, although some are also only a single sentence. The problem with using such short texts is that the assessment is likely to be based on the successful decoding of a single word. In fact, the four pictures that the reader needs to select from on the PIAT use decoding confusions as the sole basis for constructing the alternatives. So, if the sentence was "The patients were amazed by the giraffe in the lobby," then the wrong-answer pictures would depict events using a word similar to *patients*, like *parents*, and a word similar to *giraffe*, like *graffiti*. In other words, the child would be required to select among pictures of *patients amazed by the giraffe, patients amazed by graffiti, parents amazed by the giraffe*, and *parents amazed by graffiti*. Thus, "comprehension" of the sentences on the PIAT boils down to the decoding of two words.

To explain why short passages tend to be more influenced by decoding, Keenan et al. (2008) also suggested that decoding problems are likely to be more catastrophic in short passages than in longer passages. In a single sentence, there frequently are no other words for the child to use to help determine the correct decoding of difficult words, such as *magician*. In a longer passage, however, the text is likely to describe events, such as pulling a rabbit out of a hat, which would allow the child to use this context to determine the correct decoding. In fact, we found that decoding skill accounted for much less variance on the QRI measures where the passages are quite long and decoding problems can often be rectified by context.

Decoding appears to play a very small role in explaining variance on the GORT. Although the GORT passages are longer than the texts used on the PIAT and the WJPC, but shorter than the QRI, there is a factor other than length of passage that probably explains why decoding has so little influence on the GORT. Keenan and Betjemann (2006) showed that most of the GORT items can be answered with above-chance accuracy without even reading the passages. They found that the best predictor of performance on the comprehension questions when children actually read the GORT passages was not how accurately they read the passages, but rather how easily the question could be answered without reading the passage.

IMPLICATIONS OF DIFFERENCES BETWEEN READING COMPREHENSION TESTS

Given the complexity of comprehension, it would be unreasonable to expect that there would be no differences between tests of reading comprehension in the amount of variance accounted for by various component skills. However, what our comparison of tests has shown is that these differences can be quite substantial. For example, for young children, the PIAT and the WJPC are not measures of comprehension, like the other tests, as much as measures of decoding. The clinical implications are significant. If comprehension skill is tested with the WJPC or PIAT, a young child whose deficit is only in decoding skills will appear as if he or she also has poor comprehension skills. Likewise, a child who really does have both poor decoding and poor comprehension could appear as if he or she has good comprehension skills if tested on the GORT, where many of the questions can be answered without comprehending the passage by just using prior knowledge. Thus, it is important for those who perform clinical assessments to be aware of the differences in component skills being assessed by various tests. Even when component skills account for rather similar proportions of reading comprehension variance, as Cutting and Scarborough (2006) found for the Wechsler Individual Achievement Test Reading Comprehension subtest, the Gates–MacGinitie Reading Test, and the GORT, there can nonetheless be a fair degree of inconsistency across tests in whether a child is identified as having a reading comprehension deficit (Rimrodt, Lightman, Roberts, Denckla, & Cutting, 2005).

Although it is obvious how a misdiagnosis can have quite an impact on a child's life, it may not be as apparent how differences between comprehension tests can impact research. We turn now to demonstrate with our studies of the genetic and environmental influences on reading comprehension that the effect of using different tests to answer research questions can be similarly significant. First, we give some background on our genetic studies.

BACKGROUND ON THE CLDRC

Since 1982, investigators in the CLDRC have been studying school-age identical and fraternal twins to estimate the relative influences of genes and environment on group deficits and individual differences in reading and related skills (DeFries et al., 1997; Olson, 2006). The basic approach involves sorting the covariance between twins into three components: that resulting from *genes*; from their *shared environments*, such as family and school environments; and from *nonshared environmental factors* (e.g., if one twin had a head injury from falling out of a tree and the other twin did not have such an injury). We briefly describe the logic of how this is done.

Identical twins develop from a single egg and sperm, so they share all their genes. Fraternal twins develop from different eggs and sperm, so they share half of their segregating genes on average, the same as nontwin siblings. This difference in genetic similarity for identical and fraternal twins, plus the fact that our twins share their home environment, allows us to estimate the relative influences from genes, shared environment, and nonshared environment on individual variation. Nonshared environment influence can be directly estimated from the average difference between identical twins, because they share their genes and their shared family environment. Thus, any difference between them must be due to pre- or postnatal environmental factors that they did not share, including any measurement error. The remaining shared environment and genetic sources of variation are estimated by comparing the average similarities of identical and fraternal twins. For example, if identical and fraternal twins are equally similar on average, regardless of their difference in genetic similarity, it would indicate that individual differences or deficits not due to nonshared environment are entirely due to shared environment. In contrast, if fraternal twins, who share half of their genes on average, are only half as similar as identical twins, who share all their genes, this would imply that influences on individual variation, beyond influences from nonshared environment, are entirely due to genes. Differences in identical and fraternal twin similarities between these two extreme examples allow us to estimate the relative influences of genes and shared family environment in the population sampled, although not for any individual within the sample. See Plomin, DeFries, McClearn, and McGuffin (2001) for further discussion of the assumptions behind our behavior–genetic analyses.

Before the year 2000, analyses of reading in the twins from the CLDRC used either a composite measure of word reading, spelling, and reading comprehension from the PIAT (cf. DeFries, Fulker, & LaBuda, 1987; Hawke, Wadsworth, Olson, & DeFries, 2007) or measures of isolated word recognition and related component skills (c.f., Gayán & Olson, 2001, 2003). This research found that much of the differences between individuals within the CLDRC sample was due to genes; both group deficits (i.e., having a reading disability or not) and individual differences were largely due to genetic variation. Gayán and Olson also reported strong genetic influences on phonological decoding (nonword reading), and these genetic influences were almost perfectly correlated with the same genetic influences on word recognition.

BACKGROUND ON OUR GENETIC STUDIES OF READING COMPREHENSION

In the year 2000, we expanded the test battery given to our twins at the CLDRC to include a broader assessment of comprehension; up to that point, our only test of comprehension was the PIAT Reading Comprehension test, whereas now it includes the five reading comprehension tests discussed previously. In addition, it includes four tests of listening comprehension so as to have an assessment of comprehension skill outside of reading. The change in our test battery to expand comprehension assessment reflected a growing recognition in the field regarding the importance of comprehension (summarized in RAND Reading Study Group, 2002). This recognition developed in part as a result of a shift in how the relation between word reading and comprehension was viewed.

When the CLDRC began its studies of reading and reading disability, it was common to assume that difficulties in reading comprehension were largely, if not completely, due to deficits in word decoding (Liberman, Shankweiler, Fisher, & Carter, 1974; Perfetti, 1985; Shankweiler, 1989). Labored, dysfluent word decoding in poor readers was thought to result in fewer cognitive resources available for comprehension. Thus, comprehension problems were thought to be a byproduct of decoding problems.

Independence in the contributions of word decoding and comprehension skill to reading comprehension began to be recognized when Hoover and Gough (1990) proposed their *Simple Model* of reading, which stated that reading comprehension is a product of both skill in decoding and skill in listening comprehension. This view garnered significant support when researchers started identifying children who had no problems in word reading accuracy and fluency but nonetheless had problems in reading comprehension (Cain, Oakhill, & Bryant, 2000; Catts, Hogan, & Fey, 2003; Oakhill, 1994; Yuill & Oakhill, 1991). The existence of such poor comprehenders, or comprehension deficit children, suggests some independence between decoding and comprehension skills (Nation, 2005; Perfetti, Landi, & Oakhill, 2005).

The findings from our first behavioral genetic analyses of reading comprehension from the CLDRC twins, when the size of the sample was still rather small (70 identical twin pairs, 121 fraternal twin pairs), provided further strong support for the view that there is some independence between word decoding and comprehension skills (Keenan et al., 2006). In order to show that, we first need to describe the study.

In the Keenan et al. (2006) study, we used composite scores on reading comprehension, listening comprehension, and word recognition skill to assess the covariance between twins so that we could evaluate the degree of genetic and environmental influences on individual differences in reading comprehension. In particular, we were interested in determining the extent to which genetic and environmental factors that influence word reading skill and listening comprehension also affect reading comprehension. It was the first behavioral genetic analysis of individual differences in reading comprehension to assess comprehension on longer passages and thus the first behavioral genetic study of discourse comprehension.

Keenan et al. (2006) found substantial, and significant, genetic influences on individual differences in both reading and listening comprehension. Model-fitting procedures referred to as Cholesky or triangular decomposition (e.g., Neale, Boker, Xie, & Maes, 2002) showed that the largest amount of variance in reading comprehension, 51%, was accounted for by genes; 18% was due to shared environments and 31% to nonshared environment, which also includes measurement error. Genetic influences, indicated by higher correlations on each of our variables between identical twins than between fraternal twins, were evident in each of our variables: word recognition, .76 vs. .39; listening comprehension, .69 vs. .38; and reading comprehension, .64 vs. .45. We also found that genes were the main reason for the phenotypic correlation between reading and listening comprehension as well as the correlation between word recognition and reading comprehension.

The most interesting finding in Keenan et al. (2006), from the perspective of understanding the components of reading comprehension, was that, even though there was considerable shared genetic variance between word recognition and listening comprehension, each nonetheless accounted for significant *independent* genetic influences on reading comprehension. This differentiation in genes for word decoding and listening comprehension is just what would be predicted by Hoover and Gough's (1990) simple model of reading comprehension. In addition, these two factors together accounted for all the genetic influence on reading comprehension. In other words, there was no additional genetic variance to account for with possible other factors, such as processing speed (cf. Joshi & Aaron, 2000). Thus, the results provide genetic support for the simple model in terms of both the proposal that reading comprehension is a product of only those two factors as well as the assumption of some dissociation between these factors. Note that our finding dissociation in the genes associated with word recognition and comprehension provides a genetic reason why some individuals can have comprehension deficits without word decoding deficits (Oakhill, 1994; Yuill & Oakhill, 1991) and why others (e.g., the classic case of dyslexia) can have decoding deficits but not problems with general comprehension, at least when they are not reading.

Keenan et al. (2006)'s Cholesky analyses also examined whether there is a dissociation between word recognition and comprehension in terms of shared environmental influences. However, no dissociation was found. The shared family and school environmental influences on individual differences were essentially the same for all variables. This was not surprising because it is reasonable to expect that environments good for promoting the development of decoding skill are also likely to promote comprehension skill. There was no significant overlap for nonshared environmental influences, suggesting that much of these nonshared influences may have been due to measurement error. In sum, Keenan et al. showed that while decoding and comprehension share the same shared-environment influences and much of the same genetic influences, nonetheless there is some dissociation between the genetic influences on decoding and comprehension.

HOW THE GENETIC RELATIONSHIP BETWEEN WORD READING AND COMPREHENSION SKILL DEPENDS ON THE TEST USED FOR READING COMPREHENSION

Keenan et al. (2006)'s finding of some dissociation in the genes associated with word recognition and comprehension was based on analyses in which reading comprehension was defined by a composite of all five of our reading comprehension measures. However, as we became aware of the large differences between our tests, described earlier in this chapter, we wondered whether the extent to which reading comprehension shares genetic variance with word recognition depends on the test used to assess reading comprehension. In particular, we speculated that if reading comprehension was defined by performance on the PIAT and WJPC, the two tests that load more highly in our factor analysis on decoding than comprehension, we might not see any dissociation between genetic influences on word decoding and comprehension. This finding would be similar to that of Byrne et al. (2007), who used only the WJPC with first graders and found complete overlap in decoding and reading comprehension. In contrast, if we defined reading comprehension using the GORT and the two QRI measures, where the passages are longer and context can be used to resolve decoding problems, the dissociation might emerge.

To test these predictions, we repeated the behavioral genetic analyses of Keenan et al. (2006), but this time we did them separately for the two sets of reading comprehension tests. Additionally, to reduce the effects of test error on our analyses (which was evident in the large nonshared environment effects in Keenan et al.), we used latent traits of the two hypothesized types of tests. Thus, one analysis used a latent trait for reading comprehension defined by performance on the PIAT and the WJPC; the other analysis used a latent trait for reading comprehension defined by performance on the GORT, QRI recall, and QRI Comprehension questions.

As we expected, we found large differences in the genetic correlations between word recognition skill and reading comprehension depending on the type of reading comprehension test (Keenan, 2007; Betjemann et al., 2008). When reading comprehension was assessed by the PIAT and the WJPC, the genetic correlation (which measures the degree to which two variables are influenced by the same sets of genes) between word decoding and comprehension was quite high: $r = .90$. However, when reading comprehension was assessed by the GORT and QRI, the genetic correlation was considerably lower: $r = .56$.

This result demonstrates how critical the nature of the specific test used to assess comprehension is. One of the most central questions in behavioral genetic research is the degree to which there is overlap in the genes associated with different cognitive processes, like word recognition and comprehension, or different disabilities, like dyslexia and comprehension deficit. Our finding that genetic correlations can vary dramatically as a function of the test used to define reading comprehension shows how critical it will be for researchers to not base conclusions regarding genetics on analyses where the phenotype is assessed with just one test. A single test may be adequate for assessing word decoding skill because such tests correlate quite highly; in our CLDRC sample, our two measures of word recognition correlate at .88. However, as our earlier discussion showed, comprehension tests are quite different (see Table 10.1), and as our genetic findings show, these differences have significant consequences.

It is interesting to note that, although our analyses of genetic correlations between word decoding and comprehension varied considerably as a function of type of test, the overall influence of genes, shared environment, and nonshared environment on individual differences in reading comprehension was quite similar regardless of which set of tests was used (Keenan, 2007; Betjemann et al., 2008). When reading comprehension was defined as performance on the PIAT and WJPC latent trait, we found that genes accounted for 61% of the variance; shared environment accounted for 34%, and nonshared environment accounted for 5%. When the QRI and GORT latent trait was used, however, the respective values were 65%, 30%, and 5%. This suggests that if one is only interested in assessing genetic and environmental influences on comprehension, it may not matter what test is used for assessing comprehension. However, if one is interested in estimating shared and independent genetic and environmental influences on individual differences across different component skills, the specific test used can make quite a difference.

CONCLUSION

Recent years have seen an increasing interest in the field of reading research in trying to understand comprehension, as reflected by this volume and the conference on which it was based. What our work shows is that progress in understanding comprehension, both in terms of its cognitive components and the biological bases for individual differences, ultimately depends on the particulars of the instruments of assessment.

We have shown that different reading comprehension tests measure different skills, and that sometimes even the same test measures different things depending on age and ability. We have also shown how being unaware of these differences can lead to significant problems in interpretation of clinical diagnoses and research results. Having now become aware of these test differences and component skills, we hope to have taken a step closer to comprehending comprehension both in terms of assessment and etiology.

Assessment and Etiology of Individual Differences

ACKNOWLEDGMENTS

This research was supported by National Institutes of Health Grant HD27802 to the Colorado Learning Disabilities Research Center, for which R. Olson is the principal investigator, and J. Keenan is a co-principal investigator, and by National Institutes of Mental Health Training Grant T32 MH016880-25, which provided postdoctoral training for R. Betjemann.

NOTE

1. We use the PIAT rather than the PIAT-R to maintain continuity with earlier data collection on the project, but its format is identical to the PIAT-R.

REFERENCES

Betjemann, R. S., Keenan, J. M., Wadsworth, S. J., DeFries, J. C., Willcutt, E., & Olson, R. K. (2008). *How the genetic overlap between decoding and comprehension skill depends on the measure of reading comprehension*. Manuscript in preparation.

Byrne, B., Samuelsson, S., Wadsworth, S., Hulslander, J., Corley, R., DeFries, J. C., et al. (2007). Longitudinal twin study of early literacy development: Preschool through grade 1. *Reading and Writing, 20,* 77–102.

Cain, K., Oakhill, J., & Bryant, P. E. (2000). Investigating the causes of reading comprehension failure: A test of the phonological processing deficit hypothesis. *Reading and Writing, 13,* 31–56.

Catts, H. W., Hogan, T. P., & Fey, M. E. (2003). Subgrouping poor readers on the basis of individual differences in reading-related abilities. *Journal of Learning Disabilities, 36,* 151–164.

Cutting, L. E., & Scarborough, H. S. (2006). Prediction of reading comprehension: Relative contributions of word recognition, language proficiency, and other cognitive skills can depend on how comprehension is measured. *Scientific Studies of Reading, 10,* 277–299.

DeFries, J. C., Filipek, P. A., Fulker, D. W., Olson, R. K., Pennington, B. F., & Smith, S. D. (1997). Colorado Learning Disabilities Research Center. *Learning Disabilities, 8,* 7–19.

DeFries, J. C., Fulker, D. W., & LaBuda, M. C. (1987). Evidence for a genetic aetiology in reading disability of twins. *Nature, 329,* 537–539.

Dunn, L. M., & Markwardt, F. C. (1970). *Examiner's manual: Peabody Individual Achievement Test.* Circle Pines, MI: American Guidance Service.

Francis, D. J., Fletcher, J. M., Catts, H. W., & Tomblin, J. B. (2005). Dimensions affecting the assessment of reading comprehension. In S. G. Paris & S. A. Stahl (Eds.), *Children's reading comprehension and assessment* (pp. 369–394). Mahwah, NJ: Erlbaum.

Gayán, J., & Olson, R. K. (2001). Genetic and environmental influences on orthographic and phonological skills in children with reading disabilities. *Developmental Neuropsychology, 20*, 487–511.

Gayán, J., & Olson, R. K. (2003). Genetic and environmental influences on individual differences in printed word recognition. *Journal of Experimental Child Psychology, 84*, 97–123.

Hawke, J. L., Wadsworth, S. J., Olson, R. K., & DeFries, J. C. (2007). Etiology of reading difficulties as a function of gender and severity. *Reading and Writing, 20*, 13–25.

Hoover, W. A., & Gough, P. B. (1990). The simple view of reading. *Reading and Writing, 2*, 127–160.

Hoover, W. A., & Tunmer, W. E. (1993). The components of reading. In G. B. Thompson, W. E. Tunmer, & T. Nicholson (Eds.), *Reading acquisition processes* (pp. 1–19). Adelaide, South Australia: Multilingual Matters.

Joshi, R. M., & Aaron, P. G. (2000). The component model of reading: Simple view of reading made a little more complex. *Reading Psychology, 21*, 85–97.

Keenan, J. M. (2007, April). *Individual differences in reading comprehension*. Paper presented at the Workshop on Reading Comprehension: Linking Theory and Practice, Oxford, UK.

Keenan, J. M., & Betjemann, R. S. (2006). Comprehending the Gray Oral Reading Test without reading it: Why comprehension tests should not include passage-independent items. *Scientific Studies of Reading, 10*, 363–380.

Keenan, J. M., Betjemann, R. S., & Olson, R. K. (2008). Reading comprehension tests vary in the skills they assess: Differential dependence on decoding and oral comprehension. *Scientific Studies of Reading, 12*, 281–300.

Keenan, J. M., Betjemann, R. S., Wadsworth, S. J., DeFries, J. C., & Olson, R. K. (2006). Genetic and environmental influences on reading and listening comprehension. *Journal of Research in Reading, 29*, 79–91.

Leslie, L., & Caldwell, J. (2001). *Qualitative Reading Inventory–3*. New York: Addison Wesley Longman.

Liberman, I. Y., Shankweiler, D., Fisher, F. W., & Carter, B. (1974). Explicit syllable and phoneme segmentation in the young child. *Journal of Experimental Child Psychology, 18*, 201–212.

Markwardt, F. C. (1989). *Peabody Individual Achievement Test–Revised*. Bloomington, MN: Pearson Assessments.

Markwardt, F. C. (1997). *Peabody Individual Achievement Test–Revised–Normative Update*. Bloomington, MN: Pearson Assessments.

Nation, K. (2005). Children's reading comprehension difficulties. In M. Snowling & C. Hulme (Eds.), *The science of reading: A handbook* (pp. 248–265). Oxford, UK: Blackwell.

Nation, K., & Snowling, M. (1997). Assessing reading difficulties: The validity and utility of current measures of reading skill. *British Journal of Educational Psychology, 67*, 359–370.

Neale, M. C., Boker, S. M., Xie, G., & Maes, H. H. (2002). *Mx: Statistical modeling* (6th ed.). Richmond, VA: Virginia Commonwealth University, Department of Psychiatry.

Oakhill, J. (1994). Individual differences in children's text comprehension. In

M. A. Gernsbacher (Ed.), *Handbook of psycholinguistics* (pp. 821–848). San Diego, CA: Academic Press.

Olson, R. K. (2006). Genes, environment, and dyslexia: The 2005 Norman Geschwind memorial lecture. *Annals of Dyslexia, 56*(2), 205–238.

Perfetti, C. A. (1985). *Reading ability*. New York: Oxford University Press.

Perfetti, C. A., Landi, N., & Oakhill, J. (2005). The acquisition of reading comprehension skill. In M. Snowling & C. Hulme (Eds.), *The science of reading: A handbook* (pp. 227–247). Oxford, UK: Blackwell.

Plomin, R., DeFries, J. C., McClearn, G. E., & McGuffin, P. (2001). *Behavioral genetics* (4th ed.). New York: Worth.

RAND Reading Study Group. (2002). *Reading for understanding: Toward an R & D program in reading comprehension*. Santa Monica, CA: RAND.

Rimrodt, S., Lightman, A., Roberts, L., Denckla, M. B., & Cutting, L. E. (2005, February). *Are all tests of reading comprehension the same?* Poster presentation at the annual meeting of the International Neuropsychological Society, St. Louis, MO.

Shankweiler, D. (1989). How problems of comprehension are related to difficulties in decoding. In D. Shankweiler & I. Y. Liberman (Eds.), *Phonology and reading disability: Solving the reading puzzle* (pp. 35–68). Ann Arbor: University of Michigan Press.

Wiederholt, L., & Bryant, B. (1992). *Examiner's manual: Gray Oral Reading Test–3*. Austin, TX: PRO-ED.

Woodcock, R. W., McGrew, K. S., & Mather, N. (2001). *Woodcock–Johnson III tests of achievement*. Itasca, IL: Riverside.

Yuill, N. M., & Oakhill, J. V. (1991). *Children's problems in text comprehension: An experimental investigation*. Cambridge, UK: Cambridge University Press.

11

Genes, Environments, and the Development of Early Reading Skills

Stephen A. Petrill

Over the past two decades, there has been important progress in our understanding of the development and cause of early reading skills. Studies have consistently shown that phonological awareness, sound–letter correspondence, vocabulary, and reading fluency are important components of early reading (see Whitehurst & Lonigan, 1998; National Institute of Child Health and Human Development, 2000). At the same time, numerous quantitative (e.g., Pennington & Smith, 1983; Stevenson, Graham, Fredman, & McLoughlin, 1987; Olson, Forsberg, & Wise, 1994; Trouton, Spinath, & Plomin, 2002; Byrne et al., 2002) and molecular genetic (see Fisher & DeFries, 2002; Grigorenko, 2005, for a review) studies have suggested that genetic influences are important not only to individual measures of reading outcomes (Pennington & Smith, 1983; Stevenson et al., 1987) but also to components of reading processing (e.g., Olson, Gillis, Rack, DeFries, & Fulker, 1991). Additional evidence indicates that the genetic influences related to reading are correlated with other cognitive skills such as general cognitive ability and mathematics (Petrill & Plomin, 2007). Finally, researchers have also begun asking how genes and environments influence the prospective development of reading. The assessment and target skills in a 5-year-old differ markedly from those in a 12-year-old (Dale & Crain-Thoreson,

1999), and these age–related differences may be accompanied by differences at a genetic or environmental level. On the other hand, genetic or environmental influences may contribute to consistency across different skills as the development of reading progresses.

Three population-based studies have examined more narrowly recruited samples of young twins as they learn to read: A collaborative study involving samples in Colorado, Australia, and Scandinavia (Byrne et al., 2002); the Twins Early Development Study (Trouton et al., 2002); and the Western Reserve Reading Project (WRRP; Petrill, Deater-Deckard, Thompson, & DeThorne, 2006a). The purpose of this chapter is to highlight key findings from the WRRP. After a description of the sample and the overall aims of the project, the chapter discusses univariate and multivariate genetic results pertaining to the development of early reading skills. Next, the relationship between indices of the home environment and early reading skills is examined. Finally, ongoing data collection and analysis efforts related to reading comprehension and math skills are discussed.

OVERVIEW OF THE WRRP

The WRRP is a longitudinal twin study involving 400 pairs of twins (see Petrill et al., 2006a, for more information). Recruiting was conducted through school nominations, Ohio state birth records, and media advertisements. Schools were asked to send a packet of information to parents in their school system with twins who have been enrolled for kindergarten but have not finished first grade. We secured the cooperation of 280 schools throughout the state of Ohio. Media advertisements in the greater Cleveland and Columbus metropolitan areas have also been used for the effective recruitment of additional twins.

Each of the 400 pairs of identical and same-sex fraternal twins is being assessed via a comprehensive battery of cognitive, reading-related, math, and environmental measures across seven home visits (Figure 11.1). Six reading visits occur annually, within 1 month of the previous home visit. One additional math assessment occurs at the 6-month window before or after the third reading visit, depending on when the twins turned 8½. Parent and teacher reports are also collected to assess reading-relevant aspects of the home environment, school, and each child's behavior. DNA was collected at the time of the first home visit and was used to determine zygosity. Because this is an ongoing study, data collection is continuing. The current chapter focuses on empirical studies from the Reading 1, Reading 2, and Math 4 visits.

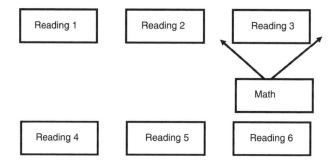

FIGURE 11.1. Home visits: Western Reserve Reading Project.

UNIVARIATE GENETIC ANALYSIS
OF EARLY READING

One of the primary goals of the WRRP is to examine the longitudinal course of reading development using a genetically sensitive design. The most basic question is whether univariate genetic and environmental influences vary at different ages. Univariate genetic effects are estimated by comparing the similarity of family members who differ in terms of their genetic similarity (see Plomin, DeFries, McClearn, & McGuffin, 2007). For example, genetic influences (h^2) are implied if monozygotic twins, who share 100% of their genes, are more similar than fraternal twins, who share 50% of their genes, on average. Shared environmental influences, or c^2, are implied if genetic similarity is disassociated from familial similarity (e.g., if identical twins are no more similar than fraternal twins or if biological siblings are no more similar than adoptive siblings). Nonshared environmental (e^2) influences are implied to the extent that the correlation between identical twins is less than 1.0. In the case of manifest variables, e^2 also includes random error.

Our first published article (Petrill et al., 2006a) used these univariate genetic methods to examine one of the most basic issues related to early reading. In particular, with the exception of a handful of other studies (e.g., Byrne et al., 2002), the vast majority of behavioral genetic studies on reading involved cross-sectional samples of twins spanning a wide age range (see Olson et al., 1994; Olson, Gillis, Rack, DeFries, & Fulker, 1991; Gayan & Olson, 2001; Knopik, Alarcon, & DeFries, 1998; Gayan & Olson, 2003; Compton, Davis, DeFries, Gayan, & Olson, 2001). These cross-sectional studies suggested that shared environmental influences on early reading skills were relatively modest in comparison to substantial genetic influences. Behavioral genetic studies of other cognitive domains, such as general cognitive ability, indicated that shared environmental influences are highest in young children and attenuate as children reach adolescence (see Petrill, 2003). Thus, our hypothesis was that the youngest readers in the WRRP sample would show large and significant shared environmental effects. Table 11.1 presents data from the Reading 1 home visit, which included twins assessed in kindergarten or first grade. Results suggested that, as expected, genetic influences are statistically significant for Word Identification and Word Attack subtest scores from the Woodcock–Johnson Reading Mastery Test (Woodcock, 1987) as well as for the Phonological Awareness Test (Robertson & Salter, 1997) and rapid automatized naming (RAN) from the Comprehensive Test of Phonological Processing (Wagner, Torgesen, & Rashotte, 1999). Additionally, shared environmental influences were significant and substantial for all reading outcomes, with the exception of RAN and Word Identification. Interestingly, the largest shared environmental effects were for those reading outcomes most closely related to direct instruction (e.g., letter identification) while the smallest were for those tapping fluency (RAN).

MULTIVARIATE GENETIC ANALYSIS OF EARLY READING

The univariate findings described previously, aside from demonstrating that genetic and environmental influences are important, do not address how genes and environments shape the relationships among reading-related outcomes. Do genes promote stability among differ-

TABLE 11.1. Univariate Genetic (h^2), Shared Environment (c^2), and Nonshared Environment (e^2) Influences and 95% Confidence Intervals: Reading 1 Home Visit

Variable	h^2	c^2	e^2
Letter identification	.05	.57*	.38*
Word identification	.67*	.18	.15*
Word attack	.42*	.30*	.28*
Phonological awareness	.30*	.50*	.20*
Rapid automatized naming	.72*	.04	.24*

Note. From Petrill, Deter-Deckard, Thompson, and DeThorne (2006a). Copyright 2006 by Sage Publications. Reprinted by permission.

*$p < .05$.

ent aspects of reading cognition within measurement occasions and across the developmental course of reading? Are dissociations between different aspects of reading, such as fluency and phonology or decoding and language, reflecting independent sources of genetic variance? Does common instruction in the environment serve to bring different aspects of reading together, or does instruction drive wedges between different aspects of reading? The answers to these questions are central to how we understand and, it is hoped, intervene in the complex gene–environment interplay, which influences individual differences in reading.

These kinds of questions are directly addressable using multivariate behavioral genetic methods. An illustrative bivariate example of this general multivariate approach is presented in Figure 11.2 (Neale & Cardon, 1992) for two reading outcomes: phonological awareness (PA) and word identification (WID). The multivariate model is based on the premise that the correlation between PA and WID is influenced by common genes (A1), shared environments (C1), and nonshared environments (E1). Additionally, the independence between different PA and WID is influenced by unique sources of genetic (a^2), shared (c^2), and nonshared environmental (e^2) influences. It then becomes possible to evaluate the significance of these common and independent effects. For example, PA and WID may be influenced by common genetic effects (A1 large and significant), but there are no independent genetic influences on WID separate from PA (A2 equal to zero). The same logic applies to shared (C1) and nonshared (E1) environmental pathways. In contrast, to the extent that WID is independent from PA, a^2, c^2, and/or e^2 would also be large and significant.

We have used this approach to examine issues of theoretical interest in the reading literature. For example, considerable debate remains concerning the phonological core versus double-deficit models of early reading (see Swanson, Trainin, Necoechea, & Hammill, 2003). One important question is whether phonology and serial naming influence reading outcomes through overlapping or independent sources of genetic and environmental variance. RAN and phonology may share common genes as they predict reading outcomes, but additional genes specific to RAN may also be influencing reading. Second, genes may contribute to a set of basic learning skills, along the lines of the Plomin and Kovas's (2005) "generalist gene" hypothesis, but environments may drive wedges between different aspects of early reading. Third, in addition to shared genes, shared environmental influences, such as the early home literacy environment, may have a unitary influence on early

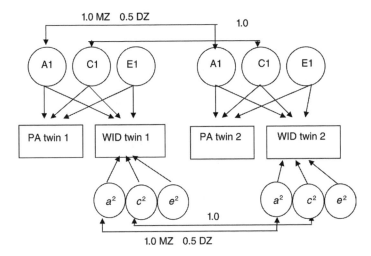

FIGURE 11.2. Bivariate genetic model. MZ, monozygotic; DZ, dizygotic; PA, phonological awareness; WID, word identification.

reading outcomes. Finally, both genes and environments may influence the overlap and independence between phonology and RAN as they predict reading outcomes.

We examined this issue using the data from the Reading 1 home visit (Petrill, Deater-Deckard, Thompson, & DeThorne, 2006b). Our results suggested a complex picture of gene–environment effects. First, phonological awareness and RAN correlated moderately ($r = .20$) and 100% of this correlation was influenced by common genetic factors. In other words, to the extent that PA and RAN correlated, this correlation was due completely to genetic effects. However, RAN possessed additional independent genetic influences separate from PA, suggesting that RAN, although genetically correlated with PA, is also somewhat genetically distinct.

What is most interesting, however, is that the relationship between PA and reading outcomes (defined as word identification and nonword decoding) and RAN and reading outcomes is influenced only by the common genetic variance between PA and RAN. In other words, only common genetic effects in PA and RAN influenced reading outcomes. The additional genetic variance in RAN is specific to RAN. As for the shared environment, our findings suggest that they influence the correlation between PA and reading outcomes independently from RAN.

Taken together, these findings are emblematic of the ongoing theoretical debate concerning the phonological core versus double-deficit models. In particular, the behavioral genetic data suggest that the double-deficit model is supported by independent shared environmental influences affecting the correlation between PA and reading outcomes independent from RAN while the core model is supported by common genetic effects across PA, RAN, and reading outcomes.

LONGITUDINAL GENETIC ANALYSIS OF EARLY READING

In addition to examining the relationship among different facets of reading, another unresolved issue is the degree to which there is stability (e.g., Catts, Hogan, & Adlof, 2005) versus instability (e.g., Chall, 1983; Dale & Crain-Thoreson, 1999) as reading skills develop. Multivariate genetic designs examine the cause of the stability and instability of reading skills across measurement occasions. For example, the correlation among reading outcomes across time may be influenced by consistent family environmental influences in the home or the school or genetic effects that tap a common set of processes as reading develops. Conversely, new environmental demands or different sets of genes may emerge as the task demands of reading change as skills develop.

An emerging set of studies are examining the longitudinal development of reading. Wadsworth, Corley, Hewitt, Plomin, and DeFries (2002) found significant genetic stability between reading recognition skills assessed at 7, 12, and 16 years. Subsequent studies have used more detailed assessments of reading in more narrowly recruited samples. Byrne et al. (2005) suggested that a single genetic factor and a single shared environment factor accounted for the longitudinal relationship between preschool print knowledge, phonological awareness, and oral reading fluency in kindergarten. More recently, Harlaar, Dale, and Plomin (2007) have suggested that genetic influences are largely responsible for the stability in reading at 7, 9, and 10 years of age using teacher ratings of reading progress. Other studies (e.g., Wadsworth, DeFries, Olson, & Willcutt, 2007) have suggested that genetic influences are also important for the stability of reading disability.

Using our twin data, we examined this issue in Reading 1 and Reading 2 measurement occasions, when twins are just beginning to experience formalized reading instruction in school. These results, presented in Table 11.2, suggest substantial shared environmental overlap for measures involving direct instruction such as expressive vocabulary and phonological awareness, whereas substantial genetic overlap was found for most reading outcomes. Additionally, there was evidence for independent genetic and shared environmental effects as children began to acquire reading skills as a function of formalized instruction in school.

IDENTIFYING ENVIRONMENTAL INFLUENCES ON READING

In sum, our data and those of others suggest that genetic influences are significant and substantial for early reading at the level of univariate analysis of individual reading outcomes when comparing different measures of reading at the same time and when comparing the same measure of reading across multiple measurement occasions. Furthermore, there is some evidence that shared environmental influences are important in early reading, particularly for measures involving direct instruction.

TABLE 11.2. Proportion of Total Variance Accounted for by Genetic and Shared Environmental Overlap and Specificity

Wave 2 variable	Total	Shared wave 1		Wave 2 only
Shared environmental pathway	c^2 total	c^2 wave 1	+	c^2 wave 2
Letter knowledge	.52*	.20*		.32*
Word knowledge	.33*	.08		.25*
Phonological awareness	.47*	.47*		.00
Rapid automatized naming	.20	.20		.00
Expressive vocabulary	.40*	.38*		.02
Phonological decoding	.21	.06		.15
Passage comprehension	.11	.11		.00
Genetic pathway	h^2 total	h^2 wave 1	+	h^2 wave 2
Letter knowledge	.27*	.27*		.00
Word knowledge	.58*	.31*		.27*
Phonological awareness	.14*	.14*		.00
Rapid automatized naming	.43*	.08		.35*
Expressive vocabulary	.47*	.47*		.00
Phonological decoding	.51*	.26*		.25
Passage comprehension	.76*	.28*		.48

Note. Adapted from Petrill et al. (2007). Copyright 2007 by Springer Publications. Adpated by permission.

*$p < .05$.

However, behavioral genetic findings are still poorly integrated into the larger literature. One reason is that quantitative genetic methods estimate genetic and environment variance components but do not necessarily identify them. Several predictors of early reading have been identified in the social reading literature, including the amount of reading-related knowledge and skills children have before formal schooling (e.g., McCardle, Scarborough, & Catts, 2001; Molfese, Molfese, Key, & Kelly, 2003), the quality of the home literacy environment (Christian, Morrison, & Bryant, 1998), parental attitudes and expectations (e.g., Briggs & Elkind, 1977; Dunn, 1981; Rescorla, Hyson, Hirsh-Pasek, & Cone, 1990), parental modeling of literacy (Taylor, 1983), as well as book-related activities such as parental involvement in schoolwork, trips to the library, and so on (e.g., Foy & Mann, 2003; Senechal & LeFevre, 2002; Bus & Van Ijzendorn, 1995; Scarborough & Dobrich, 1994). In general, these measures of the environment correlate (approximately $r = .27$) with early reading success (Scarborough, 1998).

Unfortunately, because these studies described previously have largely used biologically related family members living in the same home; they confound genetic and environmental effects. Increasingly, behavioral genetic studies are including indices of the reading environment. In our data, we have examined indices of the reading environment elucidated by the reading socialization literature to account for a portion of the shared family environment estimated in quantitative genetic studies. We originally investigated this issue using a sample of 354 adopted children ranging in age from 4 to 13 (Northeast-Northwest Collaborative Adoption Project; Petrill, Deater-Deckard, Schatschneider, & Davis, 2005). Because adoptive children are genetically unrelated to their parents, correlations between measures of the home reading environment and child reading outcomes are due to shared family experiences, not genetic overlap among family members. We found that phonological, orthographic, and general cognitive skills were correlated with parental involvement in schoolwork and richness of literacy material provided in the home. Furthermore, shared environmental influences decreased as a function of child age (Petrill et al., 2005). Building on these data, we examined the relationship among parent skills, early literacy environment, chaos in the home, and early reading outcomes in our twin sample (Johnson, Martin, Brooks-Gunn, & Petrill, in press). Our results suggest nonlinear relationships between parent skills, home literacy environment, and child reading outcomes in kindergarten. For example, degree of household organization is positively related to expressive vocabulary, phonological awareness, and word-reading skills but only for those households whose mothers are above-average readers. In contrast, the quality of the early literacy environment is positively associated with child expressive vocabulary, word-reading skills, and phonological awareness but only in families where mothers were average or below-average readers.

Given the quantitative genetic evidence, it is also possible that experiences may also influence reading through genetic pathways. In this case, genetic influences not only directly influence reading outcomes but may also have indirect effects by altering the probability of coming into contact with environments that are helpful or harmful to reading outcomes. Put another way, identical twins may be more similar than fraternal twins on reading not only because they share more direct genetic effects that influence their reading skills but also because they may share more similar reading experiences as a function of their greater similarity in reading. This, in turn, may amplify identical twin resemblance relative to fraternal twins. These gene–environment effects may have increasing influence on reading outcomes as children learn to read and gain more control over their reading environments.

We have begun to examine this issue. For example, when examining the amount of time a twin reads alone, we found substantial heritability (h^2 = .63) and zero shared environment. More importantly, when we examined the correlation between time reading alone and word identification, these two variables were correlated; r = .35. Multivariate genetic analyses suggested that this correlation was completely explained by shared genetics. In other words, individual differences in the amount of practice a child experienced through reading alone, which has clear experiential influences on reading, was mediated almost completely by genetic variance related to word reading.

These data are preliminary but may have important implications for how we think about the way in which reading is taught and learned and how we might prevent and remediate reading problems. The literature has become increasingly sensitive to the issue of treatment resistance, or a child's lack of response to educational interventions (e.g., Vaughn, Linan-Thompson, & Hickman, 2003). Fuchs and colleagues eloquently state that if "all children count, then intervention researchers must increasingly contend with the fact that a substantial number of children will not respond adequately to systematic and empirically-validated interventions" (p. 307). It is possible that genetic differences explain a portion of the variability in intervention response. More generally, the fact that h^2 is significant suggests that home- and school-based differences do not explain all of the variance in children's reading outcomes.

CURRENT DIRECTIONS

Our results to date suggest that a gene–environment model of reading development is not only tenable but likely. Currently, we are attempting to take the next steps necessary to more fully integrate genetically sensitive designs into the study of reading development. First, there is an increasing recognition of the need to examine reading comprehension. To date, a disproportionate body of work has focused on phonological awareness and fluency, with insufficient attention on oral language and the component processes of reading comprehension. This is unfortunate for two reasons. First, as grade level increases, so does the emphasis on comprehension (Anderson, Hiebert, Scott, & Wilkinson, 1985; Applebee, Langer, & Mullis, 1987), with material becoming longer and of increasing difficulty in vocabulary, syntactic complexity, and conceptual demands. To examine the intersection between word level and comprehension deficits within reading disability (RD), Leach, Scarborough, and Catts (2003) tested fourth and fifth graders whose RD was identified early and persisted, was identified early but was transient, or was identified late. The late-identified group more frequently experienced comprehension without word-level difficulty; however, the great majority of students with early/persistent and with late-identified RD experienced difficulty both with word-level skill and comprehension. Moreover, comprehension-only and comprehension with word-level RD types both showed differential vocabulary deficits, insufficient knowledge of language structure, lack of background knowledge, and weak inferential abilities. This is in line with other work (e.g., Hart & Risley, 1995; Hecht, Burgess, Torgesen, Wagner, & Rachotte, 2000; Whitehurst & Lonigan, 1998) suggesting the importance of vocabulary, conceptual knowledge, and inference making as well as other studies demonstrating the importance of working memory (e.g., Kintsch, 1988; Daneman & Carpenter, 1980; Just & Carpenter, 1992) and retrieval of information from long-term memory (e.g., Spilich, Vesonder, Chiesi, & Voss, 1979; see Paris & Stahl, 2005, for a more detailed discussion).

Data collection is ongoing, but as Reading 5 data become available (see Figure 11.1), our twin sample will allow us to test competing hypotheses concerning the convergent and discriminant validity of language comprehension, decoding, and reading comprehension constructs. First, it is possible that all three constructs are influenced by a single genetic factor. This would suggest that the differences among decoding, language, and literacy are due mainly to the environment and that there is a common underlying set of genetic risk and protective factors that bind these skills together. In contrast, it is also possible that language and decoding constitute separate genetic pathways for reading comprehension. In other words, quantitative genetics may provide a method to examine whether genetic risk for reading comprehension difficulties is a function of a single omnibus "learning difficulty" factor or multiple pathways of risk.

A preliminary study by Olson and Keenan (2005) examined this issue in a small cross-sectional sample of twins, finding that the genetic variance in reading comprehension was accounted for by independent genetic pathways related to decoding and language processing. Shared environmental influences on reading comprehension, in contrast, were the result of a single shared environmental factor across all measures. However, because these data were based on cross-sectional data, they may reflect the aggregate effect of decoding and language on comprehension across a wide age range. Our data will allow us to examine this issue longitudinally.

Another major focus has been the relationship between reading and math skills (see Petrill & Plomin, 2007, for a more thorough discussion). To date, our quantitative genetic results converge to suggest that genes and shared environments are important for the variance of different aspects of mathematics, for the covariance among aspects of math performance, as well as for the covariance between math and reading skills and other cognitive skills. Results also suggest that the genetic influences at the extremes are from the same distribution as the genes for the entire range of ability. However, as noted in a recent request for applications from the National Institutes of Health (RFA HD-07-005), "A growing body of evidence suggests that the various kinds of mathematical difficulties exhibited by children with such a learning disability can be attributed at least in part to deficits in the domain of general cognitive mechanisms including, among others, components of the working memory system (e.g., impairments in attentional and inhibitory processing). On the other hand, recent evidence also suggests that these individuals may experience even more fundamental, domain-specific deficits in numeric processing" (National Institutes of Health, 2007). Because the current literature related to math is derived from broad psychometric assessments, they are currently incapable of addressing this important issue. One of the major advances in the behavioral genetic reading literature occurred when the field shifted from studies of reading and reading disability to understanding the genetic and environmental variance and covariance among measures of process and content such as phonology, rapid serial naming, vocabulary, and so on as they related to reading.

We are currently beginning an extension of our twin study to allow us to address these issues in mathematics. This will provide important theoretical insight into the cause of the mechanisms influencing more complex psychometric math outcomes. Moreover, theoretically derived measures of math process and content will offer the potential to better explain the significant genetic and environmental overlap between math and reading outcomes as well as the significant genetic and environmental independence of math from reading performance.

CONCLUSIONS

Although much has been accomplished in the study of reading, a considerable proportion of school-age children continue to lag in reading and math performance (National Center for Education Statistics, 2008). We are still far from understanding why some children thrive despite experiencing significant challenges while others show difficulties despite exposure to what appear to be optimal environments. All available evidence strongly suggests that genetic variability not only cannot be ignored but must be embraced as we search for answers to this important issue. Reading is likely similar to other outcomes such as obesity, cardiovascular health, and substance use in that is a biobehavioral outcome, that is, a socially meaningful, complex human outcome that involves the nexus of genetics, biology, and experience. Interventions will likely be more successful to the extent that they are developed and implemented with this in mind.

ACKNOWLEDGMENTS

The Western Reserve Reading Project is supported by Grant No. HD038075 from the National Institute of Child Health and Human Development and Grant No. HD046167 from the National Institute of Child Health and Human Development, Institute of Education Sciences.

REFERENCES

Anderson, R. C., Hiebert, E. H., Scott, J. A., & Wilkinson, I. A. G. (1985). *Becoming a nation of readers*. Washington, DC: U.S. Department of Education, National Institute of Education.

Applebee, A. N., Langer, J. A., & Mullis, I. V. (1987). *Learning to be literate in*

America: Reading, writing, and reason. Princeton, NJ: Educational Testing Service.

Briggs, C., & Elkind, D. (1977). Characteristics of early readers. *Perceptual and Motor Skills, 44,* 1231–1237.

Bus, A. G., & van IJzendoorn, M. H. (1995). Phonological awareness and early reading: A meta-analysis of experimental training studies. *Journal of Educational Psychology, 91*(3), 403–414.

Byrne, B., Delaland, C., Fielding-Barnsley, R., Quain, P., Samuelsson, S., Hoien, T., et al. (2002). Longitudinal twin study of early reading development in three countries: Preliminary results. *Annals of Dyslexia, 52,* 49–74.

Byrne, B., Wadsworth, S., Corley, R., Samuelsson, S., Quain, P., DeFries, J. C., et al. (2005). Longitudinal twin study of early literacy development: Preschool and kindergarten phases. *Scientific Studies of Reading, 9*(3), 219–236.

Catts, H. W., Hogan, T. P., & Adlof, S. M. (2005). Developmental changes in reading and reading disabilities. In H. W. Catts & A. G. Kamhi (Eds.), *The connections between language and reading disabilities.* Mahwah, NJ: Erlbaum.

Chall, J. S. (1983). *Stages of reading development.* New York: McGraw-Hill.

Christian, K., Morrison, F. J., & Bryant, F. B. (1998). Predicting kindergarten academic skills: Interactions among child care, maternal education, and family literacy environments. *Early Child Research Quarterly, 13*(3), 501–521.

Compton, D. L., Davis, C. J., DeFries, J. C., Gayan, J., & Olson, R. K. (2001). Genetic and environmental influences on reading and RAN: An overview of results from the Colorado twin study. In M. Wolf (Ed.), *Conference proceedings of the Dyslexia Research Foundation Conference in Extraordinary Brain Series: Time, fluency, and developmental dyslexia.* Baltimore, MD: York Press.

Dale, P. S., & Crain-Thorenson, C. (1999). Language and literacy in a developmental perspective. *Journal of Behavioral Education, 9,* 23–33.

Daneman, M., & Carpenter, P. A. (1980). Individual differences in working memory and reading. *Journal of Verbal Learning and Verbal Behavior, 19,* 450–466.

Dunn, N. E. (1981). Children's achievement at school-entry age as a function of mothers' and fathers' teacher sets. *Elementary School Journal, 81,* 245–253.

Fisher, S. E., & DeFries, J. C., (2002). Developmental dyslexia: Genetic dissection of a complex cognitive trait. *Nature Reviews. Neuroscience, 3,* 767–780.

Foy, J. G., & Mann, V. (2003). Home literacy environment and phonological awareness in preschool children: Differential effects for rhyme and phoneme awareness. *Applied Psycholinguistics, 24*(1), 59–68.

Gayan, J., & Olson, R. K. (2001). Genetic and environmental influences on orthographic and phonological skills in children with reading disabilities. *Developmental Neuropsychology, 20*(2), 487–511.

Gayan, J., & Olson, R. K. (2003). Genetic and environmental influences on individual differences in printed word recognition. *Journal of Experimental Child Psychology, 84,* 97–123.

Grigorenko, E. L. (2005). A conservative meta-analysis of linkage and linkage-association studies of developmental dyslexia. *Scientific Studies of Reading, 9*(3), 285–316.

Harlaar, N., Dale, P. S., & Plomin R. (2007). From learning to read to reading to learn: Substantial and stable genetic influence. *Child Development, 78*(1), 116–131.

Hart, B., & Risley, T. H. (1995). *Meaningful differences in the everyday experience of young American children.* Baltimore, MD: Brookes.

Hecht, S. A., Burgess, S. R., Torgesen, J. K., Wagner, R. K., & Rashotte, C. (2000). Explaining social class differences in growth of reading skills from beginning kindergarten through fourth-grade: The role of phonological awareness, rate of access, and print knowledge. *Reading and Writing, 12*, 99–127.

Johnson, A. D., Martin, A., Brooks-Gunn, J., & Petrill, S. A. (2008). Order in the house! Associations among household chaos, the home literacy environment, maternal reading ability, and children's early reading. *Merrill-Palmer Quarterly, 54*(4), 445–472.

Just, M. A., & Carpenter, P. A. (1992). A capacity theory of comprehension: Individual differences in working memory. *Psychological Review, 99*, 122–149.

Kintsch, W. (1998). *Comprehension: A paradigm for cognition.* New York: Cambridge University Press.

Knopik, V. S., Alarcón, M., & DeFries, J. C. (1998). Common and specific gender influences on individual differences in reading performance: A twin study. *Personality and Individual Differences, 25*(2), 269–277.

Leach, J. M., Scarborough, H. S., & Rescorla, L. (2003). Late-emerging reading disabilities. *Journal of Educational Psychology, 95*, 211–224.

McCardle, P., Scarborough, H. S., & Catts, H. W. (2001). Predicting, explaining, and preventing children's reading difficulties. *Learning Disabilities Research & Practice, 16*(4), 230–239.

Molfese, D., Molfese, V., Key, A. F., & Kelly, S. (2003). Influence of environment on speech-sound discrimination: Findings from a longitudinal study. *Developmental Neuropsychology, 24*, 541–558.

National Center for Education Statistics. (2008). *National assessment of educational progress.* Retrieved May, 2008, from *nces.ed.gov/naep3/*.

National Institute of Child Health and Human Development. (2000). *Report of the National Reading Panel. Teaching children to read: An evidence-based assessment of the scientific research literature on reading and its implications for reading instruction* (NIH Publication No. 00-4769). Washington, DC: U.S. Government Printing Office.

National Institutes of Health. (2007). *Request for application: Mathematical cognition and specific learning disabilities.* Retrieved May 15, 2008, from *grants.nih. gov/grants/guide/rfa-files/RFA-HD-07-005.html*.

Neale, M., & Cardon, L. R. (1992). *Methodology for genetic studies of twins and families.* Dordrecht, the Netherlands: Kluwer Academic.

Olson, R. K., Forsberg, H., & Wise, B. (1994). Genes, environment, and the development of orthographic skills. In V. W. Berninger (Ed.), *The varieties of orthographic knowledge: I. Theoretical and developmental issues* (pp. 27–71). Dordrecht, the Netherlands: Kluwer Academic.

Olson, R. K., Gillis, J. J., Rack, J. P., DeFries, J. C., & Fulker, D. W. (1991). Confirmatory factor analysis of word recognition and process measures in the Colorado Reading Project. *Reading and Writing, 3*, 235–248.

Olson, R. K., & Keenan, J. (2005, July). *A behavior genetic analysis of reading comprehension's relation to listening comprehension and word reading*. Paper presented at the annual meeting of the Society for the Scientific Study of Reading, Toronto, CA.

Paris, S. G., & Stahl, S. (2005). *New directions in assessment of reading comprehension*. Mahwah, NJ: Erlbaum.

Pennington, B. F., & Smith, S. D. (1983). Genetic influences on learning disabilities and speech and language disorders. *Child Development, 54*, 369–387.

Petrill, S. A. (2003). The development of intelligence: Behavioral genetic approaches. In R. Sternberg, J. Lautrey, & T. Lubart (Eds.), *Models of intelligence: International perspectives*. Washington, DC: American Psychological Association.

Petrill, S. A., Deater-Deckard, K., Schatschneider, C., & Davis, C. (2005). Measured environmental influences on early reading: Evidence from an adoption study. *Scientific Studies of Reading, 9*(3), 237–260.

Petrill, S. A., Deater-Deckard, K., Thompson, L. A., & DeThorne, L. S. (2006a). Reading skills in early readers: Genetic and shared environmental influences. *Journal of Learning Disabilities, 39*(1), 48–55.

Petrill, S. A., Deater-Deckard, K., Thompson, L. A., DeThorne, L. S., & Schatschneider, C. (2006b). Genetic and environmental effects of serial naming and phonological awareness on early reading outcomes. *Journal of Educational Psychology, 98*(1), 112–121.

Petrill, S. A., Deater-Deckard, K., Thompson, L., Schatschneider, C., DeThorne, L., & Vandenbergh, D. W. (2007). Longitudinal genetic analysis of early reading: The Western Reserve Reading Project. *Reading and Writing, 20*(1–2), 127–246.

Petrill, S. A., & Plomin, R. (2007). Quantitative genetics and mathematical abilities/disabilities. In D. Berch & M. Mazzocco (Eds.), *Mathematical learning disabilities: Research, theory, and practice*. Baltimore, MD: Brookes.

Plomin, R., DeFries, J. C., McClearn, G. E., & McGuffin, P. (2007). *Behavior genetics* (5th ed.). New York: Worth.

Plomin, R., & Kovas, Y. (2005). Generalist genes and learning disabilities. *Psychological Bulletin, 131*, 592–617.

Rescorla, L., Hyson, M., Hirsh-Pasek, K., & Cone, J. (1990). Academic expectations in mothers of preschool children. *Early Education and Development, 1*, 165–184.

Robertson, C., & Salter, W. (1997). *The Phonological Awareness Test*. East Moline, IL: LinguiSystems.

Scarborough, H. S. (1998). Early identification of children at risk for reading disabilities: Phonological awareness and some other promising predictors. In B. K. Shapiro, P. J. Accardo, & A. J. Capute (Eds.), *Specific reading disability: A view of the spectrum* (pp. 75–119). Timonium, MD: York Press.

Scarborough, H. S., & Dobrich, W. (1994). On the efficacy of reading to preschoolers. *Developmental Review, 14*, 245–302.

Senechal, M., & LeFevure, J. (2002). Parental involvement in the development of children's reading skills: A five-year longitudinal study. *Child Development, 73*(2), 445–460.

Spilich, G. J., Vesonder, G. T., Chiesi, H. L., & Voss, J. F. (1979). Text processing of domain-related information for individuals with high and low knowledge. *Journal of Verbal Learning and Verbal Behavior, 18*, 275–290.

Stevenson, J., Graham, P., Fredman, G., & McLoughlin, V. (1987). A twin study of genetic influences on reading and spelling ability and disability. *Journal of Child Psychology and Psychiatry, 28*(2), 229–247.

Swanson, H. L., Trainin, G., Necoechea, D. M., & Hammill, D. D. (2003). Rapid naming, phonological awareness, and reading: A meta-analysis of the correlation evidence. *Review of Educational Research, 73*(4), 407–440.

Taylor, D. (1983). *Family literacy: Young children learning to read and write.* Exeter, NH: Heineman.

Trouton, A., Spinath, F. M., & Plomin, R. (2002). Twins Early Development Study (TEDS): A multivariate, longitudinal genetic investigation of language, cognition and behaviour problems in childhood. *Twin Research, 5*, 444–448.

Vaughn, S., Linan-Thompson, S., & Hickman, P. (2003). Response to instruction as a means of identifying students with reading/learning disabilities. *Exceptional Children, 69*(4), 391–409.

Wadsworth, S. J., Corley, R. P., Hewitt, J. K., Plomin, R., & DeFries, J. C. (2002). Parent-offspring resemblance for reading performance at 7, 12 and 16 years of age in the Colorado Adoption Project. *Journal of Child Psychology and Psychiatry and Allied Disciplines, 43*(6), 769–774.

Wadsworth, S. J., DeFries, J. C., Olson, R. K., & Willcutt, E. G. (2007). Colorado longitudinal twin study of reading disability. *Annals of Dyslexia, 57*, 139–160.

Wagner, R. K., Torgesen, J. K., & Rashotte, C. A. (1999). *Comprehensive test of phonological processing.* Austin, TX: PRO-ED.

Whitehurst, G. J., & Lonigan, C. J. (1998). Child development and emergent literacy. *Child Development, 68*, 848–872.

Woodcock, R. W. (1987). *Woodcock Reading Mastery Tests.* Circle Pines, MN: American Guidance Service.

12

Examining Sources of Poor Comprehension in Older Poor Readers

Preliminary Findings, Issues, and Challenges

Sarah H. Eason *and* Laurie E. Cutting

Reading comprehension is a skill that is necessary for successful academic performance, becoming increasingly requisite in later grades. Thus, children with underlying reading difficulties will face more and more challenges as they progress through school. For children in later grades (fourth and beyond), what cognitive and neural mechanisms are associated with reading comprehension? If a child's decoding/word-reading performance is apparently sufficient, what other skills may lead to deficits in reading comprehension? Current research aims to identify these additional skills and eventually create a model of the cognitive and neurobiological factors that contribute to the development of reading comprehension.

In this chapter, we review the previous literature on the contributing factors to reading comprehension; discuss current, ongoing research aims to expand on the extant body of knowledge; and outline the challenges and areas in which future research may be directed.

BACKGROUND

Much reading research has been focused on the issue of how decoding/word recognition skills are developed in younger children (kindergarten through third grade). The findings consistently support the importance of phonological processing and the alphabetic principle in early reading development. Although many children's reading difficulties stem from phonological processing and word recognition, research suggests that other sources of reading comprehension failure exist either with or without a word recognition deficit.

Clearly, the ability to read single words is a key component to successful reading comprehension and is supported by numerous studies (Adams, 1990; Lyon, 1995; Torgesen, 2000). Still, there are children with apparent average word recognition who demonstrate difficulty in comprehension, suggesting that there may be other processes that contribute to their ability to comprehend. However, many questions remain regarding the cognitive and neural processes *other* than decoding/word recognition that contribute to reading comprehension, which becomes an increasingly important skill as a child progresses through school.

Simple View of Reading

One of the most commonly discussed theories is the simple view of reading (Hoover & Gough, 1990), which conceptualizes reading comprehension as a combination of word recognition and listening comprehension. These two factors are found to closely approximate reading comprehension; research examining the contributions of word recognition and listening comprehension indicates that they account for 62 to 80% of the variance in reading comprehension ability.

The extent to which word recognition and listening comprehension each uniquely contributes to reading comprehension appears to shift over time, as exemplified by several studies (Catts, Adlof, & Weismer, 2006; Catts, Hogan, Adlof, & Barth, 2003; Storch & Whitehurst, 2002). When administering measures of word recognition, listening comprehension, and reading comprehension to students in second, fourth, and eighth grades, both word recognition and listening comprehension were found to account for a significant amount of the variance in reading comprehension (Catts et al., 2003). However, the unique variance accounted for by each factor differed when comparing the three grade levels, with the amount of variance accounted for by word recognition decreasing from second grade to fourth grade and decreasing even further by eighth grade. On the other hand, the amount of variance accounted for by listening comprehension steadily increased from second to eighth grade. This finding is consistent with the existing literature; in later grades, language skills other than word recognition replace decoding as the primary factor to successful reading comprehension.

In another study, Storch and Whitehurst (2002) monitored children from preschool through fourth grade, assessing code-related and oral language precursors to reading in preschool and kindergarten and then examining reading accuracy and reading comprehension skills in first through fourth grades. Code-related skills consisted of print concepts and phonological awareness, and oral language components included expressive and receptive vocabulary and conceptual knowledge. The correlation between oral language and code-related skills dramatically declined over time; in preschool, the two factors were strongly linked, yet by first and second grades there was no significant correlation. When examining the factors that influenced reading ability, there was an apparent change from early grades to later grades. In early (first and second) grades, there were high correlations between reading accuracy and reading comprehension, creating a composite measure of reading. Using this model, code-related skills in kindergarten were the strongest predictors of reading ability in second grade. As children progressed in school, however, there were more discrepancies between children's word recognition and comprehension abilities, and distinct subdomains of reading ability developed. In third and fourth grades, decoding skills remained the strongest predictors of reading accuracy; reading accuracy, in turn, was a predictor of reading comprehension, as were oral language skills (including language measured in preschool).

Research on children with specific reading comprehension deficits (S-RCD), or children with average single-word reading but difficulty with comprehension, further supports the changing contributions of word-level and oral language skills to reading comprehension (Catts et al., 2006). Eighth graders described as "poor comprehenders" (average word recognition, poor comprehension) and "poor decoders" (poor word recognition, average comprehension) who were assessed on oral language and phonological skills exhibited opposite patterns from each other. Whereas the poor comprehenders demonstrated deficits in oral language but normal phonological abilities, the poor decoders struggled with phonological processing but performed in the normal range on oral language measures. Longitudinal data from kindergarten and second and fourth grades were collected from the same eighth graders, comparing oral language and reading abilities over time. Reading comprehension performance was not consistent over time; however, oral language deficits in earlier grades were predictive of poor reading comprehension in eighth grade. Catts et al. propose that the disassociation between early and later reading comprehension scores may be attributed to the changing nature of reading comprehension in school over time; there is a greater emphasis on word recognition than listening comprehension for reading comprehension in earlier grades. A child's specific abilities and deficits in different components of reading consequently may lead to inconsistency in reading comprehension performance over time. The findings from an earlier Catts et al. study (2003) are supportive of this; it was observed in this study that in second grade, more children classified as dyslexic (word recognition deficit only) were identified as poor readers (performing at least 1 standard deviation below the grade-based mean for reading comprehension), but by eighth grade hyperlexia (listening comprehension deficit only) was more common among poor comprehenders.

Although research has long supported the simple view of reading, these recent studies are especially supportive of how word recognition and language skills contribute differently to comprehension at different stages in school. In other words, a model of reading comprehension at one point in time may consist of different predictors than those that influence comprehension in another time frame. The Storch and Whitehurst study (2002) in particular exemplifies the concept of different predictors at different "snapshots" in time. Although code-related skills, not language, were the strongest predictor of reading in second grade, by fourth grade oral language (including oral language measured in preschool) significantly predicted reading comprehension. These findings suggest the potential for a factor to appear nonsignificant at one point and yet emerge later when reading comprehension places greater demands on that skill (i.e., oral language). Catts et al. (2006) also observed this when studying language skills and reading; language was not significantly associated with reading comprehension in early grades, but by eighth grade was a strong predictor of reading comprehension difficulty, independent of single-word reading ability.

The next question that stems from these studies is, what accounts for the changing roles of word recognition and language skills over time? An important consideration is the changes in the nature of reading that take place between primary grades (kindergarten through third) and later elementary school/secondary school. Curriculum, as well as assessment, changes in a number of ways at about the time a child reaches fourth grade. There is a transition from a focus on phonics and decoding monosyllabic words to an emphasis on fluency and comprehension, with more polysyllabic words being introduced. In addition, later on, reading material tends to consist of more expository texts instead of narratives, and children spend more time on silent, independent reading rather than oral reading in a group. As a consequence, if children are capable of basic word recognition but have underlying language (or other) deficits impeding their ability to comprehend more complex words and concepts, there may be what appears to be a sudden decrease in reading comprehension performance. This phenomenon could underlie the often-reported "second wave" of reading disabilities emerging during and after fourth grade (Chall, 1983). Students with these "late-emerging" reading disabilities (including both word recognition and reading comprehension) appear to account for 36 to 46% of the children diagnosed with a reading disability (Badian, 1999; Leach, Scarborough, & Rescorla, 2003; Lipka, Lesaux, & Siegel, 2006; Shaywitz, Escobar, Shaywitz, Fletcher, & Makuch, 1992). Therefore, it appears that as children progress in school and the demands of reading change, a greater variety of skills may be necessary to successfully complete reading-related tasks (e.g., oral language, working memory, processing speed). Deficits in one or more of these areas could potentially lead to a difficulty with reading comprehension, even with solid basic word recognition skills.

Indeed, the studies on the simple view appear to confirm that listening comprehension is as important as word recognition for successful comprehension, especially for older readers. However, listening comprehension itself is composed of multiple processes, such as vocabulary and syntax. These subdomains of listening comprehension need to be further explored in terms of their unique contributions to reading comprehension. Additionally, other factors outside of language may potentially impact a child's reading comprehension. Efficiency, or speed of reading, needs to be examined; studies that have added a speed factor to the simple view have found that it contributes an additional amount of significant variance (Joshi & Aaron, 2000).

SPECIFIC READING COMPREHENSION DEFICIT

A number of children—approximately 3 to 10%—demonstrate average decoding/word recognition skills but struggle with comprehension of reading material (Aaron, Joshi, & Williams, 1999; Catts et al., 2003; Leach et al., 2003; Nation, 2001; Shankweiler et al., 1999; Torppa et al., 2007). Researchers have focused on identifying the factors linked to poor reading comprehension in children who demonstrate normal word recognition. At Kennedy Krieger Institute, we have been conducting studies on the S-RCD population to understand not only this particular set of poor readers but also processes important for reading comprehension in general. We aim to gain a better understanding of how factors aside from single-word reading impact reading comprehension by comparing children who qualify as having an S-RCD (children who perform at or above the 40th percentile on basic reading but at or below the 25th percentile on at least two of five reading comprehension measures) with both average readers (at or above the 40th percentile on basic reading and all reading comprehension measures) and children with word-reading deficits (WRD; children scoring at or below the 25th percentile on basic reading). Whereas previous studies have tended to focus on examining one factor (e.g., working memory, language skills), we are examining language skills and executive function together as well as fluency and motivation. Additionally, the current studies also connect cognitive and neurobiological findings based on results of behavioral measures and functional magnetic resonance imaging. The intention is to focus on the performance of the S-RCD group on a variety of measures and see how they resemble controls, how they are more similar to individuals with WRD, and in what ways their performance differentiates them from both groups.

Fluency

As previously mentioned, some studies have added a factor of speed when examining the simple view of reading and find that being able to read words not only accurately but also quickly accounts for additional variance in reading performance. Joshi and Aaron (2000) assessed third graders' decoding and listening comprehension skills and added the variable of speed to the model by timing the children's responses for quickly naming a list of letters. Decoding and listening comprehension accounted for 48% of the variance in reading comprehension, and an additional 10% was accounted for by letter-naming speed. Shankweiler (1999) described a "bottleneck," where progressively more difficult reading material puts greater demands on higher level processes (e.g., working memory, making inferences), and if reading is not automatic, decoding may require the same resources typically reserved for these other processes necessary for successful reading comprehension.

Previous studies on children with S-RCD have tended to study accuracy of word recognition but not necessarily the automaticity of reading. However, we have considered the possibility that S-RCD difficulties may actually stem from underlying word recognition deficits but that they are just not detectable by typical reading assessments. Our current studies, therefore, seek to measure efficiency of word recognition both in isolation (single-word reading) and context (passage reading) by stressing the word recognition with a variety of measures that focus on word recognition automaticity and to do so in conjunction with assessment of other language and executive function skills that may compete for resources with nonfluent word recognition.

Language

Existing literature is supportive of the connection between language skills and reading comprehension, especially for older readers, for whom oral language predicts reading comprehension better than word recognition (e.g., Catts et al., 2003). Within the construct of oral language, however, there are a number of skills (e.g., vocabulary, syntax, inferential language), and these skills could be unique factors related to reading comprehension. A study by Catts, Fey, Zhang, and Tomblin (1999) found that more than 70% of children with comprehension deficits in second grade had demonstrated language difficulties 2 years earlier. The majority of poor comprehenders exhibited problems with both oral language (syntax and vocabulary) and phonological processing. However, there were also children whose deficits were only in one of the two domains, suggesting that oral language and phonological processing account for unique variance in reading comprehension.

Children with S-RCD appear to have difficulties in both syntactic and semantic skills (Nation & Snowling, 1998, 1999, 2000). These deficits include performing more poorly than control when identifying synonyms (Nation & Snowling, 1998) as well as recognizing semantic relationships and understanding syntax. Nation and Snowling (1999) found that there were no significant differences between good and poor comprehenders on a task requiring the participants to identify items as words or nonwords as long as the item was primed by a functionally associated word (e.g., *broom* and *floor*). When an item was primed by a categorically associated word (e.g., *cat* and *dog*), however, poor comprehenders demonstrated more difficulty for pairs with weaker associations. Because categorical associations are more semantically demanding than functional associations, these findings may indicate that poor comprehenders have a less developed ability to recognize semantic relationships with automaticity. Additionally, Nation and

Snowling (2000) have identified deficits in syntactic awareness among children with S-RCD. A task requiring children to reorganize scrambled sentences was more difficult for children with S-RCD than for controls. This task, however, required that children retain the words as they were presented to them, adding the factor of working memory, which may have contributed to the S-RCD group's difficulty with this syntactic task.

Our current set of studies are focused on expanding existing findings related to the connections between reading comprehension and language skills in controls, children with word recognition deficits, and children with S-RCD. In particular, we are assessing children on receptive and expressive vocabulary (semantics) as well as receptive and expressive grammar (syntax), including measures that manipulate syntactic difficulty.

Executive Function

Cognitive factors outside of the area of language have also been linked to reading comprehension; in particular, reading studies have examined the role of skills in the executive function domain. As children progress in school, they are increasingly expected to read independently to learn material for numerous classes; the executive function skills such as working memory and components of inferential thinking become essential for retaining information and relating it to prior knowledge. Deficits in these areas of executive function may result in poor performances on reading comprehension. The areas that have been previously examined in relation to reading comprehension include verbal and visual memory, making inferences, and the ability to plan, organize, and monitor comprehension activities.

Numerous studies have focuesed on verbal working memory and linked it to reading comprehension (e.g., Carpenter & Just, 1988; Daneman & Carpenter, 1980; Just & Carpenter, 1992; Swanson, 1999; Swanson & Alexander, 1997; Swanson, Ashbaker, & Lee, 1996; Swanson & Berninger, 1995; Swanson & Trahan, 1996). Baddeley's (1986) model describes verbal working memory as one of two slave systems supporting a central working memory system, the second system being visuospatial memory. Phonological short-term memory failures are reflective of deficits in the verbal system, which leads to problems in working memory and finally comprehension. Still, even without problems with phonological short-term memory, children with S-RCD appear to have difficulty with verbal working memory (Nation, Adams, Bowyer-Crane, & Snowling, 1999; Oakhill & Yuill, 1996; Oakhill, Yuill, & Parkin, 1986). Whereas verbal working memory appears to consistently correlate with reading comprehension, studies examining visual working memory have been more conflicting. Some studies have found connections between deficits in visual working memory and poor reading comprehension (e.g., Swanson, 1999; Swanson & Alexander, 1997); however, other studies have not supported these findings (e.g., Daneman & Tardif, 1987; Nation et al., 1999).

Making inferences also is potentially a factor for successful reading comprehension; research supports the correlation between the two skills. Oakhill and Yuill (1996) found that children with S-RCD were able to answer literal questions about a text but struggled to accurately respond to inferential questions. Additional studies also support the finding that children with reading comprehension deficits have difficulty understanding and making references (e.g., Dennis & Barnes, 1993). Although some have proposed that inferential thinking could be reliant on intact working memory skills (Oakhill & Yuill, 1996; Perfetti, Marron, & Foltz, 1996), Swanson and Alexander (1997) found inference-making deficits in the S-RCD group independent of working memory. Still, by examining both inferential skills and working memory in our studies, we hope to be able to identify the unique contributions of both factors toward reading comprehension and further clarify this issue.

In addition to working memory and making inferences, another area of executive function that may contribute to reading comprehension is the ability to plan, organize, and monitor comprehension activities. Some studies have found evidence supporting the concept that skilled readers are more likely to engage in comprehension monitoring and use strategies such as identifying the main idea, knowing when to reread, and skimming when appropriate (Perfetti et al., 1996; Swanson, 1999; Swanson & Trahan, 1996) as well as organizing what has been read (Cornoldi, DeBeni, & Pazzaglia, 1996). However, the ability to use these skills may be confounded by an individual's verbal working memory, and it will be beneficial for future studies to control for working memory when assessing the contributions of planning, organizing, and monitoring abilities to reading comprehension.

Exploring the individual influences of fluency, language, and executive function on reading comprehension is a key first step to developing a model of reading development. However, to fully understand how and to what extent these skills contribute to reading, they must be examined in conjunction. More recently, researchers looking at factors of reading comprehension have begun to collectively examine the elements of fluency, language, and executive function together in the same study. Materek and Cutting (2007) sought to address this issue by comparing the language skills, executive function, and fluency of adolescents with S-RCD with those of adolescents with WRDs, as well as a control group with average basic reading scores. They assessed the students on measures of fluency, oral language (receptive vocabulary, receptive and expressive grammar, and inferential language), and executive function (spatial planning, inhibition, organization, and working memory). The results identified both similarities and differences between the two reading deficit groups. Although both groups performed poorly on measures of language skills, only the S-RCD students exhibited deficits in executive function. Specifically, on measures of inferential language, ambiguous sentences, combining sentences, and vocabulary, there were no significant differences between children with WRD and those with S-RCD; both groups scored lower on these measures than the control group. Grammatical comprehension was a differentiating factor between the WRD and S-RCD groups; S-RCD students performed similarly to the control group, but the WRD group scored significantly lower.

In contrast, on a measure of spatial planning, rule learning, and inhibition of impulsive responding, the WRD and control groups performed more similarly. The S-RCD group performed significantly lower than the other two groups, even when age, Full-Scale IQ, and basic reading skills were controlled for. Thus, executive function may be a potential differentiating factor between those who struggle with word recognition and those who have specific deficits in reading comprehension.

One intriguing finding was that, although children in the S-RCD group recognized words in isolation as fluently as controls, they were significantly *less* fluent than controls when *contextual* reading was measured, suggesting that isolation and contextual fluency may tap somewhat different processes. To this end, a discriminant function analysis identified the combination of isolated word-reading fluency, contextual reading fluency, and executive function as correctly classifying 94% of the control, 100% of the WRD, and 73% of the S-RCD groups. Overall, findings suggest that weaknesses in executive function may be a characteristic of individuals with S-RCD and that isolated and contextual fluency may be somewhat separate constructs.

NEUROIMAGING

In addition to contributions from cognitive factors, it is possible that neuroimaging studies may shed light on the unique profile of children with S-RCD as well as other processes important for reading comprehension beyond the word level. In particular, functional neuroimaging studies offer insight into the *neurobiological* components of comprehension, especially component processes of reading comprehension beyond the word level. (Although there have been some functional neuroimaging text comprehension studies, most have focused on sentence comprehension, and the majority of these have been limited to adult skilled readers.) Sentence comprehension studies have revealed patterns of activations that are similar to those seen with processing single words; however, the activation is more extensive, including more right hemisphere activation and bilateral activation of the inferior frontal gyrus (L yy R) and the posterior, superior, and middle temporal gyri (e.g., Caplan et al., 2001; Cooke et al., 2006; Cutting et al., 2006; Ferstl & von Cramon, 2001; Friederici, Ruschemeyer, Hahne, & Fiebach, 2003; Grossman et al., 2002; Jobard, Vigneau, Mazoyer, & Tzourio-Mazoyer, 2007; Keller, Carpenter, & Just, 2001; Meyer, Friederici, & von Cramon, 2000).

The functional neuroimaging research on sentence comprehension in groups with reading disabilities is less extensive than the research on skilled readers. However, some studies have demonstrated that individuals with impaired single-word reading show anomalous patterns of activation during sentence comprehension (e.g., Breznitz & Leikin, 2000, 2001; Helenius, Salmelin, Service, & Connolly, 1999; Kronbichler, Hutzler, & Staffen, 2006; Leikin, 2002; Meyler et al., 2007; Rumsey et al., 1994; Sabisch, Hahne, Glass, von Suchodoletz, & Friederici, 2006; Seki, Koeda, & Sugihara, 2001). One notable aspect of this research is that the anomalous patterns of activations associated with sentence comprehension in WRD have been reported in both *auditorally* and *visually* presented sentences (e.g., Leikin, 2002; Rumsey et al., 1994; Sabisch et al., 2006), suggesting that comprehension processing difficulties that are not associated with word-level deficits are present.

In general, studies of sentence comprehension in individuals with impaired reading skills report differences between WRD and control groups (e.g., Breznitz & Leikin, 2000, 2001; Helenius et al., 1999; Karni, Morocz, & Bitan, 2005; Kronbichler et al., 2006; Sabisch et al., 2006; Seki et al., 2001) in a variety of regions. For example, Meyler et al. (2007) found in adolescents that, although they comprehended visually presented sentences, decreased activation in the left middle temporal gyrus, right inferior partial lobule, and left postcentral gyrus was associated with lower reading ability. Somewhat consistent with these findings, Kronbichler et al. found that the WRD group, while reading simple sentences in German, showed reduced activation in the left lateral temporal cluster (posterior temporal cortex into inferior occipitotemporal cortex) and increased activation in the left medial temporal cortex compared with controls. However, it should be stated that most studies of sentence comprehension show relatively similar patterns of activation between good- and poor-reader groups (left temporal cortex, inferior frontal gyrus, and precentral regions). Therefore, although WRD groups are processing sentences somewhat differently than skilled readers, the global patterns of activation do not seem to be *completely* different from each other. These findings are different than what is reported when comparing WRD and control groups on functional neuroimaging of isolated words, for which substantial differences are seen. This suggests that sentence comprehension taps multiple processes, which may allow for more compensatory mechanisms to be used by poor readers.

Research projects led by Kennedy Krieger Institute and Haskins Laboratories have reported on neurobiological aspects of comprehension, particularly trying to isolate different component processes inherent in sentence comprehension. Cutting et al. (2006) showed that the patterns of activation associated with the word recognition requirements of sentence comprehension versus the short-term memory requirements of sentence comprehension in skilled readers varied: Left inferior frontal gyrus and fusiform gyrus (visual word form area) was associated with word recognition, right middle frontal and cingulate gyri, as well as left precuneous, was associated with short-term memory, and comprehension itself was associated with bilateral temporal lobe. More recently, Rimrodt et al. (2007) used a paradigm of sentence comprehension alternated with single-word reading to examine patterns of activation specifically associated with sentence comprehension in good and poor readers (with WRD) aged 9 to 14 years. When controlling for activation associated with single-word reading, both groups showed activation associated with sentences in left inferior frontal gyrus and bilateral extrastriate regions. When the two groups were compared, the group with WRD showed more activation in areas associated with linguistic processing (left middle and superior temporal gyri) as well as attention and response selection (bilateral insula, right cingulate gyrus, right superior frontal gyrus, and right parietal lobe). These patterns of activation were mostly driven by the WRD group's response to incongruous sentences, suggesting that more effortful processing was needed for the WRD group to distinguish between congruent and incongruent sentences. When reading ability was examined continuously, Rimrodt et al. found that more efficient reading of isolated words and connected text was positively correlated with left occipitotemporal activation. In contrast, poorer performance on most reading and language measures was associated with right hemisphere activation.

Overall, neuroimaging contributes to our understanding of reading comprehension by providing a way to understand brain regions/circuits that underlie comprehension. Although there are very few studies comparing various types of impaired readers at this time, conducting these types of studies may help provide an understanding of where difficulties arise during comprehension processing, especially those that are associated with word level versus comprehension (or both). These brain–behavior connections, if combined with neuropsychological findings, can help provide linkages to brain circuits or areas that may be especially problematic for some readers as they try to comprehend text, particularly texts that tax different aspects of comprehension. This approach may help determine different subtypes of reading comprehension weaknesses. In summary, neuroimaging studies of comprehension may substantially contribute to our understanding of the neurobiological basis of reading comprehension, particularly the multifaceted nature of it, helping to reveal brain systems that are involved in different types of comprehension across different reader subtypes.

MEASURING READING COMPREHENSION: CHALLENGES AND CONSIDERATIONS

One significant challenge of studying the cognitive components of reading comprehension is the issue of selecting a measure, because different assessment tools may be targeting different components of reading comprehension as well as other skills (e.g., working memory, listening comprehension). There is great variety in formats of reading comprehension measures: Some consist of cloze items, whereas others may be multiple-choice or open-ended questions. Furthermore, there are variations in whether children read the passages aloud or silently to themselves, if the passage is still in view when questions are asked, and the length and content of passages. Consequently, there could potentially be much inconsistency in children's reading comprehension performance when comparing scores on different measures. Research exam-

ining differences between comprehension assessment tools is supportive of this; tests with cloze items have more variance accounted for by
word recognition and decoding than tests with question-and-answer
items (Bowey, 1986; Nation & Snowling, 1997; Spear-Swerling, 2004).
Additionally, cloze tests appear to be more strongly linked to decoding
skills, while language skills is a stronger predictor for performance on
tests with both silent and oral passage reading, followed by multiple-
choice questions (Francis, Fletcher, Catts, & Tomblin, 2005).

A study by Cutting and Scarborough (2006) aimed to assess the
variance among different measures of reading comprehension by
comparing students' performances on three assessment tools, each
containing both expository and narrative passages. The assessment
measures used included the Gates–MacGinitie Reading Test–Revised
(G-M; MacGinitie, MacGinitie, Maria, & Dreyer, 2000), which requires
students to answer written multiple-choice questions about passages
(three to 15 sentences long) they read silently. Students have access to
the passages when answering the questions, and there is a 35-minute
time limit. In contrast, the Gray Oral Reading Test–3 (GORT-3; Wiederholt & Bryant, 1992) contains six- to seven-sentence passages, and
students are instructed to read them aloud as quickly as possible. The
passage is then removed from students' view and multiple-choice
questions pertaining to each passage are read out loud by the examiner.
The third assessment tool, the Wechsler Individual Achievement Test
(WIAT; Wechsler, 1992), measures comprehension by presenting two
open-ended questions, delivered orally by the examiner, about two- to
three-sentence passages, which are read silently, with the passage still
accessible during questioning.

The study found that word recognition/decoding accounted for
significantly more variance for the WIAT than for the G-M and GORT-
3; oral language, on the other hand, was more closely correlated with
the G-M than with the WIAT or GORT-3. When oral language was further split into two separate components (vocabulary and sentence processing), there were additional differences among the three measures of
comprehension. Both vocabulary and sentence processing were predictors for performance on the G-M; only sentence processing was significantly correlated with the WIAT, and vocabulary was the sole language
composite accounting for variance in performance on the GORT-3. The
differences among the factors accounting for variance in each of the
reading comprehension assessment tools support the suggestion that
the nature of a measure of reading comprehension will influence the
specific skills the test is actually assessing.

Another study examining variance among tests of reading comprehension yielded findings consistent with the Cutting and Scarborough (2006) study (Keenan, Betjemann, & Olson, 2008). Similarly, GORT-3 scores were more strongly predicted by listening comprehension than by decoding skills, as was the Qualitative Reading Inventory-3 (Leslie & Caldwell, 2000). Decoding was more of a factor for the variance in both the Reading Comprehension subtest of the Peabody Individual Achievement Test (Dunn & Mawkwardt, 1970) and the Woodcock–Johnson Passage Comprehension section of the Woodcock–Johnson Tests of Achievement-III (Woodcock, McGrew, & Mather, 2001). Again, these findings are indicative of the varying contributions of word level and language skills, depending on the comprehension test that is administered.

It is critical to keep in mind the issue of variance among reading comprehension measures when diagnosing deficits in reading comprehension. Which assessment tool is used can have a great impact on how a child is diagnosed; in one study, more than 43% of the participants were identified as having a reading comprehension deficit (RCD) by at least one of the tests (Rimrodt, Lightman, Roberts, Denckla, & Cutting, 2005). However, if all three measures were considered, only 9.4% (21.6% of those identified by at least one test) were consistently diagnosed as having an RCD. Clearly, in practical application, these differences need to be considered when evaluating a child's performance on measures of reading comprehension. Similarly, in research, it must be acknowledged that the assessment tools used may be testing a variety of skills or factors related to the construct of reading comprehension.

CONCLUSION

Having a better understanding of the factors that influence reading comprehension potentially could have a significant impact on how children's reading performance is assessed in both research and school settings. Existing research shows that widely used measures of reading comprehension vary greatly in terms of children's performance. There is a need to identify the specific skills that each measurement tool is targeting and determine which ones are truly assessing the most salient aspects of reading comprehension. Currently, it may be most prudent to use multiple measures to create a full picture of a child's performance, identifying his or her particular strengths and weaknesses. Alternatively, as we develop a clearer picture of what reading tests are assessing, it may lead to the development of new assessment tools that address these issues, with different formats yielding inconsistent results.

Additionally, examining the variables contributing to reading comprehension may lead to the identification of "subtypes" of S-RCD, unique deficits that result in poor comprehension but have significantly different implications for successful intervention. Clearly, a child who struggles with comprehension because of an underlying reading fluency deficit is not going to benefit from the same intervention as another S-RCD child with working memory difficulties.

Although the existing research on reading comprehension contributes significantly to our understanding of how children develop the ability to read, as well as impediments to the process, there are still many questions that remain. Areas for continuing research include (1) understanding how specific components of fluency, language, and executive function influence comprehension and how these components may interact with each other; (2) examining the neurobiological mechanisms that play a role in reading comprehension and identifying any differences in the functioning of children with S-RCD; and, finally, (3) incorporating the behavioral and neurobiological findings to develop a more extensive model of reading comprehension development. Integrating these areas of study into a comprehensive understanding of reading will assist in developing new measures of reading comprehension to more accurately identify children with deficits and, most importantly, inform us of the best methods of prevention and intervention for reading disabilities.

REFERENCES

Aaron, P. G., Joshi, R. M., & Williams K. A. (1999). Not all reading disabilities are alike. *Journal of Learning Disabilities, 32,* 120–137.

Adams, M. J. (1990). *Beginning to read: Thinking and learning about print.* Cambridge, MA: MIT Press.

Baddeley, A. D. (1986). *Working memory.* Oxford, UK: Clarendon Press.

Badian, N. A. (1999). Reading disability defined as a discrepancy between listening and reading comprehension: A longitudinal study of stability, gender differences, and prevalence. *Journal of Learning Disabilities, 32,* 138–148.

Bowey, J. (1986). Syntactic awareness in relation to reading skill and ongoing reading comprehension monitoring. *Journal of Experimental Child Psychology, 41,* 282–299.

Breznitz, Z., & Leikin, M. (2000). Syntactic processing of Hebrew sentences in normal and dyslexic readers: Electrophysiological evidence. *Journal of Genetic Psychology, 161,* 359–380.

Breznitz, Z., & Leikin, M. (2001). Effects of accelerated reading rate on processing words' syntactic functions by normal and dyslexic readers: Event related potentials evidence. *Journal of Genetic Psychology, 162,* 276–296.

Caplan, D., Vijayan, S., Kuperberg, G., West, C., Waters, G., Greve, D., et al. (2001). Vascular responses to syntactic processing: Event-related fMRI study of relative causes. *Human Brain Mapping, 15,* 26–38.

Carpenter, P. A., & Just, M. A. (1988). The role of working memory in language comprehension. In D. Klahr & K. Kotovasky (Eds.), *Complex information processing: The impact of Herbert A. Simon* (pp. 31–68). Hillsdale, NJ: Earlbaum.

Catts, H. W., Adlof, S. M., & Weismer, S. E. (2006). Language deficits in poor comprehenders: A case for the simple view of reading. *Journal of Speech, Language, and Hearing Research, 29,* 278–293.

Catts, H. W., Fey, M. E., Zhang, X., & Tomblin, J. B. (1999). Language basis of reading and reading disabilities: Evidence from a longitudinal investigation. *Scientific Studies of Reading, 3,* 331–361.

Catts, H. W., Hogan, T. P., Adlof, S. M., & Barth, A. E. (2003, June). *The simple view of reading: Changes over time.* Poster session presented at the annual conference of the Society for Scientific Study of Reading, Boulder, CO.

Chall, J. S. (1983). *Stages of reading development.* New York: McGraw-Hill.

Cooke, A., Grossman, M., DeVita, C., Gonzalez-Atavales, J., Moore, P., Chen, W., et al. (2006). Large-scale neural network for sentence processing. *Brain and Language, 96,* 14–36.

Cornoldi, C., De Beni, R., & Pazzaglia, F. (1996). Profiles of reading comprehension difficulties: An analysis of single cases. In C. Cornoldi & J. Oakhill (Eds.), *Reading comprehension difficulties: Processes and intervention* (pp. 113–136). Mahwah, NJ: Erlbaum.

Cutting, L. E., Clements, A. M., Courtney, S., Rimrodt, S. R., Schafer, J. G. B., Wilkins, J., et al. (2006). Differential components of sentence comprehension: Beyond single word reading and memory. *NeuroImage, 29,* 429–438.

Cutting, L. E., Materek, A., Cole, C. A. S., Levine, T., & Mahone, E. M. (in press). Effects of language, fluency, and executive function on reading comprehension performance. *Annals of Dyslexia.*

Cutting, L. E., & Scarborough, H. S. (2006). Prediction of reading comprehension: Relative contributions of word recognition, language proficiency, and other cognitive skills can depend on how comprehension is measured. *Scientific Studies of Reading, 10,* 277–299.

Daneman, M., & Carpenter, P. (1980). Individual differences in working memory and reading. *Journal of Verbal Learning and Verbal Behavior, 19,* 450–466.

Daneman, M., & Tardif, T. (1987). Working memory and reading skill re-examined. In M. Coltheart (Ed.), *Attention and performance 12: The psychology of reading* (pp. 491–508). Hillsdale, NJ: Erlbaum.

Dennis, M., & Barnes, M. A. (1993). Oral discourse after early-onset hydrocephalus: Linguistic ambiguity, figurative language, speech acts, and script-based inferences. *Journal of Pediatric Psychology, 18,* 639–652.

Dunn, L. M., & Markwardt, F. C. (1970). *Peabody Individual Achievement Test: Examiner's manual.* Circle Pines, MN: American Guidance Service.

Ferstl, E. C., & von Cramon, D. Y. (2001). The role of coherence and cohesion in test comprehension: An event-related fMRI study. *Cognitive Brain Research, 11*, 325–340.

Francis, D. J., Fletcher, J. M., Catts, H. W., & Tomblin, J. B. (2005). Dimensions affecting the assessment of reading comprehension. In S. G. Paris & S. A. Stahl (Eds.), *Children's reading comprehension and assessment* (pp. 369–394). Mahwah, NJ: Erlbaum.

Friederici, A. D., Ruschemeyer, S. A., Hahne, A., & Fiebach, C. J. (2003). The role of left inferior frontal and superior temporal cortex in sentence comprehension: Localizing syntactic and semantic processes. *Cerebral Cortex, 13*, 170–177.

Grossman, M., Cooke, A., DeVita, C., Alsop, D., Detre, J., Chen, W., et al. (2002). Age-related changes in working memory during sentence comprehension: An fMRI study. *NeuroImage, 15*, 302–317.

Helenius, P., Salmelin, R., Service, E., & Connolly, J. F. (1999). Semantic cortical activation in dyslexic readers. *Journal of Cognitive Neuroscience, 11*, 535–550.

Hoover, W. A., & Gough, P. B. (1990). The simple view of reading. *Reading and Writing, 2*, 127–160.

Jobard, G., Vigneau, M., Mazoyer, B., & Tzourio-Mazoyer, N. (2007). Impact of modality and linguistic complexity during reading and listening tasks. *NeuroImage, 34*, 784–800.

Joshi, R., & Aaron, P. G. (2000). The component model of reading: Simple view of reading made a little more complex. *Reading Psychology, 21*, 85–97.

Just, M. A., & Carpenter, P. A. (1992). A capacity theory of comprehension: Individual differences in working memory. *Psychological Review, 99*, 122–149.

Karni, A., Morocz, I. A., & Bitan, T. (2005). An fMRI study of the differential effects of word presentation rates (reading acceleration) on dyslexic readers' brain activity patterns. *Journal of Neurolinguistics, 18*, 197–219.

Keenan, J. M., Betjemann, R. S., & Olson, R. K. (2008). Reading comprehension tests vary in the skills they assess: Differential dependence on decoding and oral comprehension. *Scientific Studies of Reading, 12*, 281–300.

Keller, T. A., Carpenter, P. A., & Just, M. A. (2001). The neural bases of sentence comprehension: A fMRI examination of syntactic and lexical processing. *Cerebral Cortex, 11*, 223–237.

Kronbichler, M., Hutzler, F., & Staffen, W. (2006). Evidence for a dysfunction of left posterior reading areas in German dyslexic readers. *Neuropsychologia, 44*, 1822–1832.

Leach, J. M., Scarborough, H. S., & Rescorla, L. (2003). Late-emerging reading disabilities. *Journal of Educational Psychology, 95*, 211–224.

Leikin, M. (2002). Processing syntactic functions of words in normal and dyslexic readers. *Journal of Psycholinguistic Research, 31*, 145–163.

Leslie, L., & Caldwell, J. (2000). *Qualitative Reading Inventory-3*. London: Allyn & Bacon.

Lipka, O., Lesaux, N. K., & Siegel, L. S. (2006). Retrospective analyses of the reading development of grade 4 students with reading disabilities: Risk status and profiles over 5 years. *Journal of Learning Disabilities, 39*, 364–378.

Lyon, G. R. (1995). Toward a definition of dyslexia. *Annals of Dyslexia, 45*, 3–27.

MacGinitie, W. H., MacGinitie, R. K., Maria, K., & Dreyer, L. G. (2000). *Gates–MacGinitie Reading Tests* (4th ed.). Itasca, IL: Riverside.

Meyer, M., Friederici, A. D., & von Cramon, D. Y. (2000). Neurocognition of auditory sentence comprehension: Event related fMRI reveals sensitivity to syntactic violations and task demands. *Cognitive Brain Research, 9*, 19–33.

Meyler, A., Keller, T. A., Cherkassky, V. L., Lee, D., Hoeft, F., Whitfield-Gabrieli, S., et al. (2007). Brain activation during sentence comprehension among good and poor readers. *Cerebral Cortex, 17*, 2780–2787.

Nation, K. (2001). Reading and language in children: Exposing hidden deficits. *The Psychologist, 14*, 238–242.

Nation, K., Adams, J. W., Bowyer-Crane, C. A., & Snowling, M. J. (1999). Working memory deficits in poor comprehenders reflect underlying language impairments. *Journal of Experimental Child Psychology, 73*, 139–158.

Nation, K., & Snowling, M. J. (1997). Assessing reading difficulties: The validity and utility of current measures of reading skill. *British Journal of Educational Psychology, 67*, 359–370.

Nation, K., & Snowling, M. J. (1998). Semantic processing and the development of word-recognition skills: Evidence from children with reading comprehension difficulties. *Journal of Memory and Language, 39*, 85–101.

Nation, K., & Snowling, M. J. (1999). Developmental differences in sensitivity to semantic relations among good and poor comprehenders: Evidence from semantic priming. *Cognition, 70*, B1–B13.

Nation, K., & Snowling, M. J. (2000). Factors influencing syntactic awareness skills in normal readers and poor comprehenders. *Applied Psycholinguistics, 21*, 229–241.

Oakhill, J., & Yuill, N. M. (1996). Higher order factors in comprehension disability: Processes and remediation. In C. Cornoldi & J. Oakhill (Eds.), *Reading comprehension difficulties: Processes and intervention* (pp. 69–92). Mahwah, NJ: Earlbaum.

Oakhill, J. V., Yuill, N. M., & Parkin, A. J. (1986). On the nature of the difference between skilled and less-skilled comprehenders. *Journal of Research in Reading, 9*, 80–91.

Perfetti, C. A., Marron, M. A., & Foltz, P. W. (1996). Sources of comprehension failure: Theoretical perspectives and case studies. In C. Cornoldi & J. Oakhill (Eds.), *Reading comprehension difficulties: Processes and intervention* (pp. 137–166). Mahwah, NJ: Earlbaum.

Rimrodt, S. L., Clements-Stephens, A. M., Pugh, K. R., Courtney, S., Blankner, J. G. B., Wilkens, J., et al. (2009). Functional MRI of sentence comprehension in adolescents with reading disabilities: Neurobiology beyond the single word. *Cerebral Cortex.* [Epub ahead of print]

Rimrodt, S., Lightman, A., Roberts, L., Denckla, M., & Cutting, L. (2005, February). *Are all tests of reading comprehension the same?* Poster session presented at the annual conference of the International Neuropsychological Society, St. Louis, MO.

Rumsey, J. M., Zametkin, A. J., Andreason, P., Hanahan, A. P., Hamburger, S. D., Aquino, T., et al. (1994). Normal activation of frontotemporal language cortex in dyslexia, as measured with oxygen 15 positron emission tomography. *Archives of Neurology, 51,* 27–38.

Sabisch, B., Hahne, A., Glass, E., von Suchodoletz, W., & Friederici, A. D. (2006). Auditory language comprehension in children with developmental dyslexia: Evidence from event-related brain potentials. *Journal of Cognitive Neuroscience, 18,* 1676–1695.

Seki, A., Koeda, T., & Sugihara, S. (2001). A functional magnetic resonance imaging study during sentence reading in Japanese dyslexic children. *Brain & Development, 23,* 312–316.

Shankweiler, D. (1999). Words to meanings. *Scientific Studies of Reading, 3,* 113–127.

Shankweiler, D., Lundquist, E., Katz, L., Stuebing, K. K., Fletcher, J. M., Brady, S., et al. (1999). Comprehension and decoding: Patterns of association in children with reading difficulties. *Scientific Studies of Reading, 3,* 69–94.

Shaywitz, S. E., Escobar, M. D., Shaywitz, B. A., Fletcher, J. M., & Makuch, R. (1992). Evidence that dyslexia may represent the lower tail of a normal distribution of reading ability. *New England Journal of Medicine, 326,* 145–150.

Spear-Swerling, L. (2004). Fourth graders' performance on a state-mandated assessment involving two different measures of reading comprehension. *Reading Psychology, 25,* 121–148.

Storch, S. A., & Whitehurst, G. J. (2002). Oral language and code-related precursors to reading: Evidence from a longitudinal structural model. *Developmental Psychology, 38,* 934–947.

Swanson, H. L. (1999). Reading comprehension and working memory in learning-disabled readers: Is the phonological loop more important than the executive system? *Journal of Experimental Child Psychology, 72,* 1–31.

Swanson, H. L., & Alexander, J. E. (1997). Cognitive processes as predictors of word recognition and reading comprehension in learning-disabled and skilled readers: Revisiting the specificity hypothesis. *Journal of Educational Psychology, 89,* 128–158.

Swanson, H. L., Ashbaker, M., & Lee, C. (1996). Learning-disabled readers' working memory as a function of processing demands. *Journal of Experimental Child Psychology, 61,* 242–275.

Swanson, H. L., & Berninger, V. (1995). The role of working memory in skilled and less skilled readers' comprehension. *Intelligence, 21,* 83–108.

Swanson, H. L., & Trahan, M. (1996). Learning disabled and average readers' working memory and comprehension: Does metacognition play a role. *British Journal of Educational Psychology, 66,* 333–355.

Torgesen, J. K. (2000). Individual differences in response to early interventions in reading: The lingering problem of treatment resisters. *Learning Disabilities Research and Practice, 15,* 55–64.

Torppa, M., Tolvanen, A., Poikkeus, A. M., Eklund, K., Lerkkanen, M. K., Leskinen, E., et al. (2007). Reading development subtypes and their early characteristics. *Annals of Dyslexia, 57,* 3–32.

Wechsler, D. L. (1992). *Wechsler Individual Achievement Test.* San Antonio, TX: Psychological Corporation.

Wiederholt, L., & Bryant, B. (1992). *Gray Oral Reading Test–3: Examiner's manual.* Austin, TX: PRO-ED.

Woodcock, R. W., McGrew, K. S., & Mather, N. (2001). *Woodcock–Johnson III tests of achievement.* Itasca, IL: Riverside.

PART V

EPILOGUE

13

Promising Interfaces

Richard K. Wagner, Christopher Schatschneider,
and Caroline Phythian-Sence

 The chapters contained in this volume represent five perspectives on behavioral and biological origins of reading comprehension: cognitive, developmental, individual differences, behavioral genetic, and neurocognitive. One obvious reason for including multiple perspectives is that multiple perspectives characterize the existing research literature. To feature only a single approach would misrepresent the state of the field. More importantly, we believe that promising directions for future research lie not in any one of the perspectives represented, but rather at interfaces between them. Consider some illustrative examples.

A promising interface between the cognitive and developmental perspectives is represented by the work of Kaschak et al. (Chapter 1) and van den Broek at al. (Chapter 5). Studies of embodied cognition in adult readers suggest that comprehension recruits bodily systems used for perception and action planning to a much greater extent than was believed previously. Given the sensorimotor developmental theories of Piaget and others, such systems may play an even greater role in children's comprehension. For example, there is some evidence of a developmental progression in which beginning readers read aloud, then transition into silent reading but with substantial subvocalization, and finally to silent reading with relatively little subvocalization. For a second example, the motor theory of speech perception argues that speech perception relies on the motor programs used to produce speech. Although a strong view of the motor theory of speech perception has not been supported, most of the studies have used college students as participants. This theory may better characterize speech perception and younger developmental levels.

Another promising interface between the cognitive and developmental perspectives is represented by the work of Rayner and Slattery (Chapter 2) and Radach et al. (Chapter 4). Much of the recent eye movement research on adults has focused on higher-level comprehension processes, whereas the relatively few eye movement studies of children have focused on broad developmental changes in basic aspects of eye movements such as average fixation duration. As yet, eye movement methodology has not been applied to study the development of high-level comprehension processes in children.

Another potentially valuable interface between the individual differences and cognitive perspectives is provided by the work of Cain and Oakhill (Chapter 7) and Compton et al. (Chapter 3). Individual differences studies comparing good and poor readers have been used to identify skills that appear to exert a causal influence on reading comprehension. These skills are important targets for training in future intervention studies.

Nation (Chapter 8) and Priya and Wagner (Chapter 6) explore the interface between the individual differences and developmental perspectives. Studies of impaired readers have identified vocabulary as an important component of reading comprehension. Parallel studies of the development of normal reading converge on vocabulary as an important construct. Studies of poor comprehenders that include a younger normal reading age-matched control group can provide evidence about whether vocabulary development is a cause, correlate, or consequence of the development of reading comprehension.

Castillo et al. (Chapter 9) and Petrill (Chapter 11) present a promising interface between behavior genetics and individual differences perspectives. Studies comparing alternative measures of fluency on the basis of their ability to predict reading comprehension have revealed the need for these measures to include genetically sensitive designs. Conversely, the results of multivariate behavioral genetic studies have implications for rethinking the behavioral phenotype of reading comprehension.

Finally, Eason and Cutting (Chapter 12) and Keenan, Olson, and Betjemann (Chapter 10) discuss a potentially valuable interface between the neurocognitive and behavior genetic perspectives. For neuroimaging studies, a key issue is what task to use in the magnet. For behavioral genetic perspectives, a key issue is what tasks define the phenotype. Both approaches necessarily require careful consideration of measures of reading comprehension and its component skills, a challenge that can also be informed by the cognitive, developmental, and individual differences perspectives.

Work at an interface between perspectives obviously is multidisciplinary in nature. Our hope for this volume is that it serves to advance multidisciplinary programs of research on reading comprehension.

Index

Page numbers followed by an *f*, *n*, or *t* indicate figures, notes, or tables.